swings and roundabouts

Angela Douglas

Angela Douglas
swings and roundabouts

fantom
publishing

First published in 1983 by Elm Tree Books, and
republished in 1985 by Corgi

This revised and updated edition first published in 2012 by Fantom Films
fantomfilms.co.uk

A catalogue record for this book is available from the British Library.

Limited edition hardback ISBN: 978-1-78196-018-9
Standard edition paperback ISBN: 978-1-78196-019-6

Typeset by Phil Reynolds Media Services, Leamington Spa
Printed by MPG Biddles Limited, King's Lynn

Jacket design by Dexter O'Neill and Paul W.T. Ballard

Photographs appear on plates between pages 168 and 169. All photographs not
specifically credited are from the author's personal collection.

For Kenny

and in memory of
my Mother and Father

Contents

Foreword

One of the nice things about our profession is that it is constantly changing and, whatever else, it is rarely dull, for you are always meeting and working with new people. Some colleagues come into our lives fleetingly and pass like ships in the night, while others become friends for life. Angela Douglas is a friend for life.

It wasn't until I cast Kenneth More as the Lord Chamberlain in my film of *The Slipper and the Rose* that Nanette and I really got to know Angela. I had always wanted to work with Kenny, and the role required him to sing (sort of) and dance (well, a bit) but above all it allowed me to direct his unique talents as an actor for the first time. As always he gave a moving performance, for he was one of the most gifted and natural performers of my generation, able to turn his hand to a variety of demanding roles. Above all, he had an infectious sense of humour and we shared many a laugh along the way.

When we finished the location shooting in Austria and the film returned to Pinewood, we were able to invite him and Angela to a Sunday lunch at our home, Seven Pines. Of course we had both seen Angela in many British films and we were aware that, in the beginning, their relationship had given the tabloids a field day and caused them to be socially and creatively ostracised, since Kenny was married with two children and Angela was half his age. During that first lunch his pretty, bright, quirky, enthusiastic new wife entered our lives and has been a great friend ever since.

One of the things to admire about Angela is the way in which, still at a very young age, she coped with Kenny's terminal illness. Showing great strength she created a security blanket around him of love and humour, enveloping him with a care and thoughtfulness that made his last four years as good as they could possibly be.

Turning again to her autobiography, I was once more struck by her strength and perception and the way in which she has dealt with the multitude of slings and arrows we are all prey to. She has put down on paper the jigsaw pieces of her life in a way that makes a fascinating read. I thought back to that early Sunday lunch a long time ago and how it brought into our lives a new and special friendship. I am sure that when you have read the story of her life and times, you will understand why it remains a friendship Nanette and I greatly treasure.

Bryan Forbes, CBE
July 2012

A drawing of me done for Kenny in 1962 by Annika Wills

Introduction

November 1981

I am, I've been told, vulnerable to flattery, but I wondered now if I hadn't overdone it. At some time in the soft light of the autumn evening, James and I were sitting in my kitchen. A director and friend of long standing, he'd come to visit Kenny and after twenty minutes or so, I'd muttered something about 'whisky? coffee?' and led James out of the bedroom.

'Kenny tires easily,' I said by way of explanation on our way downstairs, and let it go at that. I poured coffee into two large green cups and took them to the table, apologising as it slopped into the saucers. We drank it, the slopping overlooked. I had begun to babble a bit; there was a broken quality in my voice which warned me to shut up and I did. Much as I felt the longing to unburden myself to someone, I found it difficult to reveal anything about this upheaval in our lives. How could I ever effectually outline the measure of our loss, much less go into the intricacies of the situation which led up to that loss. Our passion for each other. The wonderful companionship. And now the final agonising love. But however inconsiderably and briefly, I had made contact; this I could tell by the look of complete concentration on James's face. I felt self-conscious and turned away.

'Angela, are you keeping a journal?' I heard him say.

'No.'

'Write it all down.'

'Why?'

'Because you'll forget…' I stopped him short.

6

'I *won't* forget, James; my memories of this time with Kenny will always be vivid. I *couldn't* forget.'

'Are you certain?' he persisted. 'I'm telling you, time plays tricks with the mind. While these thoughts are with you, write them down now while it's happening – today, not tomorrow.'

In mid-swallow, gulping down my coffee, I almost choked on his words. It couldn't be true. *Forget about Kenny and me*? I felt on the brink of panic, realising that some days, just recently, I had difficulty remembering my own name. I closed my eyes in an attempt to recapture the joy of our being together and tried to pay no more attention to James. He'd made me aware that I might lose us. Precious detail. I felt flustered, bewildered. The thoughts flew through my mind like a swift.

'You've a way of speaking that demands my attention, a natural way with words,' I heard him say.

'Oh, I get by with fluttering my eyelashes, a shrug of the shoulders... and I wave my hands about a lot!' I retorted.

Hearing the relaxation in my voice, he smiled at me.

'I don't care if you throw in your big toe and your ponytail! I'm telling you, if you can write like you speak, don't bother with a journal... write a *book*. After twenty years... you and Kenny, so in love... Angela, it's a story of triumph!' he exclaimed.

'A *book*? Me write... about us?' My voice faltered uncomfortably. 'What you mean, James, is – *out with it*! "Here I am everybody, I've got something to tell you." Oh, no!' I squirmed at the idea. 'For one thing I can't spell...' I began.

'Rubbish!'

I burst into tears, although it had nothing to do with his comment. I hadn't planned to cry – it was the last thing on my mind, an image of insipid weakness, but I couldn't help it. The tears spilled as I thrust my head into my hands. If he just understood the *dimensions*, the *complexity*. Now, while sorrow over Kenny's health circled my throat like fingers, I admitted how helpless was my love for him and also how incalculable was my need to be with him. I was squirrelling away, storing up this love of ours for the wistful moments of my middle-age.

I felt his hand reach out to touch me.

'Kenny is much loved, a wonderful man, and you captured his heart. You seem to me to be unchanged, the same girl...'

'Scatty...' I began.

'An enigma,' he replied.

I muttered something knowingly unintelligible. We were silent for a moment. Finally I said, as casually as I was able, 'James... it would not be easy for me to tell about... all this,' trying to round up my thoughts, 'I don't want to harp on about how wonderful it is for us here... it's been unmitigating hell too... that sounds like a contradiction, doesn't it? But we're, honestly, so happy – Kenny's beautiful to be with. Christ, if only he wasn't so bloody *ill.*'

It helped a little to tell him. My account was vague and loose. I skimmed over the details. I felt my stomach muscles relax.

They say life begins at forty. But for me it was thirty-eight and it began the most anxiety-filled years of all. My relationship with Kenny was complete. Extraordinary. It was indeed a marriage. We were bonded together in a world of more or less total withdrawal from normal everyday life, which was not at all as dispiriting as it might seem. To have so much time for each other was sheer bliss.

Kenny was suffering from an exceedingly rare form of Parkinson's disease which can in a few cases, such as his, do everything except kill you. 'A living death, isn't it darling,' he'd said. The specialist had also diagnosed atrophy of the cerebellum, which is shrinkage of the brain at the base of the skull. My life had purpose; the very best reason for being. Kenny needed me – we were in this together.

'Get that book going, Angela,' James said after a bit, 'and give me a blasted brandy!'

He waved his glass across the table, his voice tired and affectionate.

'You haven't been able to work for three years… and when did you last go out? You can't even ask friends in. Angela, you're living on your emotions… nerves. You've just told me that this morning you were lying in the bath wondering what to do with the winter.' He sighed, nearly a laugh – 'Well, here it is staring you in the face!'

'Are you serious?'

'Never been more so.'

'Actually I'd come up with the idea of trying to compile a book of famous love letters, but Kenny thought that women wouldn't want to part with them, he said, they're funny like that. Then I thought I could take a course on interior design, one I could study here at home…'

I looked vaguely at him. 'Okay James, I'll talk to Kenny. We'll think about it… it's a bit daunting.'

'It'll be a hard slog… sure to take a few months.'

'We have months.'

I kissed him and thanked him for talking to me. 'Oh Heavens, our life frozen into words… it's frightening, but I promise you I'll think about it.'

And I did.

Eyes still closed, his head woolly from rest, Kenny must have heard the bang of the front door. He came awake and, anticipating my immediate embrace, he lazily rolled his head towards me, smiling sleepily to greet me.

'Kenny love… can I talk to you?'

He spread his hands on the sheets. 'Give me a kiss first.' His mouth whispered around the edge of my ear as he smothered me in his arms. 'What's for dinner, Shrimp?' he breathed into my ear.

'*Dinner*…' I began dumbly.

'Okay, we won't talk about dinner… I'm not hungry anyway,' he said, releasing me. 'My precious pet. James stayed late – did you give him a drink?'

'*Listen* Kenny… please,' I pleaded.

9

'Sorry, what have you got to tell me?'

I sat on the edge of the bed beside him and stroked the worryingly warm, almost feverish surface of his arm, delicately skirting the blue-black bruise from a recent fall.

'You see Kenny,' I blurted and then almost started to stammer, suddenly wondering if I dared tell him that I was thinking about spending the winter trying to write a book about us. 'I just couldn't bear it if you laugh at me, Kenny, but James said…' This and that… and I feel this and that. I must have sounded extraordinary, my voice and mind like a cricket. 'What do you think, Kenny? Shall I stop sewing and start scribbling? *Tell me*, Kenny.' My love for him was so consuming, yet at the same time determined by such childlike dependence in so many ways. I constantly needed his approval, his praise – how I lapped it up. I knew I was irrational, but cureless. As he didn't reply I turned towards him and I was truly dumbfounded to see him smiling, cheerfully unbelieving. 'Kenny,' I cried, Kenny, you're *pleased*!' I was close to him, nose to nose. 'Shall I have a go, darling… will I make you proud of me?'

It wasn't his words that I'll always remember, although they brought shades of encouragement. It was his eyes, tender, with a smile that could not quite mask the ache behind the expression. I was as near to being speechless as I ever have been. 'It'll get us through the grey mornings,' I heard myself whisper.

'I'm so frightened of the winter, Shrimp… how are we going to pass the days?' I struggled for words, the lump rising in my throat; as I talked he listened, his face still handsome and sweet. Bemused, he lightly stroked my shoulder. 'Bless you, Shrimp,' he said, glowing with feeling. 'You're very reassuring… you make me feel safe.'

'Hooray,' I heard myself cry with joy, 'we've got a job!'

I'd made my decision, sudden, firm; this would be our project to get us through the winter. Therapy for me, a lifeline for us. A diversion from our despair. However, for the time being, the subject was closed. 'I'm late with the dinner,' I said as I edged out of the bedroom. 'What would you like, sausage and chips... or a nice big blonde?'

'Sausage and chips any time.' We looked at each other for a moment. 'Shrimp,' he said, 'oh Shrimp, I do love you... could I have tomato sauce with my chips?'

I began to cry a lot as I went downstairs. Oh, Kenny, oh please Kenny... oh please God make Kenny better... we've so much to be thankful for... you've taken care of us in so many ways. God... oh, please God help us now. My brain, groggy with worry, began to swim with pictures, voices, times past and the future intermixed.

There was a sweet domestic peacefulness, largely supplied by our continuing curiosity and humour, and the happiness that we knew was ours. Home together, no more looking over our shoulders and yearning. Our days passed slowly, paced with ritual meals and television evenings. Our nest of friends overwhelming us with their kindness – they wanted to help and they did. However, occasionally, fleetingly over this scene lay a dismal cloud, a presence depressing and stifling. Life had been unkind; we were absorbed in time. Time. Too much time. Too much sorrow. It was in the walls around us, holding our life, that we faced the constant overpowering reality: that this man that I loved, who had dominated my life, was slowly dying. Slipping away from me. His spectacular spirit trapped inside a body that was breaking down, bit by bit.

I was desperate for a distraction from the relentless anxiety of the disease. The warning signals had begun to glimmer. Being with Kenny was unqualified joy, but there were days when I wanted to scream and shout, my voice high-pitched and excited. I felt bewildered – if I was so happy, how could I feel so *nervous*? I'd lose my head and I'd say things, and then the heartache that comes with guilt would engulf me. Jesus, the *guilt*. I would go to our room and shed helpless tears. Kenny, confused and frightened by the sudden eruption, would sit in

11

his chair and look at me anxiously as I came downstairs. 'Are you pre-curse, darling…? Do you want a nip of brandy?' I'd go to him and put my head on his knees, he'd gently hold my head and we'd utter futile soothing sounds. I'd feel mortified and inadequate. He asked questions with his eyes.

'All I can say is I love you, I love you Kenny… I'm so sorry… forgive me… sometimes I think I'm going nuts.' My outbursts caused us both pain.

I went out shopping and bought a bunch of felt pens and a vast wad of plain white paper. Closing the front door to our tiny hall, I reached for the light switches, click, click, aware again of the silence of the house. Dumping my coat on the back of a chair, I called upstairs, 'Only me, darling.'

'Shrimp, you were quick, how did you get on love?' came Kenny's reply. Our old hellos. I hurried straight upstairs to our bedroom clutching my shopping, past the pretty tables holding our silver photograph frames, bowls of flowers, drinks on the Victorian pub table, the fire glowing, copper and brass gleaming… our pictures and books all around us. We're lucky to have such a lovely home, I thought.

'How's my boy, then?' Looking at him I didn't need to ask. I slid my shopping on to the sofa and hurried into the bathroom to get a hot flannel and a towel. 'Another bloody sweat, darling?' I asked with forced brightness. My tone of voice and pursed mouth must have betrayed my anxiety.

'Don't worry about me, Shrimp, there's nothing to be done. He'd been sleeping and was flushed. I dried him down, plumped his pillows and planted a kiss on his shiny forehead. He pulled at my hand and kissed it. 'I feel bloody, darling, but I'm better now you're home. Enough about me, I'm boring… what have you got to show me… is that a new book?'

I motioned with my hand for him to move his legs and make room for me to sit beside him. With difficulty he changed his position in the bed. 'Yes… *sexy and sensational* the blurb said… great one for you I thought… and some chocolate and magazines.' I spilled them from the bags on to his lap; his hand shook slightly as he flipped through the book. 'All for you, darling.'

He almost sighed and waved his hands towards me. 'You spoil me... what did you buy for you?'

I laughed and held his knee. 'This stuff, Kenny. What audacity... me write a book! Who do I think I'm fooling... I'm not nearly grown-up enough!' We smiled happily and there was a long silent look between us. I started to count the pens. 'Seven – wow, darling, I've got all the props, but where do I start – middle, beginning, end?'

'Well, Shrimp,' he said reaching out for my hand, 'what sort of book do you want to write?' I sat quietly, my face a blank. 'Do you want to write about your childhood?' he asked.

'Yes.' I looked at him with slight surprise, thinking, Golly, I haven't thought about all that. It's only a game isn't it – he's really taking this seriously.

'About finding your feet as an actress?'

'Yes.'

'About us meeting and falling in love?'

'Yes.'

'Our life together, the good and the bad bits?'

'Yes.'

'About the illness, and how it is for us now?'

'Yes.' .

'A book about all that?'

'Yes, yes, Kenny,' I said, 'all that!' I was surprised at the cheek of it.

'Will you want it published now... or later?'

'*Now*, now, darling! While it's so wonderful... with you here with me, looking over my shoulder.'

'Good, *good*. That's the spirit, Shrimp!' He punched his clenched fist into the palm of his hand. 'Go for it, darling... *Go for it!*' Grabbing at my arm he squeezed it tightly. 'Blimey, O'Reilly, you and I... we can't do anything by halves, it's not in our nature.' There was a pause again, we seemed happy, sure. However, my laughter was uncertain.

'*Terrific* – budding author needs a shove in the right direction. Antonia Fraser I'm certainly not! Will you help me with the lead-in, Kenny?'

Silent for a moment, thinking, scratching his head behind his left ear, then smiling his kindly smile, he said, 'Why don't you say… "There were twenty-six years and two world wars between us" – how about that?'

'Hooray, Kenny! That's it! You're wonderful!' I exclaimed out loud. Inside me my heart thumped. He's involved – I've caught his interest. '*Perfect*, darling, just the push I needed.' I shifted up the bed and buried my face in his neck. 'You're all I need… I can't be without you Kenny… tell me you know how much I love you.' My eyes welled.

'No tears, Shrimp.'

'Cor! You can talk… look at you blubbing!' We half laughed as we reached for the box of Kleenex and mopped at each other's eyes.

'Shrimp, I want this to be your book,' he said after a moment, 'it's important to me. *Your* words. You have to write what you want to write… something of yourself, not brought about by me telling you something. If you really get stuck, then come to me. But I won't criticise or correct, because then it will sound like me, not you. Do you understand what I'm trying to say, love?' he stroked my head.

'Yes, Kenny, I do… but my spelling. You will help me with my spelling, won't you?'

He ran his fingers over my face. 'I'll always be here for that… don't take that part of you to anyone else… that belongs to me.' We scrabbled for some more tissues to smother our eyes and we blew our noses a lot. I attempted to laugh and wound myself around him tighter.

'Darling, you must have, "Kenny, how do you spell…?" engraved on your heart!'

He was suddenly still; 'I've got "Shrimp" engraved on my heart, promise me you'll always remember that.' He fiddled nervously with my ear. '*Promise* me, Shrimp.' Our tears were silent. There was too much to say to say anything. Our hearts were full. It was a time of great happiness and great sadness.

Part One
Child

I set to work very quickly.

There were twenty-six years and two World Wars between us. 1940 must have been an awesome time for my parents, Peter and Marjorie McDonagh, to realise they were expecting another baby. My sister Elaine was four, and home for them was a small flat in St John's Wood. My father was exempted from military service because of a childhood accident to his left arm. They did the best they could, but it was never easy – living in London with the restrictions of war was grim. They had strong characters and would survive somehow if only to make sure their children did. Determined we shouldn't be deprived – and we never were.

I believe in guardian angels – I ought to. Mine was called Angel Botibol. One of seventeen brothers, he was a self-made millionaire. Amongst other business interests he had a chain of tobacconist shops and a restaurant, The Rose of Normandy, in Marylebone High Street in London which my father ran for him. They became friends and on learning that a new baby was expected, he made arrangements for my mother to go to an excellent nursing home in the country, a month before I was due to be born – and all bills were to be sent to him. Overwhelmed by his kindness my parents told him, 'Angel, if our baby is a girl – we want to call her Angela after you.'

So it could be said that I was born with a silver spoon in my mouth – but it was only on loan. Sadly, I was never to know him: he died when I was only a few months old. Fortunately, I have my name and think of my benefactor very fondly, whenever Mummy asks, 'Be an angel and do something for me.'

Time brings many things to my mind and I have the clearest image of a small country circus ring. The sound of the canvas vibrating in the wind; of bunting decorating the support ropes like a shaken box of confetti. Rows and rows of wooden seats filled with happy captive faces. The ringmaster announces, 'I want the prettiest little girl in the audience to come and sit on this pony and help me do the next trick.' With an 'In you go, darling', my father disentangled me from my mother's warm lap and without hesitating lifted me up and over the front rail. I was about three years old. I had to remember that afternoon. My father had dreams and I was one of them. It is because of his perseverance and encouragement and my mother's solid support that I have a story to tell at all.

My father was a tall, slim, softly spoken Irishman from Galway. He was an extreme and witty man, gentle in his ways with a personality and zest for life that made him the centre of attraction wherever he went. He had the brightest blue eyes, the most beautiful hands and he could make music with almost anything. Wherever Daddy was you'd hear music; his toes were always tapping. Daddy was an obsessive gambler and streetwise.

My mother was English, 5'2", slim and very pretty, with a reserved but determined personality. She was a Nanny and the daughter of a lady's maid. She was lively and loved to 'tea-dance', which is how she met my father. Her family came from Surrey. She was blazingly honest, conventional and an innocent. In later years Daddy often said, 'Neither of you girls can hold a candle to your mother.' She liked to hear that.

I am one of three. My sister Elaine is four years older than me and my brother John is three years younger. I cannot recall any great displays of affection towards us – no hugging and squeezing. It might have happened. I can only say it's not clearly remembered.

Our Irish grandparents died before I was born and my mother's parents were remote figures to me. Grandpa had been badly gassed in the First World War; he was a kind, bent old man. He seemed old to me then – he was about seventy. He seldom moved far away from his chair in the corner near the door in the garden room, his books and tobacco on a small wooden table beside him and a large jar of sweets. He always had a sweet for me. Grandma was a tall, handsome and disciplined woman. I remember she had beautiful table manners. She seemed almost to be shy when she ate, and would turn her head delicately away while she chewed. 'This child aims to please,' she'd tell my mother. But she never kissed me.

The first thing I can remember with any definite clarity is standing in the doorway of a two-up, two-down terraced house in Norwich, clutching the hand of my sister Elaine; our eyes full of tears as we waved Mummy and baby John goodbye. They were going back to London, Daddy and the Blitz. We had been evacuated. We were in the custody of a kindly couple, far beyond child-bearing age. It must have been difficult for them to be asked to care for two very homesick small girls. I was there for my fourth birthday. I dreamed there was a bulky parcel on the bottom of my bed. I *didn't* dream it! There it was. Crystal clear. Brown paper and string all in knots. I excitedly tore into it – pushing my fingers into a hole in the corner, only to find that inside the large box there was a smaller one. My sense of anticipation knew no limits. Is it soft – is it pretty? – Tell me! I surrendered to tears on finding a large potato. My sister, sitting with the eiderdown wrapped around her, provided comfort with 'Grown-ups can be very silly.'

The V2s came silently out of nowhere. And they rattled my mother's already fragile nervous system. Two things she was sure of. She wished keenly for her family to be together again, and she wanted us to get out of London and away from the bombing.

She recounts a few events. The bleak bungalow on the cliffs at Peacehaven, Sussex, lent to us by a friend. So damp we all had to sleep in the sitting room; the ice on the windows was two inches thick inside the windows in the bedrooms. We were snowed in and cut off. But it was shelter and peace for us and Auntie Emmy. We were lucky; fortunate by comparison with many other families. We, uncles, aunts, cousins, survived the War.

At the end of the War, Daddy found that he was in the right place at the right time. The whole of the South Coast was opening up, coming to life. He was offered the lease on a restaurant, the Palm Court in West Street, Brighton, and he grasped the opportunity with both hands. Signed on the dotted line. And then he and Mummy set about trying to raise the money. Frantically racking their brains. They needed *everything*. China, kitchen equipment, tables and chairs: the lists were long. They wrote letters to long-lost distant relatives, to people here and there, people they hadn't seen in donkeys' years. Their courage and stamina, however, couldn't be borrowed, that was an integral part of them. They had a sort of genius for making something out of nothing.

I don't want to give us false status, but the Palm Court in West Street proved, in my mother's words, to be a gold mine. It would be no demented fantasy on my part to say that our family, at this time, appeared stable and solid. Not wealthy, but we had all the comforts of home. Elaine and I were at boarding school – St Martha's in Rottingdean, a village a few miles along the coast – and there was a Nanny for John. It wasn't just good fortune; they had to work so hard for everything they achieved. Their resolution was to survive. They were a determined, adventurous, spirited and gregarious couple.

'Peter, we'll have to send Angela as well. There mustn't be any cause for jealousy between the girls.'

A remark often repeated in answer to the question: 'Mummy, how did you ever come to send me away to school when I was only four?'

'Four and a quarter.' She said the words quickly.

'*Tell me*, Mummy.'

'You know very well the reasons – the pressure and strain your father and I were under – we had no *choice*.'

Better pack the subject in. We'll only get nervy.

Occasionally I'll look at the four-year-old children of my friends and wonder how on earth anything as tender and in need of Mum and Dad could be sent away to school. That was how it was. Perhaps my parents couldn't allow themselves the luxury of guilt.

However, being the baby of the school had distinct advantages in some ways. I was hopelessly spoilt – I suppose I brought out the latent maternal instinct that was in some of the nuns. It became obvious, quite early on, that I wasn't going to shine academically.

'Angela, where was the Magna Carta signed?'

'At the bottom, Sister.'

'Angela, you are late for your botany class!'

'Oooh! – aren't you rude!' I got fifty lines for that. Drat.

Maths? I never got to call it that – I didn't get beyond the 'sums' stage! The usual response to my desperate attempts to keep up with the class were greeted with: 'Angela, you just run along and help Sister St Gerard in the garden.'

Yes – please! Anything to wriggle out of 'sums' – or spelling – or French. As a consequence I was completely hopeless. I was perpetually willing to please; trying to impress; trying to compensate.

'I'll do the ink wells –'

'I'll clear up the mess someone's made in the loo –'

'Oh – Mary's been sick! – let *me* wipe it up.'

Elocution was high on the list of priorities. I was entered for most of the local Sussex competitions, wearing my neat little dress made from black-out material, and won enough to make my parents proud of me. Elaine and I both had pretty singing voices and were usually chosen to 'star' in the end-of-term shows. How many times did I have to sing *Mother Machree* – my father cried every time.

The bedroom at St Martha's looked down on to the small playground. When the bell rang in the morning for milk and playtime, I'd start to feel hot and sweat would trickle down my arms and leave tell-tale stains on my shirt. Was I the only girl in the school who wet her bed? Mine seemed to be the sole mattress to be found almost permanently hanging out of the window to air. I was laughed at and taunted. Accused of picking too many dandelions. Playtime was torture.

We had to queue up each morning to go to the loo. A nun would stand outside the door and issue each girl with one small square of thin shiny paper, and instruct us to 'Be quick – be quick.'

'Sister, I can't go with you standing outside the door!'

The roots were formed for a complex that was to remain with me until the present day. We were spanked with the back of a hairbrush for bed-wetting, and we were spanked if it was discovered that we were still wearing our vests under our nighties. I was spanked quite a few times, so out of necessity I became devious, careful not to get caught.

Post-war life was austere. Food rationing was very much in existence though we were more fortunate than most, because our parents were able to provide extra food from their restaurants – but I'd still steal my sister's sweet coupons. Eggs had to be supplied by your family and each egg marked with your name. There might be one orange and one banana a week, if you were lucky. I remember the horror of grey mashed potato with hard lumps – and the fun we had scooping it into our hands, moulding it into firm hard balls and surreptitiously throwing it under and along the table, aimed at an unsuspecting leg. And was she for it if she showed the slightest reaction – to be cool was a lesson learnt early. Any girl found with her elbow on the table had it pricked with a safety pin by one of the patrolling prefects. I can remember sitting alone in the large dining hall – my legs swinging to and fro, just staring down at the plateful of rapidly congealing glutinous macaroni cheese and thinking – nothing on earth will make me eat it. Not even the threat of having it served up again for supper.

We had church three times on Sundays – I didn't mind going. At least in church we got to sing. I'd stand at the altar and I would appear to be singing *Ave Maria* et al. A nice fresh face – eyes wide and attractive, my mouth opening and closing in time to the words. No one would know – or read my thoughts – except Jesus. Tapping with one finger on my small mother-of-pearl prayer book, I'd beat out the rhythm, the words banging around in my head:

'Put another nickel in, in the Nickelodeon

All I want is loving you

And music, music, music…' – slow the pace down now –

'A……… m… e… n.'

Jesus will forgive me. I was brought up by the guilt method.

Prior to my first Holy Communion I was drilled and grilled on the contents of the catechism. We had a practice confession with the friendly Father holding me on his lap, and we were shown how to kneel and pray at the Stations of the Cross. So many – I didn't linger. We would experiment with the little discs of paper, make believe we were receiving the Host. The paper would soak up my saliva and it would stick to the roof of my mouth. However, to touch the Host with your tongue, finger or teeth was a sin. So I would strain and try to suck it down. If I looked pensive and perhaps wistful on the big day, it wasn't because I thought I looked wonderful, which I secretly did think. Mine was the prettiest dress; Mummy had seen to that. She'd made it out of white crepe and it had a sash with little white silk roses near the knot. My veil came to my waist and my shoes were of white leather with small pearl buttons. My thoughts were preoccupied with, *Our Lord mustn't feel my teeth*. What would I do if Our Lord got stuck in my mouth? I walked, eyes downcast, to my place in the front pew. Along with four other nine-year-olds I knelt before the Priest. Our Lord didn't touch my teeth or get stuck.

Afterwards in the garden my fine feathers were admired and nice remarks were passed. We had photographs taken. I opened my eyes wide, hoping to gain attention, and I blinked.

'Stop blinking, Angela, and show your teeth when you smile.'

Yes, Daddy.

There was ice cream for pudding; Daddy had supplied it. I hope this photographer doesn't take too long, it might all be gone.

Sundays for good little Catholic girls – and I was – meant no books, except the Catechism – no games – no sewing or knitting – no radio. But Sunday was bath night! The amount of water was carefully monitored to just above the little toe. I recall a group of small girls waiting their turns. We stood in line as Sister Veronica issued each of us with a bar of soap. I watched her very carefully dip into a box and place a new creamy bar of Lux into the outstretched hands of the girls in front of me. I was next. Looking down I was horrified to see a muddy red bar in my hand – with 'Lifebuoy Toilet Soap' written on it. The tears didn't wait for an instant:

'Sister – you've given me *toilet* soap!'

The tears kept coming. My feelings were easily hurt. Nothing changes.

The uncertainty of childhood remains. It was very reassuring for me to have my sister always at hand. She showed me how to breathe and stretch myself in bed at night to get warm. And she read my mother's letters to me. Although it must have been tedious for her at times, she was expected to look after me to a certain extent. My hair was long and had to be plaited every morning, and if she was in a resentful mood, she'd wind my plaits round my neck, tug on them and tease me, saying that only babies had long hair and plaits were good for strangling you with!

Elaine was such a favourite with the nuns. And on reflection I can quite see why. She was wonderfully pretty with a small heart-shaped face, delicate tip-tilted nose and masses of very dark curly hair. A bright student, quiet and gentle. She gave no trouble at all. She won first prize every term for undressing under her dressing gown and showing the least – she was like Houdini. I suspect that what really endeared her to them was that she got religion quite badly. Well, *I* thought badly. She didn't just dream of being a nun, she had her heart set on becoming a saint! She was in charge of my pocket money, which she chose to spend on holy relics and pictures of Our Lady and Jesus. All I wanted was sweets, and the day rationing ended Daddy took us to a shop and bought us enough bars of chocolate, nut toffee, Palm toffee, bags of pear drops and bull's-eyes to fill a shoe box. We went to a playground. I'd eaten more than was decent, went on a see-saw – felt sick – fell off and cut my head open. But I came up smiling – it didn't seem to matter.

My relationship with John was fairly typical, I should imagine, of the second and third children. He was a joyous little boy, and I remember being distinctly jealous. Once he'd arrived I seemed to spend a lot of my energy saying 'Notice me! Look at me! You can kiss me if you like!' We fought like little animals; he once stuck his bicycle pump in my mouth and proceeded to pump me up! On reflection I can see I was tiresome – telling tales and being manipulative. I'd defy him to thump me – goad him on and when he lunged I'd go running to Mummy and say things like '*Mummy*! – John's hit me and you told him he mustn't because of my *bosoms*!'

'I'm so glad I'm a girl, Mummy, someone will always look after me.'

My mother's hazel eyes looked at me without sentiment – 'Stand still while I dress you, Angela, you're such a fidget.' A very familiar sentence. Yes, please, Mummy, you dress me, you do it best. When you dress me I feel comforted, secure. White linings under navy knickers. No one tucks my liberty bodice in my knickers quite like you do, and slips a sixpence in the little secret pocket. My elastic garters with their Cash's name tape neatly sewn over the join were slipped expertly over my feet and up my calves and snapped into position with a 'There – that's you dressed!'

Unwrapping my hair ribbons from the empty milk bottles they had been wound round all night, I handed them to her.

'Try doing it yourself, dear – you should be able to by now – remember two loops not one. Try to keep your eye on them and not lose them today – I'm running out of material.'

My ribbons were made from her precious satin nighties.

'Mummy, I wish you'd let me have Philomena for my Confirmation name – she was so brave. They tried to kill her fourteen times and she just wouldn't die.'

'You are the most morbid child I've ever known. I don't know who you take after… not my side of the family!'

Mummy always smelt so fresh with soap and scent. In the holidays she cooked all the things she knew I liked; tidied my clothes and talked to me. Nobody would ever love me again, I thought, like she did.

'Mummy, I want to be a Nanny, as you were, when I grow up.'

'Never! You'll have enough of washing your own babies' nappies without washing other people's!'

She seemed angry and sank back on her heels. I glanced out of the corner of my eye and saw that she was crying.

'Anyway, you dance and sing very well and seem to really enjoy it.'

I didn't know whether to pretend that I had not noticed her tears, or if I should hug her. I wanted to. 'We are not a kissing family,' she used to say. She began sniffing and dabbing at her eyes. She cleared her throat sharply as Daddy opened the door. He watched, seemingly fascinated, as Mummy

27

prepared and laid out our party outfits for that afternoon. Mine was a dark blue panne velour dress – with small mother-of-pearl buttons and neat lace collar. With that I was allowed to wear flat red shoes with cut-out toes and a charm bracelet – a present from my Auntie Phyllis. I used to put it under my pillow when I slept in case Elaine wanted to borrow it. 'Don't make a fuss, Angela – it isn't real silver' did nothing to moderate my enthusiasm for it. What's real silver, Mummy.

'Has she done any real harm to her leg, Marjorie?'

Mummy frowned and bit her lip. Daddy switched the light on with a quick click. Suddenly I was lifted up on to the bed and the sock on my left leg drawn down to reveal a new raw red scar on my calf – the result of a misjudged jump over a fence while out playing. The rusty nail sticking out at an angle, which took a large lump out of my calf, hadn't been taken into consideration.

'That's it, Marjorie, she'll never win a lovely legs competition now.'

It sounded like a chastisement. He shrugged and walked downstairs. He was right.

We had wonderfully happy family Christmases; we had everything and more.

I can look back at one special Christmas. Special because Elaine was given the fairy on top of the tree. Her joy I consciously tried to overshadow. I howled with envy. I expressed my jealousy by pulling some of the tinsel off the fairy's hair. And jumped around in a rage.

'Be *polite*, Angela! What are we sending you to that expensive school for if they can't teach you to be polite?' My sister's eyes shone when she looked at that doll – but not as bright as mine.

My childhood is a confusion. But looking back I can recall standing in the dark outside my parents' room staring down at the light from underneath the door, and listening fearfully to the sound of their raised voices. Tears streaming down my cheeks I tried to tiptoe back to bed, but Mummy must have heard me because minutes later I squirmed over to the cold side of the sheets as she got in beside me.

'Are you all right, Mummy?'

'Yes, dear, don't worry, I'm all right.'

My heart lightened and my legs stopped shaking. I need not worry now. If I twist a piece of satin around my index finger into a point, and pick at it until it makes a flick-flick-flick noise against my pillow, it helps me get to sleep quickly.

'Don't *do* that... make that noise... it gets on my nerves, Angela.'

'Sorry, Mummy.'

I still do it in times of distress when sleep is slippery.

Arguments between my parents were mostly about money. Not the making of it, but keeping it. Stories have been recounted. I make no criticism. They were opposites; he sanguine, she a defeatist. But both, thank God, incorruptible hard workers. Daddy's love of gambling shadowed their marriage and our lives.

My head is in a muddle, full of woolly ideals and half-digested information. I remember it was the end of the summer term of 1950 and we were walking to the gates of St Martha's and the waiting taxi, laden down with our cases, rackets, and all the paraphernalia one associates with the end-of-term chaos and commotion. I bounce around like a true St Trinian's horror, unable to contain my excitement. 'No more Mass – no more bed-making with hospital corners – no more lumpy potato! – why are you looking so fed up, Elaine?' She knew and I didn't that we were leaving the gates of our school for the last time. Many years later I returned with Kenneth More as my husband – to say the nuns were thrilled to meet him would be an understatement.

The shadows had lengthened over our young and seemingly bright lives. Because of Daddy's love of gambling, my childhood was scattered. We were never to know again the security of one school and its embracement. We moved around a lot over the next two or three years. I went to eight different schools. It was almost a standing joke between Kenny and me; whenever we were out driving around London and we passed a school, he'd invariably say: 'One of yours?'

We – John and I – were sitting, ears pressed up close to the speaker of the radio, thrilling to the sound of the *Dick Barton – Special Agent* introductory music. Surrounded by packing cases – suitcases – umbrellas – lamps – hoovers – cat baskets. I cuddled my adored cat, Panda, on my lap for consolation. We'd moved home again. The smell of frying first, then whiffs of cigarette coming up the stairs from the cafe below. Downstairs would be in full swing. My parents moving quickly. Sounds of closing up, securing the doors, stacking the chairs, clatter of cutlery and china – light switches clicking. Would the time go faster if I helped? Faster and faster – then we could all go off to the cinema. What was showing at the Gaumont, the Odeon? It didn't matter – anything to occupy Daddy's mind – keep it off the horses. We would spend at least three evenings a week absorbed in the scent of a darkened cinema. Mummy used to take her knitting. She'd sit in the end seat so that if she dropped a stitch or something, she could slip out to the Ladies' cloakroom. Sometimes she'd be in there for ages – 'Mummy, Mummy – you're missing all the best bits!'

'I'm coming… 28, 29, 30, drop one, slip one… won't be a minute dear.'

I'd be back in my seat leaving her standing holding her needles up to the bleak bare light bulb – still counting.

I was in love with Errol Flynn – my thirteen-year-old idea of unqualified perfection – brave, dashing, handsome – and I saw Mario Lanza in *The Great Caruso* four times. But I dropped off to sleep when it was Leslie Howard in one of his old films – *The Scarlet Pimpernel*. My mother stayed in her seat, eyes firmly on her hero. She didn't take her knitting that evening.

As we left the cinema one afternoon having just seen *Reach For the Sky*, I heard Mummy say, 'Good actor, that boy, didn't you think, Peter?'

'Tremendous... what's his name?'

'Kenneth More... wasn't it a sensitive, confident performance? I'm sure we'll see more of him,' she commented.

I recall skipping along beside them, no worries, no doubts, impatient to get home: there were hot sausage rolls for tea.

June with its varied weather, hot days, then oddly damp and cool, had been chosen for the Coronation. There was a conscious air of excitement in the area of London where we were now living. Enlarged photographs of Princess Elizabeth stared back at me from windows. She seemed to live such a fabulous existence, freed from contact with the real world, or so it seemed to me then.

I was sitting on a bus on my way to school when I first saw it. A man kissing a woman. In the seat in front of me. I was jammed in my usual seat, hemmed in by a man wearing an overcoat with white starched cuffs showing below his sleeves and a big winged collar, and a pork-pie hat. In June! He was much too engrossed in checking the contents of the small leather horseshoe-shaped purse he shook into his hand, to notice the gentle and affectionate outpourings of love being expressed so near to me. I began to indulge. I stole an occasional look at them. I'd never seen a live kiss before. Their profiles smudged into one another. Noses bumped – lips parted – teeth almost touching. 'Ooh, you're such a great kisser!' And she winked at him, turning her head. I reckoned she must have been lying. Actors in films didn't do it like that. I wanted to giggle. But I knew it wasn't because I found it funny. I was nervous and exhilarated. After about a minute, a

31

long minute, the conductor rang the bell and yelled: 'St Dominic's School.' My stop.

In the jostling crowd of children gathering in the playground waiting for the bell to go, I slipped sixpence into the hand of a classmate, and in exchange I was allowed to copy out my homework hurriedly. I sat on the ground beside the milk crates full of yesterday's bottles. A smell not easily forgotten. The sixpence had been 'borrowed' from the till in the cafe. I'd have to think up an elaborate lie for confession on Saturday. I must remember to add that sixpence to my list. Homework secured by a stolen sixpence lessened my fears for the day. I could compose myself. I intended to pay Daddy back someday all of the sixpences – I hope I did.

I was content just to stare at Robert Stacey from across the playground. He was tall with fair curly hair and shy. I had a helpless crush on him. I propped myself up against the railings and allowed myself to wonder: was he 'a great kisser?' I thought no more of kissing until I was home. 'John, John, quick – into my room. I think I know how to "French Kiss"!'

We sat down and I described every detail. And then I demonstrated. It made us laugh.

'Sweet Mary, what are you two up to? What are you doing with your brother ?'

I felt the blood rushing to my cheeks. I wouldn't tell Daddy anything. Sweet Mary, he'd said – was that a swear word? he seldom swore.

Mummy had been cleaning the mirrors in the sitting room. Her cheeks were flushed as she came into the bedroom.

'Go to your room, Angela, and stay there! French kissing, how *disgusting*!'

I was downcast and pushed my chair back against the wall. Why were they so agitated? People did it on buses. I hoped they didn't know about the other games I played with John.

We had everything other people had, only smaller. But the adjustments we had to make were many and I found some things difficult to take in my stride. I thought it such a terrible comedown. I always looked backwards when I got off the bus after school to see if any of my classmates were following me – they did sometimes, trying to find out where I lived – they'd lie in wait for me by the sweet shop. Chewing on my nightly bar of banana Palm toffee (eating in the street – *another* sin), I'd dawdle around looking at the various bus numbers, pretending mine hadn't come. Tut-tut my bus is late. One evening I let three buses go by before I was sure I was alone. I'll always remember:

'Do you live in a mansion?'

'Is your Dad rich?'

No and *no* again. My boarding school accent had to go, it didn't fit. I wanted to be like my new friends, and they called me posh. What's posh, Daddy. I soon learnt. I'd sit on top of the bus and sing. There was only one tune in my head, *Lady of Spain* – Spain – I'll go there one day. I'll marry a posh man with a posh job and have babies – lots of babies.

We were now continuously aware of money, it was too tight to mention. Mummy went to the sales on her bike. She knew the places to go. Harrods for Daddy's underwear, Selfridges and Daniel Neal's for us. Wasn't I the lucky girl to have a new swimsuit? And for only ten shillings! It was a dark colour with brighter spots on it and elasticated with a rolled cord around the neck. A group of us used to go swimming once a week. Coming to the side of the pool I pulled myself up the step ladder, and in reaching down to adjust my swimsuit – it always used to get caught in my bottom – saw to my horror that when wet it had become completely transparent! All had been revealed! Quickly, without anticipating it, I flopped back into the pool. Hopefully giving the impression that all I wanted to do was to swim and swim. I was trembling with cold by the time everyone had gone. Gathering the towel around me I could see the ridiculousness of it all. Another feeling arose in me a couple of hours afterwards. Would I have minded so much, being seen almost bare, if I'd had bosoms? I kissed the swimsuit goodbye, ten shillings or no ten shillings!

I was always divided and doubly insecure. Different things were said. Outside their door I'd listen to the raised voices. As a couple, my parents were combustible. I'd call up from a phone box outside the school in the dinner hour, with a 'borrowed' two pennies.

'Are you all right, Mummy? Do you want me home early?'

Anxiety. What could I do to help – to please.

I was, and still am, a person who takes things literally. I follow words faithfully. Today I think if I were told to turn right into the left-hand lane of a motorway, I might do it. I do not have a suspicious enough mind.

'Be an angel and give the sitting room a good hoovering for me – don't forget the corners.'

'Okay, Mum.'

She gave me that prim look.

'Okay, *Mummy*.'

I reflected with some satisfaction. I felt happy that I'd managed to collect so many cigarette ends from the ashtrays on the cafe tables and carry them upstairs in a large envelope. I was in two minds about looking for some more.

But no, I had enough, I thought. I sprinkled them all over the carpet and rubbed a few in extra hard with my foot.

'Don't worry, Mrs Badman, ash is good for the carpet.'

I'd heard Mummy say it only yesterday. The woman was making a nuisance of herself, sitting in our large armchair, which bore a cream lace antimacassar, tapping the ash from her cigarette and missing completely the ashtray which rested on the arm of the chair, attached to a piece of soft brown leather. I kept my eyes on the falling ash. How could it be *good* for a carpet – all that awful grey mess. Still, if Mummy says so.

My eyes were fixed on the Hoover lead as I unwound it and moved towards the point.

'Good heavens, I don't believe it.' She spoke through clenched teeth. Mummy was in the doorway. I saw her face pale. An incredulous expression in her eyes.

'My one good carpet. Peter, look what she's done now!'

I was silent. Determined to make a good impression, I'd only succeeded in making myself look a fool again.

The 'good girl' syndrome started early. If I was a good girl then someone would scoop me up and take care of me. My life would always be all right. I didn't see the catch in it.

'Is there a theatre near here?' I heard a man ask, as he put his head round the door. London was in the grips of a pea-souper fog which pressed against the city, muffling the sounds. The fogs then were filthy, so stifling and foul-tasting that Daddy made us masks out of his best handkerchiefs. 'Good Irish linen – take a look at the edges... hand-rolled... Harrods.' The buses crawled along flush to the kerb as their conductors walked in front of them holding flares which gave the streets a creepy Victorian light.

The man had been joined by another and as I took confident strides towards them I said, 'I know, I know where the theatre is.' I loved going to the Bedford. It was just up the road. I loved being able to clap and shout, 'Behind you!'

'We've got two shows this evening and we've lost our way in this bugger of a fog.' Enthusiastically I gave them the directions. One wore a pale camel-hair coat and carried a small suitcase with small gold initials on the side. And I thought, Ooh, how *smart*.

I looked at Panda's fat smiling face. He had to work for his living here. He laid his paw affectionately on my arm. I thought how much I loved him. And how much I loved these fried egg sandwiches we had for our tea. We weren't given these at the Convent. John and I would sit at the end table waiting for Mummy and Daddy to close up.

'I saw that man again this morning, in the Nazi uniform,' I whispered to John. He continued with his sandwich, feeding bits to his cat Dusty. Wanting to think his own thoughts, he only nodded.

'I see him every morning from the bus on the way to school. He stands in the window, saluting... You won't tell anyone, will you?'

Why the caution? I suppose I found secrets thrilling. John just shook his head pretending to listen. He knew I was dramatic.

We'd put halfpennies under paper and scratch out designs. We'd melt our winegums in glasses of hot water and pretend to get tipsy. We'd make small sham wine glasses out of the silver paper from cigarette packets, wet the bottoms with our tongues and toss them at the ceiling and somehow they stayed there. We'd go into the phone booth and dial 999 – he'd put his hands round my throat and squeeze – and I'd scream into the receiver, 'Help, help, police... I'm being *murdered... Aaaagh!*' And we'd collapse in a heap of breathless excitement.

Getting into the bath after Elaine – 'Mummy – do I *have* to have her water!' I'd usually sit there and sing until the water was cold.

'Angela, you've got that *wiggle* in your voice!'

'Don't come in Daddy, don't come in!'

Rapidly flinging the flannel over my budding bosom, I quickly got up, wet feet squelching on the lino, and hid behind the door.

'I'm only your father... All right, I'm not coming in.'

He'd stand five or six steps up from the bottom of the staircase. He'd listen to me. Instruct me. Tap the rhythm out with his foot.

'That's grand.' He'd sing with me. *Underneath the Arches, Sunny Side of the Street, Smoke Gets in your Eyes.*

My rapidly disappearing boarding school accent still earned me the respect of my form mistress – it couldn't have been my academic achievement.

'Angela McDonagh, would you take the class for ten minutes.'

I swallowed the lump that had risen in my throat and managed to seat myself at the teacher's desk before a twisted piece of paper that had been dipped in ink and then flicked with a ruler went whizzing past my head. Drip, drip went the sweat under my armpits. A real revolution! Twenty-eight unruly, book-throwing, jumping and thumping twelve-year-olds! I couldn't hope to control them. I fixed my eyes on the light hanging from the ceiling. I wanted to go to the lavatory rather badly – oh why hadn't I gone when I had the chance to! On impulse I stood up and burst into 'Aah – sweet mystery of life at last I've found thee – aaah...' *à la* Gracie Fields. The silence followed by their laughter was a sensational sound. I followed it with my impression of Schnozzle Durante's 'Ink-e-dink-e-dink-e-dink-e-dink-e-dink-e-do'. That earned me a patter of applause. From then on all thoughts of work went out of my head.

'Angela's got brains, she just refuses to use them,' the mistress told my mother. 'If she thought more about her work and less about the effect she had on her classmates with her eccentricity of humour, she would be a pupil to be proud of.'

Yeah, yeah. Keep them laughing. At last I'd found a way to hold my own. I was the class joker. I was accepted. A happy half-wit – a million laughs.

Robert Stacey wasn't in my class. One day I returned to my desk to find that a neat flat box had been placed on the top next to the inkwell. The words 'From Stacey' were written on the lid. It was a pen and pencil set. My heart leapt with excitement. I hurried home at the end of the day and ran upstairs to show Mummy.

'Look, Mummy, look!' – from my satchel I took the box and placed it on the table for all to see. She inspected it quizzically.

'You'll have to give it back, Angela.'

Why did she say that? I wrung my hands and put on a close-lipped look of martyrdom which usually worked. But according to my mother, unless it was 'Birthday or Christmas' we couldn't accept presents.

'You must give it back to him tomorrow. Explain. Say "thank you," but no.'

'I can't, I can't, I can't,' I said.

'I've told you, there's no such word as *can't*.'

That night I lay awake for what seemed a long time. Next day I went in search of him. I felt awkward standing outside his class. In hardly more than a whisper, I managed some sort of explanation. I was embarrassed, upset and clumsy. The bell had gone – I had to run. I pushed the box into his hand. I remember not being able to look him in the face. He was a boy. I wasn't at ease with boys. It was the nearest we ever were.

I was taught to say no to everything. Or rather, no *thank you*. Quick to reply 'No thanks' to a bottle of Tizer, a Wimpy. Later on I made a great pretence of refusing a lift when faced with the prospect of a long walk home. No to having my bus fare paid. No to a party. No to a kiss – *No, No, No!* – *Thank* you. I uttered some of those no's too hastily.

Today I can bring myself to say 'Yes, please,' when I mean it. Inside me I still hedge a bit, feel the guilt. I much prefer to be the giver.

However tough things were, the standards my parents set never dropped. The tight rein they held on us was continuous. Where did the vigorous energy they directed towards us come from?

'Elaine, your slip is dangling a quarter of an inch.'

'Angela, sit properly – put your knees together, you're a big girl now.'

'John, leave some food on the side of your plate for Mr Manners.' John used to love licking his plate when no one was looking.

We had to be gloved, overcoated and correct whenever we went out. Tidy. We were forbidden to eat anything in the streets, even an ice cream. Chewing gum wasn't allowed, ever. We leapt to our feet when an adult entered the room, almost standing to attention. When we returned from a treat – the park, a circus, the seaside, a visit to the Bedford Theatre – Mummy would whisper, 'Don't forget to thank your father for taking you.'

Thank you, Daddy.

She had been a Nanny. Never to be forgotten. We were brought up in a very hard school. I was taught self-respect at an early age. I've seldom regretted the discipline imposed. On the contrary. There have many times when their demands made me feel loved and secure. They made me feel special to them.

We were on the move again, and Mummy had told me I mustn't ask questions. Mustn't mind the discomfort, the insecurity, the strangeness. Mustn't mind having to say goodbye to Panda and Dusty. *Mustn't mind*? My first touchable loss. I wondered what Panda would think of me leaving him. How did he feel? Who'd look after him and groom his coat? I didn't know.

We had the most wonderful surrogate granny in our Auntie Emmy. She was our great aunt – my grandfather's sister. I remember her as being timid, petite and silver-haired. And very kind. She'd taken Elaine and I into her home which was a small terraced house in Clapham. When I think of Eccles Road I think of the warm kitchen, neat and shiny as a pin, facing on to a tiny yard and the backs of other houses. The backyard always seemed to be in shadow.

Auntie Emmy perpetually bustled. I can see her standing by the table with its freshly laundered cloth, her tin Coronation tea caddy in front of her. She'd open a packet of tea and pour it in. Then carefully remove the thin paper lining from the packet and tap any loose leaves of the precious tea that might have escaped into the palm of her hand, and then brush them gently into the caddy. Not a leaf wasted. She produced wonderful cakes and stews from the old kitchen range which we all gathered round. I've never seen anyone but she hold a loaf of bread on its end and carefully butter it before cutting a slice. I do it that way – and remember her. We did not have to use gas for making toast as there was the open fire of the range. And at night the glow from the fire took the place of electric light. Economy was practised for its own sake.

Daddy picked up his copy of the *Evening Standard*, yawned some more and rubbed his fingertip around the rim of his stiff collar. He folded the paper in half and then in half again, moving off the bed to get closer to the reading lamp.

My brother sprawled on the floor having a pretence war with his toy soldiers, making mock-bombing noises. Mummy was sitting in one of the two armchairs knitting, trying to salvage the yellow waistcoat she was making for my father. She seemed to pay no attention to the fact that the previous night he'd almost torn it in two during a Celtic rage about something or other. She was preoccupied, her lips moving ever so little as she counted the estranged stitches.

With the money from the sale of the business they had agreed to buy the leases on two flatlet houses in London. One in Bayswater and one near Marble Arch. The temporary lull, while waiting for the completion of contracts, was a strain. Even with Elaine and me staying with Auntie Emmy, two adults and a child living in a small furnished flat in an old-fashioned house in Streatham was also a strain. My father needed a diversion. It came from an unexpected source – the *Evening Standard*.

'Mammy' – his manner eager, his face alight as he sat bolt upright – 'come and tell me what you think of this... I've got a hunch.'

Engrossed in her knitting, she continued to count stitches as she crossed over trailing her ball of wool with her, and sat beside my father on the bed. Holding the newspaper under the light, he quickly read to her one of the adverts in the classified section.

'Wanted, bright, well-spoken teenagers with personality for stage and TV work. Valerie Glynne, Dryden Chambers, Oxford Street, W1. Tel. no... What do you think...? For Angela.'

He didn't wait for her answer. With a squeeze of her knee, he was off to the phone box to make an appointment. He was on a cloud. Checking the paper again for the number and getting the right money together for the phone. 'She could be my last chance, Mammy.'

'What, *doughnut*?' shrieked my brother. Har – har – har!'

So while I, aged thirteen, was still talking and dreaming of being a Nanny, my father had already made up his mind that wasn't what he wanted for me, and the following morning Daddy and I hurriedly made our way through the crowd to Oxford Circus and along towards Tottenham Court Road. I don't remember the time of year, but the sun was bright in my eyes as I followed in Daddy's long strides. Dodging buses and taxis and people. We had the address on a scrap of paper. There was a newspaper kiosk just in the entrance to the courtyard, and down the side there was a varnished wooden board with the names and numbers of each apartment painted in discreet gold lettering.

Valerie Glynne was small, vivacious and dark-haired. Her eyebrows were pencilled in and her mouth wore bright lipstick. We sat in a room marked 'Private', on a low sofa and looked at all the framed photographs which lined the walls, inhabitants of another world, self-assured and sleek – I wished that I was self-assured and sleek.

As she chatted, she twisted a cigarette holder between her fingers. She asked me to read a scene from a play with her – *The Good Companions* by J. B. Priestley. I read, trying very hard to sound well-bred.

'Are you sure you want Angela to be an actress, Mr McDonagh?'

'Quite sure,' he replied with courage. He really was *quite sure* now. Optimism had brushed aside all hesitation.

Are you stage-struck, Mr McDonagh?'

'Oh yes.' Out to impress. 'And so is my daughter.'

What's stage-struck, Daddy.

She pointed to my tummy.

'Well, then, we'll have to do something about that puppy fat of hers.'

It was just not to be believed. But the fact had to be faced that between negotiating the contracts for the two flatlet houses and signing on the dotted line, Daddy had managed to gamble away half our precious savings. They could now only afford the lease on one property, not two. As a result, No. 15 Upper Berkeley Street, W1, became our home. A once beautiful house, it had seen better days. However, fine cornices, fireplaces and elegant mahogany doors with original fittings remained. It was now divided into flats which my parents intended to let. That was twenty-eight years ago and I'm trying to pin down the images.

My parent's greatest asset was their ability to get on with it. The first few nights we all slept in one big room, beds in all four corners, trunks and packing cases and furniture piled high in the middle. For a while we slept and lived with the smell of fresh paint as Mummy and Daddy spruced up the house from top to bottom. Wallpaper was hung, floors were scrubbed, curtains were made. Elaine was seventeen, I was thirteen and John was ten.

Four rooms, bathroom and kitchen. Five of us living so closely with little room for privacy, and tempers were quite often lost. Arguments about the rights and wrongs of what they were doing. But, as a family, we had humour and I quite liked the crowding – it made me feel safe. Life at home centred on the kitchen. The ironing board was almost always up and the TV almost always on. The budgerigar lived in her cage on top of the television and Happy the hamster and her babies lived underneath. Cuthbert, the injured pigeon rescued by John from Hyde Park, lived behind the door, staying for nearly two years. And then there was Lady the black poodle.

I was young for my age and hadn't yet become aware that I was overweight, or, if I was aware, it hadn't yet become a problem. I had the face of a child, clear and happy. I certainly looked uncomplicated enough, but soon I was cleaning my teeth four times a day, shadowed by the horror of uncleanliness. Still now, whenever I'm unhappy, the first thing I'll do is clean my teeth.

We grew up in a madhouse! Hounded with, have you done this – have you done that – don't lisp – don't gape – sit up straight – get out of that bed – don't answer back – take that look off your face – go outside the door when you blow your nose – don't talk with your mouth full – stop squeezing that spot – turn that record player down – aren't you ever going to bed.

There were twice-weekly play-reading sessions for a small group of us held in Miss Glynne's apartment. We'd read drama or recite pieces that had been set for us to learn. I remember that sometimes Anne, Gillian, Luanne, Tony and I used to go together from a one-room school in Ealing. It was affiliated in some way with Valerie Glynne's Agency. It was a spacious room with several windows which can't have been opened often. The air in the room seemed stale. There were a couple of large leather sofas with flowered cushions to match the curtains. And several rugs covering the worn patches in the carpet that covered the floor. The three tables were big and we sat around them on an assortment of different chairs; surrounded by volumes of textbooks, reference books, school books, books of verse, algebra, French and spelling. The occasional well-thumbed book on the 'art of make-up for the theatre' didn't seem out of place, nor the out-of-date copies of *Spotlight*.

The lady who presided over us looked more like a dealer in books than a teacher, but nevertheless she took all the subjects herself. There didn't seem to be any set pattern for the lessons. Almost haphazard. And relaxed. To say the least, she was a sizeable lady. A shapeless shape. Her wispy grey hair drawn loosely back into a bun at the nape of her neck. She dressed in mauvish soft dresses with drapey sleeves and lace at the neck and light shawls around her shoulders that kept slipping. Her plump feet squeezed into little black button shoes. There would be a great show of work, our young heads bent, eyes only a few inches away from the text and a flurry of books handed around – 'I haven't copied that bit yet!' – when the education inspector from the Council was due to visit, as he did periodically to see that our work was up to scratch.

Luanne's family were well off, I thought. She was very tall for her age. Blonde, pretty, vivacious and extremely confident. She came top of the class in almost every subject. I was so envious of her – I almost hated her. I don't think she ever guessed. I used to run around after her, trying to please or impress, currying favour. She said, 'Mummy reads *The Times*.' And Luanne was voluptuous.

Gillian was absolutely beautiful. Short, naturally blonde hair and a gentle, sleepy face. She could have been Kim Novak's younger sister. She was quiet and blushed easily. 'I've come on,' she confided in me. She was becoming voluptuous.

Anne seemed insecure and didn't mind talking about it. 'I'm so dweadfully depwessed' – and cruelly we laughed at the way she spoke. What's depressed, Mummy. She was indulged by her mother, a large, dominant, formidable but kind woman. Anne had lovely legs and a wonderful figure. Voluptuous.

Me? I had a good look in the mirror, my breasts scarcely formed. When would they *show*?

I could do better, I *could*.

'Thankew dear,' came the voice of the director from out of the dim subterranean grotto of the auditorium. The shaking in my legs started as I walked towards the wings. My auditions took very little time. Mass auditions for Tennent's. For movies. For 'B' movies. Commercials for the cinema, and TV plays. I was either too young, too old, too short, too tall, too fat or not quite fat enough.

There were fifteen of us in Ronnie Curtis's waiting room. He was a very popular man, known to give more work to actors than anyone else. We sat on bentwood chairs and a bench. On a small table in the centre of the room was a large tin lid filled with cigarette ends and several back copies of *The Stage*. There was an older girl sitting beside me flicking through her folder of studio stills. The floor was uncarpeted and I counted the bare boards to help pass the time and to try and keep my mind off the butterflies in my tummy. There was an office beyond, with a strip of cardboard stuck on to the door which read *Private*. The rooms were linked by a hatch with a sliding glass window. Mr Curtis put his head through the hatchway.

'Sorry about the delay, loves.'

He looked in my direction. 'What's your name, dear?'

Was he talking to me or the girl by my side? He had a 'lazy' eye and I couldn't be sure.

'Angela McDonagh,' I said rather too loudly.

He looked down at the piece of paper he was holding.

'There must be some mistake… I can't find your name on my list,' he smiled; 'can you see yourself out? Now who's next?'

I descended the stairs with speed. My cheeks were smarting. That's a new one. Not even on the blinking list! I arrived home depressed and locked myself in the loo. Such prompt, immediate rejection hurts.

Having washed my hands and cleaned my teeth, I picked up a stub of pencil from the toffee tin near the telephone and searched for a space on the note pad.

'Dear Mummy, home early to change for an audition. Commercial for soap powder. Fingers X. Got my bus fare. Love A. x'

Lots of us stood in a straight line in a large dingy gym. The director and his assistant looked us over and talked to a few. He talked to me – I can't recall now what about except he turned me around with a 'Look left, look right.' And, 'You've got a very pretty smile.' He asked me to leave my name and address and agent's telephone number with his secretary who was sitting at a table with one arm full of envelopes and her chin nursing a telephone to her neck like a fiddle. I went straight home and the kitchen was a-buzz. Miss Glynne had called. I don't know how it happened but they had chosen me.

Mummy was not one to show great excitement, bounce up and down. But you could see she was delighted. Daddy was laughing; then I began. John and Elaine joined in. Once we'd started we almost forgot how to stop. Daddy allowed himself to get quite carried away. 'We're winning, Mammy, we're winning!'

Miss Glynne talked to my father about the contract and advised him 'not to tell Angela how much she's earning. It's best the children don't know… They'd only discuss it amongst themselves and make comparisons, and that could lead to jealousy… We don't want that, do we?'

He trusted her completely. I wondered whether my fee for the day's filming covered the cost of the new dress Mummy bought me for the occasion. It was cotton and sleeveless with a blue and white diamond design. The skirt was full and had little clowns standing in spotlights. Most appropriate, she thought. The call came through, I had to be in Sudbury at 7.30 a.m. A car was sent for me. Pulling dressing gowns around them, Daddy and Mummy waved me off.

'Don't forget to show your teeth when you smile.'

Oh, Daddy, I wish I had a penny for every time you've told me that. But I tried to look suitably grateful for his advice. It was a clear crisp morning, and as the car sped towards the location, I read and reread my lines. I thought Omo was such a strange name for a washing powder. But I didn't care very much what they called it. I felt terrific and peered out of the window. Hey, I'm an *actress*. Why isn't everyone looking at me!

My mother never mentioned sex. The girl next to me in the playground at school had whispered to me one day that she'd heard you had to be with a boy to have a baby. I replied fiercely that it was 'a dirty lie', and ran off quickly so she couldn't catch me up. I swished my plaits over my shoulder and snatched at my socks which had slipped down to my ankles. I stood quite still for ages. I was dazed. It couldn't be true. Not Mummy and Daddy. I knew boys had winkies, but surely girls couldn't be expected to look at one, *touch one*! *Filth*! It just had to be a lie. And a lie was a sin.

I used to blush and my pulse would quicken whenever I got to the written word *breast*. It made me squirm. And I'd read it over and over again. But I couldn't say the word out loud. When we sang hymns in church, and it came to 'Our Lady, Mother of God, on whose sweet breast...' Oh golly! I'd keep my gaze lowered and my lips tightly closed. I'd be embarrassed. And I didn't know why.

I'd listen to the raw quick bursts of laughter from Mummy and Auntie Phyllis as they categorised men: drunks – gamblers – womanisers.

Mummy's version of the facts of life only went as far as periods, which meant bleeding from your privates, having packets of pads hidden in the cupboard by your bed, and funny belts with large safety pins. She told me that babies grew in your tummy and how it could all be beautiful if you loved someone. But she never mentioned that men had anything to do with the process. She said that some girls were 'man mad' and you had to feel sorry for them. Periods were still two years away from me, but I did once take some pads from where Elaine kept hers. I put them in my satchel which I left open by my desk, hoping my classmates would notice and the word would get around. Partly I wanted to be thought one of them. Partly perhaps, to show off.

There was a large room to the back of the ground floor of the house. It had been divided into two, as bedrooms for John and me. A big window looked out on to the walls of the back area, and down below on the basement level Mummy had built an aviary for the budgerigars that she bred. The raucous screeching from dawn till dusk would echo up and jangle the nerves. John, in desperation for some peace, would hurl his shoes out of the window and on to the wire net roof with a 'belt up will you!' And for that momentary respite I'd have to hang on to his legs while he dangled out of the window trying to retrieve his collection of shoes.

I had to go through John's half of the room to get to mine. I pulled the door to my small haven behind me. A bed with my doll, Maureen, and Teddy on it, a little Lloyd Loom chair and table, a fitted cupboard, a hanging shelf for my collection of much loved but modest china ornaments. I had been allowed to choose the wallpaper and I'd fallen for a huge blue and white rose design. Overwhelming in a room the size of a closet. But I couldn't blame the choice on anyone else – I had been insistent.

It was always a rather cold room. I lit the oil stove and lay curled up on my bed. Retrieving my satin flick rag from under the pillow, I coiled it round my finger and started to flick, flick against my cheek. Fourteen and still sucking my thumb. I looked down at my thumbs and compared them. My 'sucked' thumb was broad and white with a small red lump on it from where my teeth dug in. 'I'll lay even money that you'll still be sucking your thumb on your wedding day!' Daddy was right – I was, and still am.

I had a lot to occupy my mind. Yesterday we had been to the coast. Daddy had heard that for ten shillings you could cut a record in a booth on the pier. For days before he had put me through my paces. I found my self-consciouness difficult to overcome and refused to sing if he were in the room.

'I can do it when you're not watching me, Daddy!'

I practised in the sitting room. I'd stand and face the closed door and Daddy would stand on the other side and listen to me.

'Not bad, not bad at all.'

'I can't make that note, Daddy.'

'You took your breath too early, and the words weren't clear.'

'Only you… can make the wo–orl–d seem right…

Only yoooo–uuu…'

'You see, you can do it when you try.'

Then there pierced into my mind the scene with Daddy straight-faced directing me through the keyhole and me singing my heart out to a closed door! I felt an unbelievable fool and giggled a lot.

We decided that the 'A' side of our record would be *Only You* and the 'B' side, *Underneath the Arches*. We sang together in some sort of harmony and emerged capsizing with laughter! It was so *awful* – it was almost wonderful.

I treasured that little record for years, but sadly it was lost along with other sentimentally valuable possessions in our last house move.

I stretched out and reached for a pair of nylon pants and tossed them on to the top of the oil stove to warm. Sizzle. Sizzle. They disintegrated before my eyes. I smiled that I could be so stupid. I looked in vain for another pair. All in the wash. Oh, well I'll have to make them last another day. Footsteps were heard on the stairs. I finished dressing and left the room. I looked over the banisters, and saw that Mummy was coming up carrying the baby in her arms. One of our neighbours had been married to an Indian and she had a beautiful little boy of about ten months old. And I was trusted to take him to Hyde Park in his pram. Strapping him in, Mummy shot me an anxious glance and reminded me to 'only cross the road on the crossings.'

Outside in the street I briskly pushed the pram, and in just holding the handle I began to feel the part. My back straightened. My head got higher. *My baby*. He was black and I was white. A fourteen-year-old with plaits, short socks, sandals and freckles. It was quite a long walk to the Serpentine. Since it was a weekday the park seemed almost deserted. I sat myself down on a bench beside two women – their heads close in whispered conversation. And I waited. I rocked the pram, coo-cooed and tut-tutted. The women ceased to talk. They had started to watch me. I could feel it.

'Lovely baby.' Her companion nodded in agreement.

'Ow, thankew sew much… isn't he the cutest thaing? He's ma furst baby an' ahm sew *threeled* with hym… he's the image of ma husband.'

The women sort of shifted on their bottoms and exchanged wide-eyed looks. Then they carefully focused on me. The lady sitting nearest to me pursed her lips and leant forward moving her legs apart, planting her hands firmly on her knees. I could see her knickers.

She said rather formally, '*Your* baby? A *husband*? But you're so young!'

'Ah,' I pronounced. 'Ah, yes, wheel ya see, ahm from Tennessee.' I paused for maximum effect. 'The United States, you know… we mayrrie verry early baack home.' In the silence of utter astonishment that followed I smiled and said, 'Ma little one's goin' to need feedin'… ah think bottle feedin' sew bad, don't yew?' And pulled my cardigan close together across my chest for emphasis. 'Goodbye, y'all,' I said without looking back.

I delivered the baby boy back safely to his mother.

'Thank you, you are an angel to take him out. Perhaps you'd like to come back later and give him his bath, and if...'

I cut her short with, 'So sorry I can't... homework to do.' I put out my hand and patted the baby's head and hurried off. *Bath* him! Oh golly – no. I'd have to look at his *winkie*.

As the young mother said, help yourself to anything you want in the fridge and we won't be late, I replied coolly: 'That's okay, thank you... Hope you have a nice time'; but it was only with immense difficulty that I kept from grinning crazily at how perfectly I was playing the role of my dream, to be a Nanny. Only this was much better than my dream. The apartment of this American couple was vast and more luxuriously furnished than I'd ever seen. The air smelt sweet with all the lovely summer flowers. The mother in her chic dress was more beautiful than the aristocratic English woman of Knightsbridge whom I'd seen striding through Harrods, three paces in front of Nanny and pram. This was solid, unimagined, with two solid unimagined children in their cots for me to sit with all evening.

I went into the nursery to check on them. And to kiss them. I hovered around them, a little boy of about two and a half and a five-month-old baby girl. One more kiss, I decided, bending over the cot, just one more and perhaps she'll wake up and need a cuddle. In a hushed, childish little way I said, 'He–llo baby, he–llo pretty baby.' She didn't wake up. But her brother did! He pulled himself up in his bed, and on seeing me, he opened his mouth and wailed, '*Mommy*' as his tears started to flow. I threw some words of reassurance and endearment to him and hurriedly scooped him up in my arms. He wanted none of it: 'Mommy, my Mommy,' he cried.

Oh *blimey*. 'Here, darling... suck your thumb.'

He was getting ready to be hysterical. I took his blubbering, drooling face and kissed him and squeezed him tight. He pelted me in the eye with his fist and gave me a header on my nose as he lapsed into sobs. I prayed, *shush* – don't wake baby, please... too late! I left him jumping up and down shrieking and hurried to the small baby. My nervous system was by this time flickering with alarm. All sorts of squalling boohoos emitted from the nursery as I ran to the telephone tensed up. I needed my 'Mommy'.

'They just woke up, Mummy' – that was a lie. 'They're both screaming and I don't know what to do!' That wasn't.

Mummy said not to panic and to make a bottle of sugar water for the baby, and that the little boy would probably be calmed down if *I* did. And that no catastrophe could happen so long as I made sure he didn't go near any plug sockets or fall down the lavatory. 'Just don't leave them unattended!'

I propped the baby up on some silk cushions with a bottle of warm sugar water and then stood in front of the boy and hitched my dress up and down to get his attention, in a desperate endeavour to break into his unhappiness. 'Hello, hello,' I called to him, bending over and speaking between my legs. I stuck my tongue out and rolled it round making clucking noises. I stayed like that offering him chocolate and toys until I felt as though I was going to conk out. All of a sudden his little face fell into a smile and he joined in with the game.

I tucked some tissues into the neck of his pyjamas and fed him what he asked for, 'chocolate and 'nanas,' and when he said he wanted to go 'number two', I groaned inside, perching him on his potty with his toys around him. I faced the baby, asleep by now with the bottle, like a dummy, in her mouth. So sweet. I looked at the little tufts of fair hair on her head. It looked matted, spikey. I touched her, *lightly* this time. *Stiff!* So was her nightie. All sticky and rigid. I blinked at the empty bottle; the sugar water had run out of the top – I hadn't screwed it on properly! – all down the baby and on to the cushions. The small boy was by now slinging his toys all over the room.

Chaos. The door latch went. Mr and Mrs Beautiful America had timed it perfectly. I heard her say, what an angel I was and... for-heaven's-sake-what-*had*-we been up to! She hurried over to her son and in a sham scolding tone she drew her eyebrows together in a waspish frown, saying, 'And what have *you* been eating?' I quaked as she moved towards the baby. I heard her suck in air between her teeth.

It was all settled. I smiled – over-smiled when I was handed my ten shilling fee. I hung my head and tried not to take it, but she was insistent, tight-lipped and polite, pressing it into my hand as she hurried me through the door. I was red with embarrassment and sick with nerves. I couldn't remember getting to the bus stop, but I could remember wanting to get away from Swiss Cottage as quickly as possible. Wow – what a night!

The atmosphere at home was always stimulating. A good day for my father meant he'd hit a streak of luck with the horses. Whenever I worked or went for an audition he'd say, 'Be lucky.' And sometimes *he* was.

I remember one evening he came into the sitting room and his pockets were bulging, pulling his trousers out of shape. He'd only allow his trousers to be out of shape for large, white, tissue-thin five pound notes! He had to lift his pockets up and inwards to sit in his chair, there really wasn't enough room for him *and* his pockets! John and I were on the rug in front of the fire playing draughts. I sat cross-legged at Daddy's feet, my chin cupped in my hand, wearing a fascinated expression on my face as he pulled out the precious bundles, and just dropped them on to the rug. Rolled up and captured in their rubber bands. Daddy seemed tired, put his head back and closed his eyes, and then quickly lent forward picking up the nearest bundle, took aim at the fire and – whoosh! It missed the hot coals by about two inches.

'There, who needs money?' *Whoosh* went another lot.

'Pass me that one – I won't miss next time.'

A chorus of, Oh, Daddy, don't – Oh, Daddy don't tease – Oh, Mummy come and see what Daddy's doing – brought my mother rushing in to the room with 'Daddy, are you touched?'

'Whatever you say, dear.' He pulled at his collar, leant back and looked at the ceiling. We were then all smiles.

I caught sight of myself in the jewellery shop window, and preened. I smoothed my hair with the flat of my hand, and then rubbed my hands down the sides of my dress. Tightening the belt to grip my waist, hoping to make it appear smaller. I went into the shop wearing my most serious expression. It was like an Aladdin's cave. I gave the male assistant a half smile.

'Can I help you?' said he.

'Erm, yes please. You – er – have some very pretty – um – er – engagement rings on – em – tray 27 in your window. Could I see them?' Very debonair.

At close quarters the velvet tray came to life. The twinkle. The shimmer. The sparkle. The *romance.* I looked at the assistant and pointed to a small single diamond.

'I'd like to try this one… and perhaps that one.' I'd spotted a sapphire and diamond hoop.

No response from the other side of the counter, save a sigh. I'd already passed *two* jewellers' shops. It had taken real courage on my part to get this far. I couldn't move. Then with great reluctance the younger man took the rings from their little slots and placed them on a plush mat in front of me.

'Certainly. Would Miss like a chair?' Hooray! He was playing the game.

I pushed the little diamond on to my engagement finger and, noticing the ink stains all down the side of my forefinger, I curled it inwards and held it tight against my thumb. I felt a deep thrill and while appearing to examine the ring, holding my hand in front of me and slightly up, I was imagining, picturing, getting engaged.

I went outside with a 'Good afternoon and thank you… I'd like to think about it,' aware that my socks were slipping down around my ankles.

Next Saturday I think I'll go to another jewellers and try on a *wedding* ring, see how that feels. I was fourteen and I can't say how many Saturday afternoons in my life were spent trying on rings, waiting until it came to my turn.

On Sundays we three would go to St James's Church in Spanish Place for Holy Communion. John used to keep the money, twopence, that he'd been given for the collection. I suppose I told on him. He says I was a terrible tell-tale. Sorry John. We would return, hoping to find Mummy in the kitchen preparing the Sunday lunch. Oh! her roast potatoes were *special*! A happy Sunday meant a delicious smell from the kitchen and *Family Favourites* blaring out from the radiogram. Daddy would stand as close to it as he possibly could. Bent down from the waist, never bending his knees for fear of creasing his trousers, his ear to the speaker. He would play his harmonica, his right foot tapping out the beats. He taught Elaine and me all the dance steps and said, 'You'll never be considered a lady unless you can waltz!'

What about rock and roll, Daddy.

Mummy was usually to be found up a ladder fixing curtains, hanging wallpaper, painting ceilings. The open cracks on her fingers and the rough dry skin on her hands were such a contrast to my father's hands, so smooth and elegant, his nails beautifully manicured by the girl at 'Moishe's', the barber shop at the top of Upper Berkeley Street. He'd go there almost every morning to have his hair done and be shaved; and of course to talk to the boys – Moishe, Dickie and Sammy – about the day's form in *The Sporting Life*. Sometimes he'd blend some warm olive oil and sugar in a bowl and he'd gently massage my mother's hands. 'Oh,' he'd say softly, looking down at her, 'this is sure to help, Mammy.'

'You've got Daddy's hands,' she says to me with evident delight – flying at me if I go to do the washing up without my rubber gloves: 'Your *hands*, child – your *hands!*'

When my mother was seventeen she was told that in London prostitutes were known as 'birds'. So on a day trip to London she walked up Regent Street and looked for women wearing feathers in their hats! When she was forty-four she put a notice on the iron gate leading down the steps to the basement. 'For Sale. Young cocks, various colours. Finger tame £2. Tel. No. Ambassador 0528.'

Daddy and John thought it a huge joke and purposely didn't point out to her that if she wanted to sell her young budgerigars, she could perhaps phrase it a little more delicately. John answered the phone the first time it rang; he listened for a second, then holding the phone in the air he called, 'It's for you, Mum.' She eagerly reached for the receiver, 'Hello, can I help you! Excuse me what di…' – her voice trailed off. She looked up in surprise. The more hotly indignant she became, the more Daddy and John roared with laughter. She was livid and tore up the steps and pulled the note from the gate. But there were at least six more 'dirty' phone calls that evening. '*Men!*' she said.

H. M. Tennent were casting a new play called *Anniversary Waltz* written by Jerome Chodorov and Joseph Fields who was also directing. It was an American comedy. A fat, pert fourteen-year-old was needed and Valerie Glynne thought I fitted the description.

It was a mass audition and I arrived at the theatre and stood on the bare stage along with about thirty others. A handful of us were singled out with: you in the red jacket, forward; you, third from left, forward; you with the plaits, *me*? forward, you dear, you, and yes, you. The others were thanked for coming and we, the happy half-dozen, were asked to leave our names with the stage manager. I was recalled. I couldn't believe it. They wanted me to read for them the next afternoon.

I headed for Miss Glynne's office where she dressed me in jeans, sneakers, T-shirt, a shiny baseball jacket and peaked cap. She did a full stage make-up on my face. Panstick, pencilled-in eyebrows, carmine on my lips and pink dots in the corners of my eyes. I must have looked a fright. But it was fun to do.

With the chaperone I walked to the theatre and found the stage door. I walked quickly to the wings where the stage manager was waiting, checking off names on his list. He handed me the script and, finding myself in the midst of so many others, it was difficult to find a quiet corner to read it. I managed to glance through it twice and practised a couple of gestures which I thought might impress. I stood in the wings and watched as another girl read. I quickly moved away putting my hands over my ears. I didn't want to hear her inflections. If I listened to her I might lose the spontaneity of the written word on first reading.

Finally my name was called. A harsh light focused on the stage and my stomach felt tight with nerves. As I walked downstage, I knew that Joseph Fields, Hugh 'Binkie' Beaumont, Bernard Braden and Barbara Kelly were sitting beyond the orchestra pit in the darkened auditorium. There was a confused impression of figures, voices and cigarette smoke. I was terrified and felt ridiculous in the make-up and borrowed clothes. I'd done it all wrong. I didn't feel anything like *me*.

I got through it. However nervy I felt, I had confidence that my voice was clear and that I could be heard. My American accent was good and came easily to me. And I was certainly fat enough! At the end I tried to remember to smile, but my legs were shaking so much I even had difficulty doing that.

From the dark of the auditorium a gentle American voice asked, 'What have you done in the theatre, Angela?'

I stepped out of the brightness of the spotlight and said that I was sorry but I hadn't done anything. Without being asked, I said, 'Goodbye' and 'Thank you'. The excitement that ran through me was tempered with the feeling that I'd been too hasty in admitting my inexperience. I went home and shared my impressions of the afternoon with my family.

Auditions for the theatre are torture. You expose everything you are in the glare of a cold spotlight. Packaging your pride and handing it over to strangers. H. M. Tennent rang Miss Glynne and said they had been impressed, but I wasn't experienced enough, plus I wasn't quite fat enough. But would I like to understudy? At last something. At fourteen-and-a-half, farewell school, and I was more than content. The play was to go out into the provinces for eight weeks, starting in Manchester and then into the West End: the Lyric Theatre, Shaftesbury Avenue. My fee was to be eight pounds a week and an Equity card and a chaperone.

Tony – Anthony Valentine – had been chosen to play the son. He was Valerie Glynne's client too; also we were in class together. I don't think he liked me very much, he was always very casual. But I found it reassuring to know that at the first rehearsal there would be a familiar face.

A cluster of events. Daddy was to be seen more and more frequently with his head in his hands. His depressions made my mother tense, but we were all on his side. It was suggested that perhaps he should go home to Galway for a while; Mummy got out the tin of chocolate marshmallows, his favourite thing, saved specially for him. It was discussed and plans were made in a civil way. He was in the kitchen doing up his tie and asking for more tea; we sat stiffly trying to think of something to say. Mummy smoked a lot, for her bad nerves. When he left for the airport, the pulse of the family flickered with a new insecurity.

Real actresses changed their names, didn't they? I changed mine to Douglas.

Rehearsals began. This was indeed a new world. This was a surprise. It was quite a large cast headed by Barbara Kelly and Bernard Braden. On the first day we were all given new red covered scripts and coffee in paper cups. The principals sat around a big table in the middle of the stage. The chairs were set on all four sides. As an understudy I was told to sit behind and slightly to the right of Maxine Aslanoff who was playing the role of the daughter. She was about four years older than me and had the confidence of experience. In a way, I was happy that she had landed the part and not me. I wasn't sure if it was the prospect of appearing on the West End stage that frightened me, or whether I intuitively felt I wasn't ready, wasn't good enough. Anyway, who knows, Maxine might break a leg or something, and *then* I'd be ready, *then* I wouldn't be frightened.

For the time being I was happy to scurry around taking messages here, there and everywhere. I slid between the seats in the stalls towards Hugh 'Binkie' Beaumont. He was sitting with his camel-haired coat around his shoulders in a swirl of cigarette smoke. I hoped he hadn't noticed my hand shaking as I handed him a telegram: 'For you, Mr Beaumont, it's just arrived.' He was very important in the theatre world, so highly thought of. Squinting through the smoke, he smiled his thanks. In a decade's time I was to make this witty, intelligent man bacon sandwiches in my kitchen and call him 'Binkie', but I wouldn't have believed you if you'd told me that then.

Another chair? Tea? Coffee? Running around in my short socks, flatties and full felt skirt with its fashionable coloured patches on, I was only too willing to be everybody's dogsbody. So many new faces, but I felt I belonged.

I'd sit at the back of the theatre in the stalls and watch rehearsals. Marking my script, noting the moves. On my way home in the evening I'd sit in the bus and hold my script up high, close my eyes, and with a tortured expression on my face I'd silently mouth the lines, hoping someone would notice and think, Gosh, that girl's an *actress*! I was on cloud nine. I'd read about Mr Braden and Miss Kelly in the glossies, and I was overpoweringly star-struck – but I tried hard not to stare.

For me, the three-week rehearsal period went quickly. The company call was Euston Station 10.30 a.m. It was a chilly but bright morning as actors, stage-management, wardrobe mistress and chaperone laughed and joked their way on board the train. Mummy sent me on my way with a squeeze and a hug. Our tears started to come. I held mine back. And she did the same. I wasn't going to see her for six weeks. 'I'll come and see you in Oxford, for your birthday.' She patted my cheek. She seldom showed her emotional attachment. But the bond that existed between us was potent.

The train started to pull out of the station and I hung out of the window for as long as I dared, blowing kisses and waving. The rush of the train took my breath away and, sitting back in my seat, my mind lingered on my family. Would Mummy be all right? Hoped John wouldn't play all my records. And Daddy. How was Daddy? Then little by little I began to look ahead. I thought how different I felt. New clothes packed neatly in the suitcase in the rack above my head. New friends around me. New places to see. To be precise, Manchester, Liverpool, Newcastle, Leeds, Nottingham, Coventry, Oxford, Bournemouth and Brighton. New *life* here I come!

Away back in my memory now are the sounds and sights as I first sensed them. The resounding echo of feet clumping, clicking, running up and down endless flights of backstage stone stairs. The crackle of the Tannoy: five minutes, ladies and gentlemen – five minutes please. The excited chattering from the auditorium simmering to a hush as the swish of velvet announced the curtain was up.

Across the noise, the nerves. Life on tour is hard. To survive you have to become almost a gypsy. The pressure to get the show 'right' is constant. Daily rehearsals. Nightly performances. The adrenalin pumps away and you keep going largely on hope.

'Mummy – Mummy!' I ran away from the window of my 'digs' in Oxford and down the stairs into the street towards my mother. I shouted out '*Mummy!*' She had come to be with me for my fifteenth birthday. How I had missed her. It was *Mummy*; my head pounded with excitement. I felt a surge of tears and flung my arms joyfully around her.

'Angela, oh dear! You nearly knocked me over! You're so heavy. Goodness, dear, you *have* put on weight.'

I was silent for a moment. I wanted words of love, not censure. Again the urge to cry.

'Angela?'

'Yes, Mummy?'

'What's wrong dear?'

'Nothing.'

'Are you sure?

'Yes Mummy,' I smiled, 'nothing's wrong.'

I felt guilty at being so easily hurt.

The next day I was fifteen years old! Mummy bought me my first lipstick: Gala. Italian pink. My first bra, not exactly padded but definitely stiffened, looking rather like ice-cream cornets. (I once leant up against a wall and the tips of the bra became inverted – I walked around all afternoon totally unaware!) And a waspie for my twenty-five inch waist. I was allowed to wear my hair up now. It was indeed a milestone day! I'd bought myself five birthday cards to swell the numbers. To escape detection I signed them with my left hand using fictitious names. I wished myself lots of love and birthday kisses.

I leaned back in my bath pushing my hair away from my neck. I looked at my nails and resisted the urge to bite them. I wondered how I could ever have been gullible enough to coat my eyelashes with clear nail varnish. 'You've got such lovely long eyelashes,' Maxine had said. 'Why don't you put clear nail varnish on them. They'll look beautifully silky.' So I did. And they all stuck together in a clump and fell out. I felt with my finger around the rim of my pink eyes that stared back at me from the mirror. Stupid fool, I whispered to myself. But nobody had heard me for the noise of their laughter – no more than I deserved.

Immersed in warm water in a dingy little bathroom, lit by a naked light bulb which cast a dismal eerie light over the cracked and discoloured basin and bath, my voice rang out:

'Oooh, Rose-Marie, I *love* yoo-uuu,

I'm always think – ing of *you*'

– that sounds *good*. Forgetting completely where I was, I got control of my voice again.

'No matter what you do I can't for – get you,

Sometimes I wish-that-I-had-never *met* you.'

The door burst open and there stood the stage manager, out of breath and scarlet in the face.

'So *there* you are – finally I've found you…! Have you taken leave of your senses!'

I looked up – my pink eyes wide and innocent. Holding my flannel tightly to my body.

'The Bradens are in the middle of their big love scene; we've got a packed house and all that can be heard is *you* singing bloody *Rose Marie*!'

I winced. And I wished I were invisible. Everyone was a bit silent with me for a couple of days.

When the tour finished, *Anniversary Waltz* opened at the Lyric Theatre. I don't have endless memories of this period, but I do remember being very conscious of the fact that my attitude towards the long queue of nameless, faceless men invariably to be found outside the entrance to the Windmill Theatre was one of sharp disapproval. Our dressing-room windows overlooked Great Windmill Street. I used to save my empty Coca Cola bottles and keep them full of water on my window sill. And on a rainy evening I'd empty them on to the hats and umbrellas of the unsuspecting men waiting in the street below. I'd duck behind the curtains as bewildered faces looked up to see where the deluge had come from. I thought if they got wet enough they'd go home to their poor little wives – prissy little miss.

On matinee days I'd go over to 'The Nosh Bar' opposite our stage door. Famous for its delicious salt-beef sandwiches. My favourite, however, was hot chicken on rye bread with a cup of coffee. At home coffee was only for guests and grown-ups, and Christmas. Forbidden fruit tasted extra good. Maxine and I would sometimes walk around Piccadilly Circus trying to prompt some of the American servicemen that seemed to have almost invaded London at the time into a wolf whistle. With my pony-tail swinging and my short white socks I suppose the ones we did get weren't meant for me. We'd run back to the theatre for the evening show and rush up to the dressing room. Breathlessly we'd both start to talk at once.

'Oh, did you *see* that fat blond one giving you the eye.'

'Not *me* he was looking at, it was *you*!'

'There were seven whistles in all.'

'How about the dark-haired one with the moustache?'

'I got four whistles.'

'Oh, one asked if he could buy me a Wimpy. I said *No*! Will I ever get asked again?' It was fun.

Maxine never did break a leg or catch a cold. The show closed. I went back to the theatre the week after we had all said our goodbyes. I just walked around the empty dressing rooms – I couldn't bear to leave the fun behind.

Mummy nodded and stood up. She shook hands with the elderly gentleman and smiled her weary smile. My heart felt for her: she had so many responsibilities.

'Right, Angela, we hope you'll be happy with us and we'll expect to see you at nine o'clock on Monday morning.'

It was odd, I thought: an aspiring actress one minute, a messenger girl in an advertising agency the next. I didn't know anything about this new world, but I was willing to learn. For two pounds and five shillings a week I would make tea, help with the switchboard and take copy to Fleet Street. I was told it was a job with prospects. Mummy had pointed out, not for the first time, that even though people said, wasn't I a scream, and obviously I was destined to be an actress, now that I was fifteen I really ought to think about a proper job. And she considered starting from the bottom of Kingham's Advertising Agency to be a proper job.

I was spurred on by the thought that maybe one day I'd sit at the reception desk saying, 'Can I help you' and manipulate the switchboard with a neat 'I'm putting you through' as I'd watch Fleur do. She was lovely, with waist-length naturally blonde hair which she swore she'd never washed. She was engaged to a young doctor. He bought her a Victorian opal hoop engagement ring. She talked of him and her eyes shone. This I thought is love. This is what it will be like.

Then there was Helen – we became close friends. Older than me by about two years, she was a typist whose personality matched her haircut. Bubbly. She was fun. We shared a dream – to be singers. We'd work on our routine in the ladies' loo in the lunch hour. Our lunch breaks were spent singing, jiving at the Cafe de Paris in Piccadilly, or looking round the shops. She bought me a five-shilling 'silver' medallion on a chain from a street trader and I bought her an identical one. We'd wear them at the same time and believe we'd be friends forever. Sometimes we'd while away the hour sitting in the Cafe Roche in Oxford Street. It was my introduction into the free and easy atmosphere of the coffee bar world. A cup of frothy espresso coffee in a glass cup was ninepence and we'd make one cup last as we chatted and flirted with the continental students from the school of languages close by. I'd try my best to sound sophisticated which isn't easy to do at fifteen. Over the hiss of the coffee machine the jukebox would blare out *Jailhouse Rock* again and *again please*. I continued venting my dreams on Elvis Presley. There was Bill Haley, Buddy Holly and Fats Domino – and mostly and for always, there was Elvis.

I looked apprehensively at the people hurrying around and I felt myself becoming nervous again. What was I doing here? Helen had said it was about time I went to a dance and how she knew of one being held that Saturday at Harrow – why didn't we go together? I could stay the night with her. Mummy said all right and Elaine lent me a dress. Standing by the door looking into the crowded dance hall my legs began to shake. As I knew they would. How am I going to get through the evening? Of course, I'd never been out on a date. Fifteen was still too young for boys and I'd only ever danced with Daddy and John.

I remember he had a moustache and tight wavy hair. And I thought he was old. At least twenty-four. He made a bee line for me as the band started to play; he had his arm around me; and my first thought was, good, I'm not a wallflower. Then I looked at him and I didn't know how to behave. As well as having awful hair and a moustache, he was wearing a cravat. He wouldn't do. I was revolted and regretted being so close. I looked down at his feet and pretended to listen as he talked about my blue eyes, and where did I live, and about his car outside and taking me home. I was horrified to hear almost a sense of command in his voice. I looked towards the ladies' toilet sign as he said something about the next dance. I'm talking to this man as though I *like* him, I thought. Can't dance any more... don't like it, terribly sorry... I really must go to the loo. It was so spontaneously said that surely he couldn't doubt my sincerity. He responded with, I'll wait here for you. He smiled as I fled, and I felt guilty in some obscure way.

'Angela, what are you doing hiding in here?' It was Helen to the rescue.

I almost wrung my hands from my wrists and cried, 'Oh, I can't go back in there... did you see that awful man – he's so old and wearing a *cravat*! He wants to have every dance and take me home.' I cringed into a corner as girls with clenched waists pushed past us in full skirts of net and petticoats, cuddled into their mohair stoles. California Poppy filled the air. 'I can't go back out there – he said he'd wait for me... I'm having such a miserable time,' I wailed.

'What rubbish,' said Helen pulling me from behind the door. 'You can't spend the evening hiding in here! I've been looking everywhere for you, I've met some friends and we can join up with them.'

She was laughing as she pushed me, flushed with tears and fright, in front of her. I was tempted to turn and run, but just then the band stopped and one of Helen's friends leant towards me and said, 'Do you rock?' I grinned and my voice rose – 'Oh, yes!'

He took my hand as the band broke into *Blueberry Hill*.

A group stood round and clapped in rhythm as we rocked. My shoes came off. He twirled me around, over his head, between his legs, into the air and down again. My feet were in automatic. We rocked the night away. My feet hurt badly and my stockings were in shreds. As Helen and I walked home, we moved away from the dance hall knowing that the boys' eyes were following us. But I was mindless of their eyes and my torn stockings. I was on a high. I had had a wonderful time.

Nice girls from good homes stayed virgins until they married. They saved themselves for the men they were going to spend the rest of their lives with. If you made a mistake and allowed a man to make love to you, then you had to marry him. And a man wouldn't want to marry you unless you were a virgin. You must never ever go out with a married man. You wouldn't be allowed to bring a married man home. These were the golden rules Elaine and I were brought up on.

I stood a suitable distance away at the top of the stairs. I was eavesdropping. There were certain things I heard and certain things I couldn't. Elaine appeared from the kitchen.

She had broken one of the rules and the home was in an uproar. Mummy asked in the same urgent tone of voice if she was sure she knew what she was doing. Yes, yes, replied Elaine. She was in love. The radiance that was hers couldn't be touched. Mummy sobbed steadily. Elaine was silent. I heard my mother say how she bitterly regretted not having allowed Elaine to become a nun as she had wished. Her talk was dispersed. She cried saying she'd lost a daughter and that this man was married and an American. What did she know about him? Daddy would blame her, saying it was all her fault. Sounds of my mother's dismay filled our home. I crouched at the top of the stairs and could almost hear my heart beating. Mummy's voice wailed – you could have gone out with him, but you didn't have to *sleep* with him. I shivered and went into my room, and out of habit I reached for my flick rag. At fifteen I couldn't distinguish between the rights and wrongs of moral behaviour. I lay on my bed until it got dark, pressing the pillow over my ears, but it proved impossible to escape my mother's anguish. I vowed that the most important thing in the world was that I should never be the cause of this sort of stress to my mother. I swore that I'd never hurt her – hoped she wouldn't cry these tears over me. I promise, I *promise* Mummy I'll never go to bed with a man until I'm married.

Elaine left home, half in happiness, half in sadness. I ran around saying, Oh please Elaine, please don't upset Mummy. But she wanted none of it. She just wanted to be with Lewis. She held fast. If she didn't have my mother's blessing, then she'd go it alone. She returned home briefly to collect some clothes. I eyed her. She was nineteen now and a woman. I'd never seen her look so beautiful.

My mother continued to be exasperated, worried and nervy. I tidied up, thumped the cushions, hoovered a lot, making endless cups of tea, so anxious to give her that little sign of my loyalty.

She bought me a record called *Stay as Sweet as You Are.* That was her way.

Old Mr Kingham was a kind, friendly man. Perhaps I thought he was nice because he seemed to like me. He had called me into his office, patted my head and given me a bunch of roses from his garden. He spoke to me about childish things and I wasn't sure how to reply. Most grown-ups treated me like that; they made me feel young and silly. I *was* undeniably young, and silly too.

That year moved along. I managed to give my mother a little money. I yearned to be able to give her more. She encouraged me to try and save a little; we actually worked out a budget. She was keen for me to learn the value of money. 'Save for a rainy day' – a lesson I've yet to learn! The first thing I ever bought out of my savings was a pair of 'Baby Doll' pyjamas. White with little red hearts sprinkled all over. I was so thrilled I took them to the office to show everyone.

But my two pounds, five shillings salary wouldn't stretch to singing lessons with Maestro Mario who held classes on the fourth floor in a house in Bond Street. I didn't want to go to my mother for money. We'd already discussed it. I knew there was none to spare. My mother was the voice of reason, urging me to do my best in life, but not pin my hopes too high. However, she always did her utmost and found the money from somewhere. She came with me and climbed the stairs to the fourth floor. We sat outside the door to the studio listening to the sounds of a singing lesson in progress. My nerves began to jangle, I'd only sung to Daddy. Would I be able to sing in front of a stranger? Better find out now. After waiting a while, the door opened and Benny Hill walked towards us. Mummy was thrilled to see him – you could tell. He smiled and hurried away.

Maestro Mario was smallish, fattish and wore a red hairpiece. When he moved his head sharply, it used to almost slide off his head. I had a few lessons with him, but I felt uncomfortable. That slipping, moving hairpiece was too much for my sense of humour.

There had to be more. I wanted to get on with my life. My *real* life, whatever that was. As the office drudge I had no interest in the firm and was becoming restless.

'Why did you, Angela?' – confronted by two stern faces a foot or two above my own.

'I didn't think about getting found out,' I said and immediately regretted my words. The previous day I'd been handed three envelopes and told to take them to different addresses in Fleet Street. One required an urgent answer that I was to bring back. I was told that meant a probable two-hour wait. Oh blow it! Unknown to anyone I opened the drawer where the stamps were kept, took three and put the box back with extreme care. Then I walked away quickly to the post office, and slipped the precious envelopes in the box. I spent a happy afternoon wandering aimlessly around Bourne and Hollingsworth trying on hats and costume jewellery. My half a day's freedom cost me my job.

'*What*? Don't sit there staring at me... tell me!'

I wondered what else to say to her. In dejection – 'I've got the sack, Mummy... they've given me my cards.'

I kept a very stiff upper lip while Mummy told me how dishonest I'd been. How I'd let her down. How could I add to her worries. I was silenced. Getting the sack was not fun. But I was sackable.

'I do hope God will forgive me,' I thought, a little insincerely.

In this partly humbled mood I sat down on my bed feeling deflated. Whenever I wanted to think, or when I was miserable or anxious, I'd go to my little room and I'd remain there waiting for something to tell me what to do next. The idea of being found out just had not occurred to me. I'd acted on impulse. I thought only of getting out of the rut. A brief escape from tedium.

I was sorry to say goodbye to Helen, but deep down I was happy to be shot of the job. It was quite formative to learn so early in life that I was not cut out for office work, any kind, any place. Vowing to remain friends, I was however off at a trot, leaving the advertising world firmly behind me.

Daddy was home. *Daddy was home!* I remember we all went to see a Doris Day film and returned on the top of the bus singing the theme tune: 'Que sera, sera, Whatever will be, will be.' Abandoning ourselves to the joy of having him back with us.

I write now and try and describe what it meant to have a determined father, forever optimistic, who wanted something else for his daughter. Not *just* something else – he was more specific. He wanted me to be an actress.

'No daughter of mine is going to bury herself in an *office*.'

He had so much enthusiasm, and thought I was special. He made me believe that perhaps I did have talent, enough to survive.

'But Daddy, shouldn't I take a hairdressing course, a quick one?' I asked tentatively. He wouldn't hear of it – no half measure. I wasn't aware of Mummy's feelings at the time. She seemed neutral. A realist at heart, she must have wondered if any good would come of it, but she kept silent. They both stood behind me all the way. I can recall a few members of my family, on my mother's side, tut-tutting and thinking we were mad; saying things like, 'Not a proper job.' Daddy's eyes used to shine when he looked at me – he couldn't see that I was under-developed and overweight. He refused to accept that I couldn't achieve everything in life he wanted for me. His philosophy was, you only had to want what you wanted badly enough, keenly enough, to succeed. He gambled to live and lived to gamble.

My parents sent me to Aida Foster's Stage School in Golders Green. They went without to send me there. Daddy put the bit between my teeth and I was off. But the winning post seemed a distance away.

With her parents' approval, in August 1956 Elaine married the man she loved. She became Mrs Lewis Spencer. I lived in a world of my dreams; all my love flowed towards my family. On their wedding day I cried bitterly at the thought of the McDonagh family breaking up. I couldn't give up on any of us. I had the strongest family feeling. Wanting us all to stay together.

Almost from the start I knew that for me stage school was a mistake. Sitting back in the students' Green Room I was soaked not only in sweat, but in embarrassment. I concentrated on my damp leotard, pulling it down into a roll around my ankles. I heard a voice – 'Gosh, Angela, you've got terrific legs.' Thanks. But they won't work in class. I was okay up to a point, but I knew I'd never make a dancer. I was very disappointed. I was usually good at anything I really wanted to do; and I wanted to dance, I loved it. But I wasn't ever going to be good enough. My co-ordination was weak and I lacked stamina. It didn't do anything for my confidence that I looked fairly awful in leotard and fishnets. I felt self-conscious. And I'd say to myself, Daddy, this is a *mistake*. I feel like a fool. Looking around at some of the other girls changing in and out of bras and slips, whatever their size they seemed so shapely. *Voluptuous*. I watched them backcomb their hair and apply their make-up. Grabbing at chic fashionable clothes, they'd be off in a flurry – whoosh! To photographic sessions. To studios. To auditions. They all seemed reasonably uncomplicated to me. They talked about acting, modelling and marrying Mr Right. I wanted all that.

They were friendly and I got along well with them. I was one of the youngest students, and certainly the most unworldly. Listening to the older girls who seemed to know so much about life, their casual conversation seemed to centre around sex. Of which I knew nothing. So to shield myself I continued along the high road to saying amusing things. Be sharp, be funny. I felt protected by the diversion of laughter. I hoped they would respond to me as 'funny girl' rather than 'fat girl'. I was anxious about my weight now. I spent the whole of that year being anxious. And more. I started on a series of diets. And I bought a drug which was then readily available over the counter at any chemist shop. You can't buy it now. Apparently it produced a similar effect to 'Purple Hearts' which hadn't been heard of then – well not by me. Whatever it did for me was wrong. I was light-headed and shaky. But *thinner*! So I didn't care about feeling awful.

I started to skip classes. Sitting in the Green Room with some of the other girls, we'd practise the steps of the latest dance craze, the Cha-Cha. But left on my own I'd sit and watch my bosoms grow and examine my face in the mirror, leaning across the broad rim of the old-fashioned wash basin. I'd cover this fresh young face in heavy make-up with blue shade for my eyelids and bright pink for my lips. I'd experiment with movie-starrish hairstyles – I must have looked a ruin. With my painted lips I'd kiss the mirror: I'd practise with mouth pursed, mouth slightly open; this way and that, I'd practise and pretend. I'd carry on whole conversations in front of that mirror. I'd act to the mirror. Quite ridiculous. But very consoling. Skipping classes made me feel guilty. My parents were investing their hope and faith – and their precious money – in me. They were more than entitled to be angry and disappointed if they ever found out. But the drama classes frightened me. And I found my self-consciousness difficult to overcome. I remember feeling an unbelievable fool. And I giggled a lot. But I just felt that even though some of the others thrived and blossomed, it wasn't right for me. How did I know! A seventeen-year-old kid who'd done nothing. I didn't want to *pretend*, pretend. I wanted to pretend to act. I knew I must learn my craft outside the classroom. I'd have to wait.

I stumbled through a few restless months. There was a Canadian girl; I can't remember her name now, but she took a shine to me. She was Jewish and asked me if I thought her nose was too big.

'Do I *look* Jewish?' – she seemed anxious. I was surprised. I didn't know what 'look Jewish' meant. She asked me home to meet her mother. The ornate furniture and the obvious luxury of their apartment brought home my sense of social inequality. I felt out of my depth. On my birthday she gave me a bottle of French perfume. My first. It was called 'Je Reviens' by Worth. I never opened it. It was lovely just to have.

One absurd scene has stayed with me. There was a package for me on the kitchen table. Hooray! Huge excitement! My fur-backed leather gloves and my inflatable blow-up bra from Sears and Roebuck had finally arrived. I sat on the corner of my bed with the new bra firmly in position. It had come supplied with a plastic straw which you inserted into a small hole in the lining and if you gently blew air into the cavity, you could choose your dream size. With awe I watched myself grow, making certain that my puff was equally distributed. I pressed the little valves closed and pulled on a sweater – of course! I left the house and ran for the bus. It wasn't that I was late for class. I ran because I wanted to see if they'd bounce – they didn't.

I arrived at the school to find the Green Room filled with girls getting ready for the next dance class. A couple of my friends were there and on noticing my new shape, exclaimed, prodded and giggled. I slipped into my fishnets and blue leotard and eyed myself for a moment in the mirror. I was impressed. And thought, if those bosoms were only mine. There were a few titters from my chums as they watched me struggle to get through my bar classes. My new bosoms bulged and got in the way. But disaster struck when Miss Fox instructed us to lie on the floor on our stomachs, 'close to the boards girls, close to the boards!' To say the least I found it difficult.

'I want you to stretch and deep breathe, stretch… two, three… four and stretch two… three, four. Bottoms in and squeeze…! Tighter…! Good, good.'

I squeezed and pressed. And strained. I started to giggle. The girl next to me giggled. Miss Fox hovered over me.

'Angela Douglas, when I say get close to the floor, I mean you to be like *this*.'

Firmly she placed her hands on my shoulders and pressed down to emphasise her point. As I bonged off my pogo bosoms one small balloon squeaked into oblivion as I floundered. The high-pitched tone reverberated over the floor boards. The class dissolved with laughter. One of my happiest memories.

The desire for a bigger bosom was with me. I was seduced by advertisements. Wondrous charm is the undeniable advantage that girls with big busts have.

Miss Foster walked out of her office and down the corridor. I stood aside to let her pass. She was a nice old lady with a lilac tint in her silver hair.

'Good morning, Miss Foster,' I said cheerily.

'Good morning… You're new here aren't you…? What's your name, dear?'

No, I've been here seven months, silly old crab! I'd obviously made a *great* impression!

Miss Foster was reading quickly the relevant information for an audition that was being held the next day. Four of us stood in line in front of her desk, wearing our best, eager-to-please faces. My first thought was what a waste of time – I didn't fit the description of the girl they were looking for, for this particular commercial. My next thought was what an awful hat she was wearing on her red hair.

'Nice hat, Miss Foster.'

The untruth was quick to leave my mouth. I was pretending to be a self-assured girl with confidence.

'That won't get you work,' she retorted.

I opened my mouth to answer, but my response of *What will then*? remained unsaid.

At the end of that term I cleared out my locker, said goodbye to my chums and was home within the hour. I had decided that if I ever wanted to get anywhere as an actress, then it was up to me. The time had come to go it alone. To stop hiding behind the protective skirts of a drama school. I discussed it with my parents; we all knew that there was no more money. They were upset and had hoped for so much. 'Don't worry, I'll make it.' I seemed so sure of myself. But where would I start?

I had asked a girl called Anne how to find an agent and she said that she had been to see a young woman called Joan Gray at the Premier Agency in Great Newport Street, and that she seemed keen to find new faces. Why didn't I start there? Why not!

Walking up Oxford Street I was shoved and pushed. It was noisy and alive with the throng of people that fill that hectic street. Down Charing Cross Road and left at the bottom – it took me over an hour to get there. I climbed up the small staircase to the third floor and pushed open the door to an outer office and waited for a while. Summoning all my courage, I tap-tapped on a door marked 'Private'. From the quiet, a voice called out, 'Come in.' A blonde woman looked at me, her hand cradling a telephone. She asked me what I wanted. I told her I was looking for Joan Gray.

'You've found her, that's me,' and she smiled. She said she was sorry she couldn't see me right now, perhaps I would like to come again tomorrow. I mumbled something about clearly she was busy and thank you and yes of course, tomorrow. I backed out of the door. She called to me:

'I don't know your name.'

'Angela Douglas.'

I walked down the stairs and into the street and only then did I realise how frightened I'd been, and how nice she'd been.

Full of false bravado I presented myself at her office the next day. The same clear voice answered my tentative knock on the door. I'll never forget that she turned to a man sitting at a desk and said, 'Darling, this is Angela Douglas. I told you she came to see me yesterday.' I thought, she's remembered my name. My God, she's remembered *my name*!

The rapport was immediate. 'You have an Equity card? Good. You'll need new photographs.'

The small office buzzed. I emerged an hour later. Big step. I had an agent!

Will you do this job? That job? Yes, why not! One line in a TV play. Then two. A day's filming here. A day's filming there. I spent my time going from interview to interview. Studio to studio. I was knocking on lots of doors and squeezing my foot in. I rushed around in a generally happy and excited state. I was earning very little money. But enough.

Joan rang to say that they were looking for a new girl, a new face to front a Crunchie Bar commercial. The audition was the other side of London. I spent the morning going through my scant wardrobe trying to decide what to wear. I was getting myself into a nervous state and the tell-tale trembling started in my legs. Daddy told me to relax, said it was a 'cinch' and slipped his hand into his pocket, taking out a ten-shilling note. He pressed it between my glove and hand with a 'take a cab, darlin'.' I knew it was his last ten shillings, but he wanted me to take it. So I did. But I couldn't kiss him, thank you. I was still so *diffident* with men.

I got the job, Daddy! I got it, I *got it*.

A few days later I was standing on a largish boat in the Thames in front of Humphrey Lyttleton's Jazz Band singing the praises of this chocolate bar. While I free-jived around, a group of other teenagers stood in a circle clapping in time to the music. The filming was scheduled for three days and in between the inevitable showers of rain, we'd all go below decks and drink coffee and listen to each other's stories. Roy Hudd was one of the boys – he made me laugh till I thought I'd drop.

'You're so funny, Roy, I love you.'

'Everyone loves me, but nobody *loves* me,' he said glumly. Then he winked.

When I cast my mind over some of the work I did with such enthusiasm during that period, I can see that, to say the least, my career was slow going! Christmas Day 1958 saw me at the Cumberland Hotel dressed as a fairy, handing out presents from around the huge and gaily decorated tree to a swarm of what I deemed to be privileged children at the annual tea party. I danced around trying in vain to dodge the sticky fingers that tugged at my tutu. I gaily waved my wand and smiled all afternoon. For three pounds.

Miracle of miracles – I was such a success, the management asked me if I'd like to work on New Year's Eve. Yes, please! For another three pounds I was dressed in a brief swimsuit with five different coloured hula hoops wired to me, and at the stroke of midnight I had to burst forth through a paper replica of Big Ben on to the top of a grand piano. Dong, dong, a roll of drums, spotlight glaring, and woosh, I burst forth! Clutching a small basket filled with bunches of violets I had to wind my way through the tables, murmuring 'Happy New Year', pressing a cluster of flowers into some of the outstretched hands which reached at my hula hoops and beyond. The occasional male tugged so hard that when his fingers were finally prized open, I sort of boomeranged! Fresh remarks were made. Wearing my prissiest smile I fled to my changing room. The head waiter gave me an iced cake in a box, and a dish of petit fours. I hurried home with my goodies and my three pounds, to find Mummy and Daddy waiting up for me to see the New Year in. We sat round the fire clutching cups of hot chocolate, and cutting into the cake wishing each other lots of good things in the coming year.

I had a day's filming at Twickenham Studios. Five pounds! Riches! The scene scheduled for that morning was a photographer's studio, and I was to be the model standing prettily in the background in a bikini – the dieting worked! – holding a large coloured beach ball in the air. I went into the make-up and hairdressing rooms and then was told to wait in my dressing room until I was called. Standing in front of the mirror in my bikini, I started gradually to pad my bra from the roll of cotton wool I'd brought with me. I pushed a little more in there, tucked more under that one. Push, pull, squeeze. That's okay I think, as I looked this way and that. To all intents and purposes I had two pretty full mounds plumping over the top of my bikini. I stroke them proudly. That'll fool them. I definitely felt more confident walking on to the set.

The director said good morning and placed me in position. The actors appeared, the scene was lit, all seemed ready to go. I stood on tiptoe, holding my tummy in and the beach ball high in the air. I smiled brightly. What was the holdup? Why were they waiting? Come on! My arms were beginning to ache and my smile to freeze. From behind the camera, the first assistant walked towards me. He seemed nervous. All became horribly clear as he whispered in my ear, 'Angela, you've got – erm – a string of cotton wool hanging out – erm – from your – er – er – bra.' I glanced hastily down in horror and there it was, like a baby lamb's tail. It had slipped out. I was mortified. I scuffed it off with a smart remark. I could defend my feelings with a joke. That little wall I was building around myself was getting higher.

Associated Rediffusion were doing a series of Edwardian music hall shows called *The Jubilee Show*. Very lively with famous guest artists and lots of the wonderful songs from that period. The producer, Peter Croft, wanted about ten girls who could prettily decorate the set and sing. Auditions were held and my turn came – I gave my name and sheet music to the pianist. I was so frightened, I couldn't sing a thing. My knees were trembling, of course, as I hung on to the side of the piano. I sang the last verse first. I seemed glued to the spot and couldn't move at all. I got through it somehow. At the end they asked me my name and thanked me. I groaned inside. Oh, don't thank me for *that*! They called out the next name.

I got the job.

It was two days' work a week and the fee was £16. Fantastic! The first day we'd rehearse around the piano learning the songs – *On Mother Kelly's Doorstep*, *Joshua, Joshua* and more. The next day we would be in the studio. The show was to go out 'live'. Dressed in long twirling taffeta and silk dresses, clinched in tightly at the waist with low-cut revealing fronts, we'd make our way down to the studio from our dressing room. We were ribboned, buttoned and bowed. Hair piled high with false pieces and our young faces painted, we'd troop on to the floor, chorusing our good mornings to the boys in the orchestra. Mr Croft would be there to position us.

'Pam, darling, you sit there... You look wonderful.'

'Lisa, you beautiful thing, over here love.'

That was the general shape of the dialogue, until he came to me. He was always very nice to me, but seeing the front of my dress stuffed with small artificial flowers where two luscious bosoms should be, he'd put his arm around my shoulders and shake his head as if he'd had a mental aberration. How did this little thing slip through the net? He'd smile and place me towards the back of the set, invariably next to a potted palm. I loved doing the show, singing those wonderful songs. The other girls were fun to be with, especially the beautiful Pam. However, Daddy wasn't quite so happy. I'd go home after the show and be greeted with:

'You were at the *back* again! What were you *doing* sitting at the back?'

'The director put me there, Daddy.'

'Well, that's no good – push yourself to the front! Who's going to see you stuck behind a bloody palm tree?'

'Daddy, the director is the *boss*! You don't understand.' I'd laugh. Mummy would laugh. But Daddy thought it a fine old 'malarkey'.

I can't clearly remember what it was for, but I went for an audition and I'd been told I'd have to sing, so I went prepared with my music. A spreading man said, 'Good morning,' and would I lift my skirts up so he could see my legs, and then slowly around please. I said good morning and walked out of the room. When Daddy asked me why I'd been in such a hurry to leave, I replied smartly, 'Because I don't sing out of my bottom!' Oh, *good* one, Angela.

I was eighteen and a half and had to be home by 10.30 p.m. I was brought up by rules. My standards were expected to be thought respectable and decent. I had to show it. Prove it. I was still friends with Gillian who lived in Hampstead. I used to feel thrilled at being seen getting off the tube there – I thought it was thoroughly bohemian. Wearing a pair of Mummy's glasses I'd hang around the library in the hope that I was looking clever.

Gillian was 'in' with a crowd and there were lots of parties. When the jiving stopped and the lights dimmed, that was my cue to leave. When I saw couples pairing off for heavy petting sessions, girls squirming on to laps, I didn't feel comfortable. I'd creep away towards the tube station, my mother's words ringing in my ears: '*Anyone* can do it, Angela, there's nothing clever in it.' But it wasn't just morality or temerity on my part. Nobody seemed desperate to roll all over the floor with me. Nobody whispered, 'Let me!' If a boy asked if he could kiss me, I'd answer, no. And think – oh just *do* it. Don't *ask*. I can't kiss to order. And if the boys don't try, they don't try.

The first time I was kissed was in Highgate Cemetery. He'd taken me there to see Karl Marx's grave! I was sitting on one of the tombs, gazing around and swinging my legs. He was twenty-one, dark-eyed and gorgeous.

'I'm soft on you,' he'd said.

But when he leant towards me and kissed me, the bells didn't ring, the earth didn't move, and my legs didn't tremble. So I didn't do it again.

I was doing quite a lot of modelling – fashion and photographic. One of the girls remarked on the length of my eyelashes. She thought my legs were good too. We all used to compare our 'bits and pieces'. Someone called me legs and lashes as a joke. But it stuck with me. My first tag.

For my nineteenth birthday Daddy bought me a white Revelation vanity case and had my name put on it. I'd wanted that case so badly, and had talked of nothing else. It was the most generous present and I was wild with delight. But I still couldn't kiss him thank you. I cried into my pillow; I wanted to show him affection – why couldn't I?

By now I was the doting Auntie of two little girls, Lynette and Allison. There was one year and four days between them and they became the centre of our family. They were adored. When the time came for Elaine and Lew to move to a new posting in America, we thought our hearts would break. Daddy was silently desperate, staying in his room for two days. He couldn't bring himself to say goodbye.

I overheard my Aunts Phyllis, Kathleen and Muriel talking to my mother in the sitting room. Well, actually, I didn't *overhear* – I was listening at the door.

'Strange girl, isn't she, Marjorie? Funny, I mean, nineteen and no boyfriends... there isn't anything wrong, is there?' Cluck, cluck, cluck.

I'd learned the reality at nineteen that love isn't all it appears to be; it was only for glamour girls with clear skins, who married as teenagers and then abandoned themselves to walking round Harrods all day in a fur coat, murmuring 'Charge it to my husband's account.' At nineteen I accepted that those of us with puppy fat and minus the social graces despairingly stayed at home. I played charades in my head making up boyfriends on the telephone. I was a blue-eyed girl, living a life of mixed emotions.

For me there was Little Richard, Fats Domino, Jerry Lee Lewis, Chuck Berry and Elvis. The extent of my social life was one night a week jiving my heart out at the Whiskey-a-Go-Go in Wardour Street. John and I would jive at home in the kitchen. He was the best dancer ever. But if he wasn't there, I'd jive all on my own with the door handle!

At last I had what could be regarded as a proper part. An episode of *Dixon of Dock Green*. Look, John, three pages! I'll *never* be able to learn it! I read and re-read the script. I went over it until the pages looked positively dog-eared. At the appointed time I presented myself at the rehearsal rooms – Sulgrave Road Boys Club, Shepherds Bush. I had to play my scene with a young blond actor called Michael Caine. We went home on the same number bus and sat upstairs. I declined, of course, his offer to pay my fare.

'How much are you getting for this job?' he asked.

'Twelve guineas.'

'I'm getting fifteen.'

He asked me about myself and looking down at my script with its thumbed pages resting on my lap, he exclaimed, 'Gawd, are you a bloody swot?'

By this time Joan had moved to a new office in Wardour Street. She asked me to go there to meet a film director who was looking for a girl to play the lead in his next movie, a 'B' movie, but nevertheless a movie. I was introduced to Mark who was sitting with his back to the window. The light wasn't good, but as I peered discreetly at him, I could see he was rather boyish looking, with a pleasant face. I gently stamped my feet. They were cold and wet. Had my shoes let in water? I looked out of the window. The rain had stopped, thank heavens. I sat tight, waiting for the inevitable questions. They never came. Mark talked quickly to me making the interview relaxed, enjoyable almost. I listened carefully as he described the character of the girl in the film. He took a watch from his pocket and got up quickly from his chair, and with a show of concern, helped me on with my coat, apologising for having kept me for so long. I was conscious that he was not that old really, mid-thirties maybe. Not that tall either and not my idea of a dish. I came away thinking, that was painless.

The part was mine.

I started filming the following Monday. Getting this part gave me a lift. I had no pretensions. But it was experience. Precious experience. Mark took me through my paces. Taught me about stillness, concentration. How to look at a script and work on it – read between the lines.

'How long did you work on this scene last night?' he asked one morning.

'Twenty minutes.'

'Don't tell me you want to be an actress, and then say *twenty minutes!*' He was angry. I was a comparative stranger in this field. So I cracked a joke, it was my nature to make people smile; it seemed to ease the tension; it helped. But I didn't know how far I dared go.

Quiet, please. Action. Cut. Print. Next set-up. Hit your mark. Kill the lights. Hair in the gate. I began to understand. I began to feel more of an actress.

A couple of days later, Hilda Fenemore, who was also in the cast, turned to me and said, 'You do know that Mark has fallen for you?' She laughed and continued, 'I've never seen anything happen so fast!' I was about to answer when she said, 'He's one for the girls, you'd better watch out!'

One for the girls? I thought. Don't be silly; I mean, he wouldn't be interested in me.

At the end of the day Mark offered me a lift home. He dropped me off at the door, saying he had tickets on Saturday for the movie *Gigi* and would I like to go with him? Think about it, he said. In bed that night, my mind racing, I thought about it. I liked him well enough, the little I knew. He had a quick sense of humour, we kidded around. I'd learnt that he was thirty-six years old and separated from his wife. Technically a married man, which meant I wouldn't be allowed to take him home. But physically I didn't find him remotely attractive, and I certainly wouldn't be tempted to go to bed with him. Locked into my moral straitjacket, he seemed to be the perfect answer. I was nearly twenty and had never had a date. I was a virgin and untampered with.

Mark said I was tantalising. I had to learn the meaning of the word from the dictionary. He'd look in my eyes and say, what a girl. 'I'm silly with love,' he admitted. And we still joked, kidded around.

One day we were having tea in his flat in Shoot Up Hill, when he suddenly leaned over and kissed me. That was the moment our relationship changed.

'I promise I won't hurt you.' 'I love you.' 'I'll be careful.' 'Come on please.'

Interrupted with sounds that resembled alarm. 'I can't.' 'I mustn't.' 'Let *go* of me!'

One evening my protests came to an end. I ceased to struggle, refuse. I let him. I plunged into the unknown. My eyes never looked, they couldn't.

My mind filled with images of Mummy, shaking her head, crying, saying, Daddy, look what our daughter's done. Mummy, Mummy, I'm sorry.

Hours may have passed, or minutes. My head turned to the wall – I was only aware of thinking, I've done it. Have I? Was *that it*? I didn't know what was happening. Is this really me? I felt so foolish, so degraded lying there in his small room on this creaky single bed with my skirt all crumpled. Trembling and in dismay, I searched the bed for signs of my virginity. Oh, Lord, he won't believe I was a virgin. He'll think I've done it before!

It was a disappointing non-event. For me coitus wasn't the joy that kissing was. I had felt no pain, but no magic thrill either. Essentially I was riddled with guilt. And fear. The real terror of feeling the police would be after me and getting pregnant in spite of taking frenzied precautions was ever with me.

I'd given myself to this man that I didn't love. Couldn't love. But I was a true product of a Catholic upbringing. I had sinned and therefore would have to pay the price. Having allowed him to make love to me, I'd have to marry him. I'd broken the rules.

I thought Mark was exactly what I needed – reassuring and kind. And he loved me. Oh God, *love*. The tone of weary disbelief in my mother's voice could not be misread. She'd tut-tut and purse her mouth with eyebrows raised to emphasise her point. 'Never trust a man, they're only after one thing and when they get it, they won't want you any more, I mean if you want a good man, you'll have to grow one!' Well, Mark was a good man and he says he'll never leave me, always love me. But I couldn't dwell on that now, acting was what I had to find out about. Words like 'happily ever after' were far from my mind.

I was by now almost always in work. I had dreams and longings. My father's enthusiasm for the world of theatre had spilled over into my imagination and stayed there. It had been handed down. This world of make-believe couldn't be called *work*! I was so excited by it all and that feeling hasn't altered to this day. Sometimes I'd have to get up at 3.30 a.m. to catch a tube, then a bus and then another tube to be at the studios by 6.30 a.m., and was thrilled to do it. I realised then that it wasn't enough to *want* to be an actor, you had to *have* to be. Sick with nerves and fright, you still love it. It is work of love, it has to be or you don't survive.

I'd hug my script to me, curled up on the front seat of Mark's car as he drove me to rehearsals. He took care of me. He was the first man in my life to make me feel helpless. He decided what I should do and when and where. I referred everything to him. At twenty anyone of thirty-six, with his own *car*, had to be a man of experience. I was young and gay and happy to be dependent on him for advice and friendship. He wanted us to marry and to emigrate to Australia – 'I couldn't go that far from Mummy and Daddy...' For me it never turned to love.

One day Joan asked me to go and talk to Stuart Lyons, the casting director on the epic film *Cleopatra*. Off I went. He gave me a big smile and explained that he wanted twelve actors to go and live in Rome under contract to 20th Century Fox for four months and to be on hand to play small parts if and when they cropped up in a script that was continually changing.

'I've seen your work on TV,' he told me, 'and probably all I'm offering you is the chance to be a glorified film extra.' He paused mid sentence, reaching for a sheet of paper. 'Here's the list of names of other actors who have said they'd be interested.'

I thought for a minute. What an adventure! It struck me as a marvellous idea. Four months in Rome! I replied, 'Yes, please, I'd love to go!'

And I went home elated, threw open the door and announced the news. I'd worked in Ireland at Ardmore Studios and I'd been to France once on holiday, but at the prospect of working and living in Rome my eyes almost popped out with excitement.

Mark I knew would have a fit. I'd just washed my hair and was sitting on the floor in front of the fire drying it. He sat in a chair looking unhappy.

'You can't go and leave me,' he said.

I thought what a silly thing for him to say, but replied, 'You can come out and see me... it will be wonderful fun.'

He tried this way and that to influence me. But I wasn't, and I was determined not to be. I couldn't cope with his feelings; I could hardly handle my own. My parents, much to my surprise, were all for it too, and raised no objections. I was to learn later that they hoped my going to Rome would break my relationship with Mark. They disapproved of him as a suitor for their blue-eyed daughter and wanted me away from him at all costs.

Mark drove me, with my mother, to London Airport. Joan was already there and introduced me to the other actors. Saying my goodbyes to Mummy and Mark I felt confused as to who should have the last kiss, the final wave. I loved my mother and felt warmth for Mark. But were they competing? I stifled my anxiety and boarded the plane.

Rome! Arriving in Rome was almost like something out of a wonderfully happy dream. I lived in a pensione in Via Gregoriana and if I opened the shutters and leaned out of my bedroom window I could see the pale terracotta tiles of the roof tops and hear the noise of the city, its people and traffic. I was overwhelmed by the climate, the twisting narrow streets, the beautiful graceful squares with their splashing fountains. I'd sit with the sunshine on my face on the steps of St Peter's and abandon myself to the sense of antiquity and the colour and warmth of this eternal city.

I have a precious photograph in which I look so joyful it is unbelievable. It was taken at my twenty-first birthday party which was held in a little noisy restaurant where there was music and people danced. My friends gave me a delicate gold bracelet engraved with the words, 'love from the Rome Rep '61'. It's tucked away in the corner of my jewellery box and when I look at it, I remember being twenty-one, being free, being intensely happy. And being in love. Chris took hold of my heart and drove a demented Mark from my side. We were bold, we took risks. But the relationship was under wraps. Trying not to be seen was like a French farce; the slightest noise and I'd hide in the wardrobe. For the first time I knew the meaning of the word desire. I wanted him. At the beginning of November my contract came to an end and I had to return home to London. Chris took me to the airport and I stood at his side, my eyes searching his face.

'Oh Chris, I feel so fragile.'

He silently held me. I was so sorry. Sorry to leave him. Sorry he was married. My tears began…

'Sssssh,' he whispered, 'I can't leave you this way.'

I remember very little really about my brief love affair with him, but in my diary for November 4th 1961 are the words, Chris and Rome. They are underlined.

The call from Joan came through at ten in the morning. I was in the middle of cleaning out the hamster cage and had to put Happy and her two babies inside my jumper for safety to take the call. Joan said had I got a piece of paper and a pencil and that there were two interviews for me that day. She gave me the details, telling me to come into the office when I was through. 'There's a letter for you from Rome.'

'Thank you… yes… yes… I'll come in.' A letter from Chris! I was about to say more but stopped myself. I replaced the receiver. Two interviews and a love letter! I gently shook the hamsters from the warmth of my sleeves and back into their nest, went upstairs to do my hair and sort what to wear. Pulling a dress from my cupboard, would this look right? No. Maybe. Yes. I had a feeling about today. It was a good feeling. I wondered why that was. Interviews weren't ever easy, but some were easier than others.

The director Shaun Sutton leaned back in his chair; his long pensive face wore a shy smile. 'I saw you in an episode of *No Hiding Place*,' he said. Oh good, I thought, I wasn't bad in that. 'If you've been away in Rome you probably won't have seen the new series we're doing, it's called *Z Cars*, and we're all very excited about it.' He asked me to read a scene and I did.

'Oh, it's a smashing part,' I bubbled. 'I want it, can I have it?' I'd blown my cool. I was no good at the cover-ups actresses used.

Shaun stood up, pulling at his knitted tie. 'I'm delighted to hear that, Angela, the part's yours.'

I hugged him. *Goody*!

I was out and hurrying for a bus now. Oh, to hell with it! I guiltily hailed a taxi. 'Berkeley Square, please driver.' The cab sped along. As always I was excited when I'd landed a good part. I couldn't ever believe my luck. I flipped through the script that Shaun had given me. I took a deep breath. If I got overexcited my control went. Another deep breath. Now *calm down*. The awful thought that I might be late for my next interview had me peering out of the window. The taxi was stuck behind a lorry and started to hoot vigorously. Fretting at the slowness of the traffic I opened the door and got out.

'How much do I owe you driver? I'll try walking the rest of the way.'

Stupid move number one, I decided, as the rain started to fall. I scurried along, hugging the walls for protection. I looked at my watch. I'd be on time. But first impressions count with directors and producers. I peered around for another taxi. Nothing doing. Either arrive late, looking reasonable – or be on time with frizzy damp hair and rain-splattered stockings! In my panic I almost ran up to the reception desk. I'd started to sweat and could feel the perspiration suddenly wet on the small of my back. God help me, how I hate bloody interviews. And now I had the shakes.

'Could you tell me where the ladies' cloakroom is please?'

The rain was coming off me like steam! The receptionist, all false eyelashes and backcombing, asked me my name and ticked me off from a list in front of her and pointed me in the right direction. I fumbled in my make-up bag, dusted myself with some talcum powder and patted some precious L'Aimant behind my ears, backcombed my hair and felt a little better. I turned and walked towards the large mahogany door with smart gold lettering on it. It read, James Archibald. The name amused me. I knocked.

'Come in,' came the reply.

Grinning from ear to ear I blurted, 'It can't be for real…! Not Archibald…! Nobody has a name like *Archibald*!'

Tripping in, wearing my new stilettos, I slipped on the polished parquet floor and ended up on my bottom. The two men smiled at each other and as I was helped to my feet I was introduced to the director, Clive Donner, and clapping his companion on the shoulder, he turned to me and said, 'May I introduce James Archibald, our producer.'

I looked wildly from one to the other. 'Oh, golly, I'm sorry to be so rude.' I flushed and felt an absolute fool, making an exhibition of myself like this. Stupid move number two. 'Can I go out and come in again?'

Clive Donner smiled and looked at me frankly. 'Don't worry, Angela, we are looking for an extrovert, bubbly girl. Your entrance was perfect. Tell me, can you sing?'

I nodded my head and shut up. I tried to look relaxed by settling back into my chair, but my knees hurt and I'd laddered my stocking. Oh dear. I listened as they told me the outline of the story of the film they were going into production with. There was a lot of excitement in their voices. The film was to be called *Some People* and made entirely on location in Bristol. A story about five teenagers, street-corner kids, whose lives were changed and given colour by their involvement with the Duke of Edinburgh's Award Scheme. David Hemmings, Ray Brooks, Annika Wills and David Andrews had already been cast, and apparently Kenneth More had agreed to do a guest appearance, 'for free, because he believes in the principle of the Scheme'. The idea was that perhaps I'd be right to play the part of Terry, a girl full of spirit, who sang with the local pop group and roared around on the back of a motor bike.

'Can you do it?'

I wasn't at all certain. How could I decide there and then if I'd be able to do something that I'd never before attempted? Sing in a pop group? In a *movie*! Ooh Angela, don't do it. The Irish Gremlins inside me urged – *do it*!

During the meeting it was agreed that I should do a film test on the following Tuesday. I did the test, knees knocking and a few days later Joan was told that I'd got the part.

'Are you *sure*, Joan...? Tell me *again*, do they really want me to do it?' I was delighted, so was she, everyone seemed happy. I was by this time in the middle of rehearsing my episode of *Z Cars* and my contract for the film was to start three days after the recording. Perfect timing. I was a very happy girl.

On a cold morning in February '62 I took a train from Paddington Station heading for Bristol. I arrived at the Grand Spa Hotel to find a note from Annika saying that she and the two Davids were having dinner in the dining room; would I like to join them. None of us had met before but the rapport was good. We sat around the table talking over endless cups of coffee. New people. All friendly.

An entry in my diary, Feb. 20 '62: Start of our second week of rehearsals. Have slept with my script under my pillow every night. Annika says it helps the words sink in. She's so pretty and I'm feeling unconfident about everything.

And on Feb. 25: I have no insides left. Unbelievably nervous. Have never worked so hard. And love it. Just want to get it right. Do my best. But is my best good enough.

Four days later another entry: The crew are arriving today. So are James Archibald and Kenneth More. *Strangers*. Clive Donner says don't worry, you're good. But why can't I eat?

We'd rehearsed at Filton Church Hall and today, waiting for everyone to arrive, I sat on the edge of the small stage and watched all the activity. It was exciting to see everyone getting ready to impress. I slipped into the ladies' cloakroom and cleaned my teeth *again*. My mind was racing. I repeated my

91

lines over and over to the door, the mirror. I wanted to be sick. Were the others going through all this? Was it only me? I slipped back into the hall and lolled up against the piano trying to look calm. I fiddled with my hand microphone.

'Mmmm – mmmm – Some people think that kids today… Mmmm… have gone… astray…'

Ron Grainer brought me a cup of coffee and put his arms around me.

'Don't worry, love, we're all very pleased with our Terry.'

It seemed that nearly everyone had arrived, the atmosphere was humming. The swing doors were pushed and in strode Kenneth More with rolled up shirt sleeves and his jacket slung casually over his shoulder. He smiled that wonderful smile.

Part Two
Lover

We were all introduced. I whispered my nervous hello, smiling, bobbing about.

'Angela Douglas,' he said. 'Oh, yes, of course, I know your cheeky face!'

He knows my face! He must have seen me on the telly! But no bells rang. No claps of thunder. His how-do-you-do's were warm and friendly. I wrote to my mother saying how amazingly normal he seemed. Without a sniff of the grand old man of the theatre act. But his *clothes*, Mummy! He wears a pink and green striped tie that reminds me of salmon and cucumber sandwiches! You can see with half an eye he's a square.

The film was a happy one. A fun unit. We worked long hard hours but, as I flopped into bed each night, I thanked my lucky stars.

A letter from Chris, still in Rome, was nice. The occasional phone call was even nicer. One night he called and we decided we would say goodbye. Our brief time together was up. Goodbye. Good luck. We were not especially sad at the parting. No matter. Forget it, surely that was the sane adult thing to do. But oh! That brick wall. It loomed so close – and seemed insurmountable. I would have liked to sit with my mother and confide in her, but I didn't dare.

I'd been brought up to believe that even true love didn't justify carnal experience. And yet I was only twenty-one and had already been to bed with two men. I knew nothing of passion. Or love. Or about sex. I stumbled my way through instinctively. I proved to be a valiant, able, albeit monosyllabic student of my hard-won, guilt-ridden sexual freedom. I would emerge tousle-haired; my principal sexual instinct had been to furnish satisfaction and ego-fodder for my lovers. Did they suppose that because I *had* satisfied, I would *be* satisfied? Female orgasm wasn't a phrase I'd ever heard of. Without doubt I knew a lot about unsureness. Guilt. And anxiety. But there could be no special pleading of 'It was true love, Father,' for absolution. Correspondingly, I loved the feeling of specialness. Those delicious moments when the focus is narrowed. When a man that I am attracted to makes me aware that his energy and attention is all for me.

I felt sullied. I had one foot on the bottom rung of the wrong ladder. I required more of myself.

But I needed to be in love. Just a little – every day. It didn't matter one jot if the object of my affection was unaware of me. My thoughts were all astray.

Who was totally unavailable? Out of reach? Kenny More. I'll have a crush on *him*, I thought. That'll get me through the day. He won't even notice. He was a flirt. He flirted with everyone. But he was known to be happily married; not to fool around. *Perfect.* I'd heard him say, 'I'm a bloody good husband,' and he'd added, 'If you can survive the first ten years, marriage is okay.' *Ten years*! Can it be worth it, I thought. I was a flirt who perhaps appeared more knowing than I really was. I flirted with him. It would be untrue, a lie, to say that I was drawn to him by a strong physical attraction. It was so wildly fantastically improbable that he would look my way. It was a game. A caprice.

Annika and I were leaning out of her bedroom window one night, talking quietly. It was around midnight. She was very much in love and was waiting for a phone call from *him*.

She was nervy and needed to talk. Suddenly we saw Kenny leave the entrance to the hotel and walk towards his car. We watched as he stopped and drew with his finger the outline of a heart in the frost on the bonnet. 'Annika,' I mumbled, 'doesn't he look lonely.'

He's married, I reminded myself. Leave him alone, he's a family man. What do I care, my tiny voice came back. It's only *fun*. So simple. So matter of fact.

We were always one of a crowd. We were never alone. Sometimes he'd stand a discreet distance from the camera and watch me play a scene. He'd offer words of advice, encouragement. He was known to be a generous actor. And a generous man.

'Blimey O'Reilly, it's St Patrick's Day tomorrow... Let's have a dinner party!' He arranged it all. He'd saved a seat for me next to him at the table. My mood was gay. It was lovely to celebrate. Something. Anything. I'd worried a bit about what to wear and had settled on a short green dress.

'Hey, listen,' I buzzed, nudging him in the ribs, 'do I look all right?'

'Angie, you look good enough to eat! Just like a greengage!' He laughed. I felt awkward. Was he laughing at me? I was never to be certain.

Pushing his chair away from the table, he took my hand with a 'Let's dance.' On the small circular dance floor he put his arms around me, but we didn't move. *Couldn't* move.

What was happening to me? It came out of nowhere. I don't know how it happened. My hand began to tremble, slightly, in his. Not wanting him to feel the vibration I put my hands on his shoulders and gently pushed him away. I felt so shy. (A sure sign.)

'I think we'd better sit down,' he was saying over the noise of the band as he led me to the table. I bit without looking, didn't I.

'It's not because of who you are, you know,' I said that night as he kissed me. 'You could be Joe Bloggs for all I care.'

'I *am* Joe Bloggs,' he said, pulling at his tie.

We lay in his single bed looking out of the window. It was a bright clear night. In the moonlight we could see the suspension bridge which spans the gorge and the River Avon.

'What's your middle name?'

'Josephine. What's yours?'

'Gilbert.'

What a stuffy name, I thought. A name that belongs to another age.

'Nights like these are what memories are made of... You store them away for when you are old,' he said quietly.

'Kenny, look, the moon's gone pink,' I managed to say as my cough caught in my throat. 'I'm sorry' – urgent splutter – 'I've had bronchitis and I can't get rid of this cough.' I barked again.

'Oh, my God,' he sounded concerned. And suddenly he was on top of me with a refreshed single-mindedness. Pressing his chest into my face he said, breathlessly, '*Christ*! Clive Donner's on the other side of that wall and David Hemmings is across the corridor! If they hear that bloody cough they'll know you're *in here* with me!' Rough sympathy.

I whispered faintly, 'I can't *breathe*' – squeezed, exhale. Struggling to stop and gulping desperately for air, it proved nearly impossible to seal off my rasping, or his frantic embarrassment.

'*Sssh*! Angela *please!*'

'Ow. Ow! I can't help it,' I gasped, my voice full of self-pity and snorts.

That night I slept with my pillow over my head.

'Good morning, how are you?' he asked, softly lifting the corner of my pillow. Opening my eyes I remembered where I was.

'I'm all right, thank you.' I felt timid. I smiled but felt chilled. I'd actually slept all night with a man. A first for me. I felt a slight feeling of panic. Kenny was speaking and I listened as he said, 'Coo! We were a bit naughty last night, weren't we!' His smile broadened. And I watched as he pulled on his socks.

'Don't tell anyone, but I'm having dinner tonight with the Queen… Private dinner party with the Astors… They're all scared stiff I won't behave myself!' Chuckling, he reached for his shirt and I caught my breath, seeing for the first time a livid purplish scar that ran like a crayon line from the centre of his back to his tummy button. He must have heard the sound. Turning towards me and seeing my gaze quickly slide away, he casually pulled at the skin. 'Oh that wasn't anything, just a kidney stone! The bugger cut me in half!' he grinned. I looked at him quizzically: 'Operations are nothing,' he attempted to reassure me, 'you either get better or you die!'

Holding my hand lightly he turned to go.

'Are you sure you can slip back into your room without being spotted?

I nodded. But looked around worried. He tightened his grip. 'I'll be in London for three days.'

'Who's counting?' The best thing I could come up with.

It was the last thing he heard as he closed the door quietly behind him.

During the three days I tried to put everything to the back of my mind. I concentrated on my work. Clive Donner was marvellous to work with, so patient and inventive. But in the evenings alone in my room full of the sweetest scent Boots could offer, I'd tune my radio in to Luxembourg and pad across to my bed and stretch out. I looked at my body with some amazement; it was as if it belonged to someone else. I was astonished at how aware I was of it these days. I pulled my blanket up around me like a shell, covering my breasts and shoulders. I didn't feel comfortable thinking my thoughts naked. I could still hear the words Mummy had spoken as she'd hung up my hooped petticoats on the back of my bedroom door the night before I'd left for Rome.

'It's going to be strange around here without you. Three months is a long time... I suppose you'll get tempted. Just remember dear there's nothing special in it. *Anyone* can do it.' I looked innocent and said nothing. Instead I leaned forward on my bed and examined my toes with immense interest. I had an insane impulse to tell her the brutal facts of Mark and me. Mummy cut into my thoughts: 'I just want you to be happy, dear.' She squeezed my hand. I couldn't squeeze back.

Happy? I hadn't expected me to turn out this way. Waves of despair, compounded by the after-effects of the long day's work, a glass of wine on an empty stomach, and most of all my relentless Catholic guilt and feeling of cheapness made me think I was not separable from those foolish girls I'd heard about, referred to as 'easy'. I'd heard about one-night stands and felt desperate. I was a *nice* girl. He was a *married* man. And we'd had a one-night stand. He'd done *that* with me. I felt like crying. Loathing myself, I wanted forgiveness. Sipping at the wine I felt hungry, but my stomach curled at the thought of food, so I pushed my liquorice allsorts back into their box. I sat in my bed hugging my knees – my head full of thoughts. Was I being foolish, excessive? I didn't know.

'Ow, ow,' I cried; my eyes filling with tears. I pulled at my damp tissue. '*OW OW!*' I struggled to fight my rising sense of panic as I grabbed for the new box of Kleenex. I began to sob steadily.

Help me, someone. Now what was I to do.

I could not shake off the feeling of unease. I stood and stared out of my bedroom window down into the street below, bright in the winter sunlight. People hurrying by. A boy and girl, both in leather studded jackets, were kissing on a motor bike. I wondered if, like me, they felt the burden of guilt. Hopefully not. I reddened as I watched the soft blue grey of Kenny's MG move into a parking space. God, he's back! Could I face him? A feeling of apprehension flooded over me. The telephone rang and I jumped; it was Annika.

'Kenny's back! I've just met him in the hall, he says he's going to unpack and rest for half an hour, and then he wants to take us all out to dinner!'

'I'm sorry. I don't feel up to it.'

'Don't be a wet, Ange! We're all meeting at 7.30 in the bar.'

The line went dead. I reproved myself. I'm being a wet! I had the door of my room slightly open and could easily hear Kenny's distinctive voice thanking the porter for bringing up his luggage. I waited for the silence to tell me the coast was clear, and then hurried along the corridor to his room, 157, and tap-tapped against his door.

'Darling little girl...' Kenny was lying on his bed, fully dressed, his arms folded behind his head, looking up at me. The bedside lamp made his eyes glint faintly and I noticed for the first time the tortoiseshell speckles of hazel and amber.

'Please,' I started to cry, having aimed not to. My cheeks were burning and my palms started to sweat. 'Please, Kenny,' I begged, 'I'm frightened,' which I was; 'I'm losing my way.'

My voice broke and rose as my fingers shredded the damp tissue I was clutching. He touched my knee with the back of his hand, gently moving it up and down as he said, 'Oh, are you feeling bad about the other night?' He gestured for me to slip off my shoes and lie down beside him.

I blurted out my heartache to the warmth of his comforting shoulder. It wasn't a speech I had prepared, an outline for love. 'I'm only twenty-one, starting in life... *a one-night stand...* I can't handle it. Please Kenny... would you... would you have an affair with me? Just for the rest of the film... what do you think?' I finally ventured.

He cleared his throat, his arms giving me a gentle spasmodic squeeze.

'You're asking me to have an affair with you?' he said cautiously, 'for the next three weeks?' He raised himself up on his elbows. 'Will that make you feel better?'

'Oh yes, Kenny, yes... anything but a one-night stand,' I said helplessly.

'Okay,' he said abruptly, 'let's do that...! We'll have a three-week affair!'

I threw my arms up around his shoulders, burying his neck with my kisses. He broke away and looked hard at me.

'Angela, you must promise me one thing. At the end of the film when we all go back to London, there'll be no phone calls, no letters, nothing. No contact. Promise me.'

I nodded. I understood. I promised. He'd made me an offer. I knew the rules. A brief affair with complete discretion. Cut and dried.

'Oh, that sounds perfect,' I said co-operatively. My gaze flitted over his face; his hair had begun to grey at the temples, and my fingers traced the two small lines in his skin by his ears. That beautiful mouth. How divine, I thought, to be kissed by that mouth.

'Do you feel calmer now, little one?' he asked, studying my eyes, concern rising in him like a flush. More tears, unashamedly wet, in reply to the look in his eyes. Smiling at me with sudden unexpected warmth, he whispered, 'We'll have fun.'

I pulled myself together. 'Thank you,' I heard myself say as audibly as I could. I'll be a good girl. I wiped my eyes on his pillowcase. My gratitude was the real thing, the genuine article. He'd liberated me from my guilt.

The three weeks were full of variety and gaiety. Everyone chatting and laughing; who could notice our shy half smiles to each other. All that mattered for me was working through the day and being with him at night. I didn't feel the need to sleep. We had the secrecy bug. We told no one. Any affection between us in public was restrained. But late at night I'd peel off my eyelashes, smear my make-up off with cream, and creep into my small bed and listen for Kenny's light footsteps in the corridor. We'd make love. He would smoke his one cigarette of the day, the small brass ashtray balanced precariously on his stomach. Flick, flick went the ash, never missing or spilling. He'd talk. I was content to curl up and listen. He'd tell me stories about people I was later to meet. And some who'd refuse to meet me.

He had to dash back to London for two days on business and on the morning of his return, I was alone in the make-up caravan going over my lines for the next scene. I had the door open so I could listen for his arrival.

'*Aaahh* – what a bloody long drive!' Him, him! My pulse quickened. 'Where's Angie?' and in he walked.

I got up intending to greet him with a hug and a joke, but I didn't.

'Have you missed me?' I pulled that one out of *nowhere*!

'Yes I have, I have.' Twice he said it. 'I'd be lying if I said I hadn't.' His response threw me. He patted his pocket excitedly. 'I've a present for you… here,' and he started to pull out a package. I jumped in quickly and shoved his hand back into his pocket.

'No, no I can't accept presents…! Please no presents,' I pleaded. I was getting ready to be upset and Kenny looked at me as though he was studying a foreign body.

'What do you mean, you can't accept presents!' he said finally.

'Mummy says only Christmas and birthdays.' I proffered a weak little smile.

'Well I'm blowed… you really are a well brought up girl.'

Later on that night, the well brought up girl was lying in his arms wrapped in a small towel and squeezed up against the wall.

'This bed is falling apart, you'll be pleased to see the back of it won't you!'

His sweet smile broadened.

102

'I wouldn't say that exactly,' he said reaching out to the chair where his trousers lay neatly folded. 'Look, I want to give you your present now.'

I shut my eyes tight.

'Oh that, *no, no* thank you.'

'Stop saying that – listen to me.'

Finally, when he had my attention, he whispered, 'Open your eyes.' I did. He handed me a small red leather box. Oh golly, only big presents come in such small boxes. I opened it gently. I studied the gold four-leaf clover nestled on velvet. Could I accept it? I looked at him and took a breath.

'Oh, oh,' I began brightly in a tiny voice, 'it's from *Harrods*!' I was embarrassed and my tongue felt stapled to my lips. I lifted both ears off the pillow and pulled up to kiss him.

'Do you like it, are you pleased?'

'It's beautiful… Thank you… A lucky four-leaf clover.'

'No, Angie, it's a shamrock, because of St Patrick's night.'

'But Kenny it's got four leaves!'

'Well, I'm sorry…! It was the nearest thing Harrods had to a shamrock!'

The words 'Bristol '62' and 'J.B.' were finely engraved on it. Joe Bloggs.

'It's to put on a gold chain, you've got some haven't you?'

'Yes, yes, of *course*,' I lied. Some? I didn't have *one*. I'd save up. And until I could afford it – well, what was wrong with a piece of string. As he backed away from the bed and turned towards the door, I said, 'I haven't a present for you.'

'You mustn't spend your precious money on me… Good-night love – or rather good morning,' he laughed softly.

'I do like you Joe.'

'And I like you.'

I watched him leave my room and close the door.

Two days after the 'shamrock' night, Clive Donner's voice calling out 'It's a wrap, everyone' brought the film to a close. Kenny was half in and half out of the boot of his car, making little reflex motions towards his suitcases. I was propped up against the wheel.

'We're off to the South of France tomorrow. I have a place down there… We'll be on holiday for four weeks – it's glorious at this time of year. Then I start a new film, *We Joined the Navy* – my old friend Wendy Toye is directing.' I was trying to be interested. 'We have three weeks' location at Villefrance. Aren't I a lucky devil!' he chuckled.

There was an awkward pause as he reached for his green canvas handgrip and shoved it in. We kissed each other on the cheek.

'Angie, here is my agent's address' – he slipped a folded piece of notepaper into my hand. 'I'll be back on the nineteenth of May – write to me care of him and let me know how you are.'

I shrugged nervously and said abruptly, 'Okay… fine. Yes. okay, Joe,' and nodded in agreement. But his words of three weeks ago were repeating in my mind. No letters. No contact. He'd made me promise. Weren't we meant to break away clean? He put his arms around me and as he hugged me, he whispered, 'Be professional.' I stood on the pavement and put my head straight as an arrow up in the air and smiled as Kenny revved the engine and drove away. Be professional, he'd said. I knew what he meant by that and I was resolute to be. Strong, brave, seemingly easy-going. My outlook being that I was responsible; as good as my word. But here we go again with that empty feeling.

I headed for home. I wore my shamrock round my neck on a fine piece of string under my sweater. I was aware that it was always there. At night at home alone in my room I'd take it off to dangle it between my fingers and look at it. Kenny was so entirely gone, never mentioned, that without this palpable solid proof, I might have wondered if our brief secret affair had really taken place. I had no doubt that I'd liked him. I filled my mind with his smile and sparkly eyes; the laugh in his voice. But there was no question of love. I knew I did not love him nor had any idea of loving him. It had been a game; love hadn't found me.

'Will you turn that thing down...! Oh! for God's sake open a window somebody, there's no air in here.'

My mother in the throes of a hot flush stormed into the sitting room, clicking off the television, tripping over Daddy's legs ('always sticking out – never marry a man with long legs') and throwing open a window. Daddy, who had been dozing in his chair in front of the fire, his head hidden under a copy of *The Sporting Life*, jerked to animated muttering: 'I wasn't asleep Mammy, I was just watching the filim... You like Earole Flynn,' he continued, pretending conversation.

'Look Dad, you've been in London for almost thirty years,' John said, 'and you still pronounce film – filim, and Errol – Ear-ole!'

I leant up on my elbows, squinting against the bright light of the standard lamp. I was on the floor half behind Daddy's chair, wrestling with the letter I was attempting to write to Kenny. I re-read my third endeavour. The reason for my writing to him at all eluded me, except that he had said he'd be back in London on May 19th and he wanted to know how I was. Well, today was the 17th and my diary for the past six weeks didn't make for dizzy reading exactly. I'd shuttled between rehearsals and home. Lots of work, I know I'm lucky. Annika is in Spain with her mother – we spent a desperate afternoon together in the Heaven and Hell coffee bar last week drinking endless cups of cappucino. She's pregnant and is frantic as to how she'll cope. It's all very worrying. She had to miss out on the visit to Windsor Castle (so did *you*!). The Duke of Edinburgh thanked us all – he likes the film. We had sherry in a small stateroom – he was so smashing. I forgot to curtsy I was so excited. Straightforward and nice and he gave us a quick tour of part of the garden. Hey listen! Guess what! I saw the Queen! She appeared around a corner wearing a belted raincoat, flatties and a headscarf, stopping briefly to look in our direction, and then hurried off to peer into Prince Andrew's pram. I think I was the only one to spot her and it would have been rude to nudge and point, but I was so excited! I splashed out on an outfit, top to toe – everything new! My winklepickers (89/11d!) killed me! I went to a party last week. Can you do the twist? It's great fun – you feel so much thinner! And I was fine, thank you. Really on top of things, feeling very good actually. I hope you have enjoyed France and that the filming went well. And if I don't hear from you in a few days, that's okay, and I understand perfectly.

Seemingly all I had to rattle on about was my work and my life. I laboured towards an attempt to be articulate. There appeared nothing more to say. I'd exhausted myself as a subject. I jammed the letter into the envelope and put it with the rest of the mail for posting, and joined John in teasing Daddy about his Irish-isms. We let him have it from all sides. 'You may laugh,' which we certainly were, 'sure you'll be missing me when I'm gone…' He broke off as the phone rang. I cringed my usual cringe.

'Hello Ange, it's me, Jill.' Jill was my best friend.

'Jill,' I echoed and listened. 'Yes, please, love to. Will you give me half an hour to tart up and I'll meet you there.' I could feel Mummy bristle behind me.

'Peter, did you hear that…? *Tart*…! She used the word *tart*!'

His reply of, 'Have you seen my cigarettes dear?' did nothing to help my case.

'How you've changed,' she wailed.

'Mummy, the word "tart" doesn't automatically mean what you think it means!' Ease the tension, crack the joke. 'Did you hear the one about the treacle tart falling in love with the apple…'

Cutting me off with: 'It's the people you're mixing with. Sometimes I wish we'd never let you go in for this acting business,' she continued on and on. Her tone was unmistakable. I sat down on the carpet. Oh, screw this for a lark. What would she say if I said *that* out loud?

I had no unruly emotions. I was content. Happy to be home again and to be working. To be suddenly in such demand was tremendously exciting. I had no time to look over my shoulder. I was moving on. I was twenty-one, keen-eyed and confident, and I was waiting for something to happen to me.

I was wakened by the sound of the telephone. I grumbled as I directed horrible thoughts at the alarm clock – eight-twenty – so *soon*. I got out of bed spontaneously and noticed that I felt thinner. I pushed anxiously at my thighs with my hands. Great! Those astronomically expensive little pills were beginning to work. *Answer* that phone someone for heaven's sake! I heard my mother's voice as the phone pinged into silence. My first thought was narrow. I'd been given a late rehearsal call which meant the luxury of a lie in. More sleep, give me more sleep. I lay down again burying my head under the pillow, but still listened. My mother's voice, low and surprised, came up from downstairs.

'Angela, it's for you. Who on earth would call you at this time of the morning?'

I put on my dressing gown, one of my mother's but it fitted well enough, and went through John's room – he was sitting cross-legged in a T-shirt on his bed, silently fiddling with a magneto from the car he was building. Fair hair, thoughtful solemn eyes, too large for his seventeen-year-old immature face, concentrated. Sweetheart. I stubbed my ankle on a piece of jutting-out crankshaft. I scraped my leg and cursed. *Not* such a sweetheart. I wished that someone in this house had a fervour for order. I went downstairs into the sitting room and picked up the phone.

'Hello, who's this?' I said matter-of-factly.

'Wheee…! It's me…! Am I too late?'

Kenny.

107

'Oh,' I squeaked, paralysed.

'Don't say a word! I know exactly how you feel... I was ten days late in returning from France – the filming overran and I've only just got your letter!'

'Uh-ooh-oo!' I managed.

'Have you got a flat?' he asked.

'No... well... no.' I shook my head, confused.

'Fuck it,' he said shortly. 'Never mind... Are you free on Saturday night?'

'Yes.' My throat felt dry. 'Yes I am,' I said hoarsely.

'Good, there's a Variety Club Carnival at Battersea Park in the afternoon... I'm hosting... It's a thing we do every year. It means I can get out for the evening. Do you know the River Club?' he continued.

'Yes' – I hesitated, because I didn't.

'Okay. Longing to see you little one. Seven o'clock?' He made a kissing noise. 'I've got to go,' he whispered. 'Saturday – *wheee!*' he repeated and was gone.

I thought I was probably a little crazy. Standing by the bus stop, eyes tightly shut, I moved around in a happy little jig. I felt calmer now. I don't know how I got out of the house. It took just one phone call to have me out in the street and blowing free. Cars drove past and I felt as though I was dancing on them. I felt like whirling round lamp posts, the proverbial three feet off the ground, the talked-of, fantasised-about sensation. I heard the bus arrive and hustled behind the others and took out my money. My eyes felt sparkly and bright – they didn't look, they beamed. Energy vibrated through from some untellable new source of seized strength. My mind was full of Saturday – what to wear? A present for him! I had to find a present for him. And my hair... buzzbuzzbuzz... I was on a high!

The date was for seven o'clock and I didn't want to be a minute early.

'Will you drive round the block for three minutes please, driver?'

He looked at me through his mirror and said, 'I saw you on the telly last week, didn't think the play was very good.'

'I'm sorry, I can't quite hear – did you say, did or didn't?' I enquired.

'Didn't.'

'Oh! Thank you so much.'

I'd had 'perfect manners' drilled into me for so many years but inside my head was, 'Bloody hell, thanks a bunch!' I'd had the jitters all day. My stomach was fluttering with butterflies and heavens look, now it had started to rain. My *hair*! I peered out of the window anxiously. I'd slept, or tried to, with my hair in large rollers, lying on my tummy with my forehead pressed on my folded hands. I vowed never to tell Kenny that I'd gone through all this to look pretty for him. I'll *never* admit it. I'd put on a tight-fitting black silk dress and jacket that I'd had made in Rome. It was beautifully simple and well cut, and I prayed as I did up the zipper that this wasn't one of my 'chubby' days. It wasn't. I had a tiny gold and diamond watch Daddy and Mummy had given me and my adored single string of pearls that had been my twenty-first birthday present from Mark. *Smart*! I'd thought as I checked in the mirror. Twenty-one going on forty-five – in a rush to get old. I was concerned that the small red suede box was still safely tucked into the corner of my black clutch bag. I checked. Yes it was there. I'd had such unbelievable luck in finding the perfect present in the very first shop I'd gone to on my hunt. Lying on a velvet tray with some others, I'd spotted a pair of antique gold cufflinks with small diamond shamrocks in the centre, in the window of a jeweller's shop in Bond Street. They were enchanting. Of all the luck. I'd had them inscribed 'Joe Bloggs'. If this was to be our only sneaked meeting in London, then at least we'd both have our shamrocks to help us remember that special St Patrick's night.

Having paid the taxi I quickly ran in from the rain, took a couple of deep breaths and pushed the door open into the bar. I looked curiously around the room. Through the haze of cigarette smoke I saw him; over the noise of chatter I heard him, laughing. He was sitting surrounded by people. I took hold of my nerves and pushed my way over to his group. 'There she is!' He looked at me – 'Don't you look pretty' – and the smile remained on his face. It was decided that a few of us would go for dinner at a restaurant in Mayfair called Harry's Bar, and a few minutes later we walked out to his car. He held the door open for me and as I got in he said, 'It's new – yesterday – do you like the colour?' He climbed in, closed the door and switched on the ignition and sat there. We watched in silence as the others drove off.

After a minute I ventured, 'Shouldn't we follow them?' A forced little laugh was surprised out of me.

He put his arm on the back of my seat and we both felt the intimacy of the moment. We were sitting close together and he said, 'I love you.' My heart shot up in my throat. 'I can't help it – I've fallen in love with you. In France, I've thought of nothing else… I realise that if I haven't got you, then I haven't got anything… Without you my life is empty.' He looked like someone who had waited to say something for a long time. He took my hand and then let go.

'Oh, please don't let go, hold my hand again.'

My eyes were shut tight. 'Hello darling,' he said and kissed my shut eyes.

'Hello,' I said and when I looked at him I was in love with him and everything turned over inside me.

'Shall I order for you?' Kenny suggested lover-like. Faced with a dauntingly large French menu I thought thank goodness! *What* a good idea! And acknowledged my immense relief with a smile.

By now there were at least eight of us clustered round the table. Robert Mitchum sat on one corner leaning with his head on his hands as he held a sort of walking stick, his famous hooded eyes hardly open. Next to him was Judy Garland. I watched her fascinated for as long as I dared. She was so gay and enchanting. The red plush room with its soft lighting dazzled around me and I thought, quite cheerfully, heavens, I'm out of my depth.

'Asparagus and grilled lobster all right for you, Angie?'

'Yes please, how mouth-watering. Delicious!'

A little while later I wasn't thinking delicious. I was thinking disaster! I'd never eaten fresh asparagus before and hadn't realised that if you ate the green part, or rather attempted to, that it would catch in your teeth and that no amount of polite pulling around of your lips and tongue would dislodge the wretched stuff. Feeling humiliated I rather incoherently mumbled my way to the ladies' cloakroom. Ugh, what a mess I saw in the mirror when I opened my mouth. I scrambled in my bag for my toothbrush – owing to my phobia I always carry one – and within a minute I was able to smile back at myself in the mirror and see the me I wanted to see reflected, and not an image of a cow chewing the cud!

All things considered I didn't think much of lobster. I peered down and reflected, here is this poor creature cut in half and grilled and placed on my plate. My God, look – it had had *veins*. I shrank from having to eat it but in spite of my reluctance I falteringly made a stab at it, and only succeeded in pushing a piece round the plate, this-a-way and that.

'Darling, you're meant to eat that bit,' he pointed out, 'that's flesh… actually the piece you've got on your fork… is part of the shell!' He leant over and squeezed my hand. 'Ooh, you're so adorable… I want to cover you in diamonds!'

All at once I didn't feel like food. Who could eat when one felt so exquisite.

In the car, awkward though it was, we hugged and kissed with nervous impatience. After a few minutes Kenny moved a little away from me, palmed his hair down and straightened his tie.

'I don't like being this way with you,' he mumbled. 'I should have arranged a hotel room I suppose... but I didn't feel I could presume that you...'

'Nor did I.'

'I wish there was somewhere for us to go,' he said.

'Well, I've got the key to a girlfriend's flat, she's away and I know she wouldn't mind... is it all right for you to stay out late?' I asked.

'No woman's telling me what time to be home,' he said.

I nodded. 'I see.' But I didn't really. I knew nothing. But I thought husbands and wives did everything together, certainly went to sleep together every night. I had a lot to learn.

He looked at me and came back from wherever his mind had been. 'God Almighty...! What the hell are we doing sitting here...! You've got the key to a flat? You're not joking, are you? Why on earth didn't you say?'

'I don't know... I feel shy... ridiculous isn't it?'

Do you really want to sleep with me, I wanted to ask, and did you mean it when you said you loved me? But before I could say anything less insecure, Kenny had pushed the car into gear and we were thundering towards my friend's flat in a large block called Park West, only minutes away.

We glanced at the porter slumped asleep sitting at his desk, and silently rejoiced in our luck as we hurried to the lift and up to the second floor. I sat down next to Kenny on the bed and, while I looked at him, he opened his present.

'You've spent some of your precious money on me? – little one, can you afford it?' His mouth dropped.

'Yes. Absolutely,' I said.

'Look, are you *sure* you can afford it?' He turned his eyes to me.

'Don't keep saying that! Please, please... do you like them?'

'All right, sorry love,' he said. 'They are perfect,' he sighed. 'Little diamond shamrocks... enchanting. You are a clever girl. Come here – let me thank you properly. Push the door to.'

His arms were around me. A tug of his tie, a slip of my strap. So simple, so easy.

In bed we talked over cups of cocoa. He didn't lavish a detailed autobiography on me. I learned a little about him. He was born in Gerrards Cross, Buckinghamshire. 'Wait a minute, Kenny, you won't believe this, but so was I!'

'Well, I'm blowed, that's got to be a good omen!'

He told me about his marriage to 'Bill', as she's known. How he'd 'more or less just fallen into it. She's been good for me, rubbed off my raw edges. She's a marvellous hostess, filthy rich. But I've never said, "I love you" to her.'

At this moment I interrupted. 'Kenny, this may seem a funny thing for me to say, but you've got to know... I've heard you banging on and on about how happily married you are and yet here we are in bed together.'

He squeezed me and said, 'Understand something about me. You mustn't believe everything I say in public; some things are expected of me.' I heard the words and thought. Please the people. Reassure them, that this great actor with his talent and wonderful smile – really has it all. If he's got it... then it exists, and all's right with the world.

'You mean actors *have* to excite interest?' I said. 'Is that a clause in the contract?'

He shrugged, 'I've never admitted, even to myself, that there are times when I'm excruciatingly lonely. Until you, I've lived for my work.'

That all took me by surprise. Watching him lying quietly by me talking into the shadowy spaces, I saw him now for what he was: a nice man with immense charm who was admitting his life was a lie. His life which had seemed like glossy photographs. He went on: 'My little daughter, Sarah, spoilt I suppose, but lovable – a super little companion.'

He'd been married once before, in his early twenties, to an actress, Beryl Johnstone. They'd been working in rep together. 'I climbed up the drainpipe to her room every night and the

113

landlady never caught us out!' Then the war had been declared. 'We all rushed into marriage with our current girlfriends. A sort of statement I suppose. We didn't believe we were ever coming back.'

They had had a daughter Jane – 'Christ, she's the same age as you!' – conceived on one of his leaves. They had been divorced when Jane was a baby and she had been brought up in Herefordshire. 'She's a nurse. I'm told she's a wonderful girl.'

He asked: 'You…? What about you?'

At that moment I didn't want to cry out, this is the *real* me! I gave what I believe is known as a dismissive laugh. 'Well, Kenny,' I said staring into the enclosed distance, 'I can't spell at *all*. I cry at sad films. I have one close friend, Jill. I'm allergic to men who wear cravats and hush-puppies… I like rock and roll and eating grilled chicken and chips and jam doughnuts. Hate getting my hair wet in the rain. Will never tell the exact truth about how much things cost. I don't drink… I don't smoke… I've had two lovers… No details. So I can't go to Mass any more. I want desperately to be a good actress. I love it and love going to art galleries and going to the theatre when I can afford it, and I love my family.'

'Family. How will they take it, you moving out to a flat?'

'I can't lie… I'll have to tell them the truth… Mummy reads me like a book.'

'Will you start looking for a flat? Tomorrow? I'll pay the rent.'

'No you *won't*! I'll pay my own rent… I couldn't bear *not* to!' I didn't want to be part of a sugar-daddy ding-a-ling scene.

'Excuse me, I want to go to the loo.' Draping the bed cover around me I disappeared into the bathroom. Catching sight of myself in the mirror, I was staggered to see me looking like a demented poodle! My hair all tousled and frizzed out and my eye make-up collapsing down my cheeks. Heavens, I look as though I've been out on the tiles all night! *Ahem*! I tried to open the medicine cabinet, prising it open with my thumb nail, as there wasn't a latch, searching for some eye make-up remover, or cream – *nothing*! Panic! Then I spied a box of Brillo pads by the bath taps – they'll do, better than nothing I thought. Angela, you thought *wrong*! Sitting on the side of the bath I thought, who'd believe it? Here I am, draped in a bedspread, hair a mess of matted knots, raw Brilloed crimson eyes, three o'clock in the morning with Kenneth More declaring his love for me. I looked at my watch again. Ooh, how delicious – I'd been in love for seven hours!

What would my parents think of all this? I hadn't given them the smallest sign. I'd spent most of the morning in my room poring over the Sunday papers, all the papers, all I could get, searching the small ads for a flat. Where would I live? How much could I afford? I could only think of Kenny and being with him whenever it was possible. I wanted to be free to love him. Lord knows I hadn't aimed to fall in love with him. I had not aimed to fall in love with anyone. But Lord knows I had and I lay on my bed and all kinds of thoughts passed through my mind. Finally Daddy came in, knocking first.

'Are you decent? Lunch's nearly ready, sweetheart,' he said. 'Are you coming down to help your mother?'

'Yes, Daddy.'

'Didn't hear you come in last night… were you late?' he questioned.

'Yes, Daddy.'

'A party was it?'

'Mmmm yes.'

'Enjoyed yourself did you…? Well, well, I don't know, twenty-one and still going to parties.'

He went out and I lay there. Oh, I'm sorry, Daddy, it's going to hurt.

On the Monday morning the phone rang very early, Kenny, of course, from the studio. Would I come down and spend the afternoon with him – 'we can talk' – he'd send his car for me. I didn't pause. Yes, yes, I'd be there.

Daddy was leaning over with one foot on the boiler polishing his shoes. As I came in pulling on a sweater, he stuck his head up.

'Who was that calling? Where are you off to so early?'

'It was Kenny More, Daddy,' I blurted, 'and I'm going out this morning to find a flat.'

He slumped into a chair and shook his head. 'Really? What's this you're telling me?'

'Look, Daddy, *please* don't worry,' I pleaded. It was somehow a frozen moment fraught with a confusion of emotions. I longed for emotions I could understand. I felt inside me a chaos of fear and joy.

'Have you taken leave of your senses?' said Mummy. Furious. I tried to explain things to them.

'Not only is he married, but married *twice!*'

'He says that…'

'Kenneth More – he's the Battle of Britain! He must be nearly as old as Daddy!'

'I know all that, Mummy, it doesn't matter,' I ventured.

'Are you coming between them?'

'He says not, Daddy!'

'Doesn't matter, she says! I warned you Peter… *Show business.*'

There was a silence, followed by a round of questions.

Mummy warned, 'If you break up a marriage, Angela, you'll pay the price.'

'He's not leaving his wife for me… He says he'll never do that… Never leave the home… He wouldn't do it to Sarah,' I said, trying to sound mild. Mummy was frightened and was sniffing into her hanky. I recognised their feelings. It was completely understandable that the idea of their daughter being 'a bit on the side' was heartbreaking for them.

'He says he's in love with me, Daddy.'

'Of course he's in love with you, darling... You're class. We've always brought you up to believe highly of yourself.'

The air crackled. I was in the wrong and had failed them. But nothing they could say would make me change my mind. I was resolute. Mummy was crying now and saying to Daddy – she's gone the wrong way.

Thinking back to that day I do remember the initial excitement of independence. Of being released to a life which was waiting to develop. The pitfalls were perfectly obvious and if I didn't want to think about them, then I didn't have to, did I? My objective was to find a flat as quickly as possible. Where would I go? How would I manage? I found for the first time that organising comes naturally to me.

I opened the door to No. 3 Cross Keys Close, off Marylebone High Street, and directly in front of me was a short flight of stairs. At the top of them and to the right was a minute kitchen and on the left a good sized bathroom, two bedrooms and a sitting room. I squinted against the bright light streaking into the small hallway and thought, it needs painting, and carpets, shelves and window boxes – golly, it needs everything. And I thought – lovely, this is it.

The estate agent asked me to step into his office. He rubbed his nose and pushed his skinny hands into the pockets of his jacket, making them bulge out of shape.

'I just wanted to say, Miss Douglas, that it's the first flat you've looked at. I've got others, perhaps you'd like to think about it... Best not to hurry into these things.'

I looked at my watch and thought – *hurry*! I must hurry – it was almost twelve-thirty and Kenny was sending his car for me at two o'clock.

'Thank you for your help... I love the flat and want to have it... Can you give me the details and I'll come and see you to discuss everything tomorrow.'

I said all that in a voice I did not recognise, crisp and urgent. I walked home and thought perhaps he's right, maybe I should take my time. But if he only knew, if he only knew how I loved a man – and how this man loved me. I didn't care what I was getting into.

My immediate reaction to the gleaming sleek brown and beige Rolls Royce waiting outside our house was one of embarrassment. Kenny had said he would send his car for me, but he hadn't mentioned the word Rolls. A first for my house – I'm sure I saw the net curtains twitch as the chauffeur, Beint, opened the door for me. I struggled with my rising sense of panic and asked if I could sit in the front with him and would it be all right, please, as I hadn't had time for lunch, if I ate the Marmite sandwiches my mother had made for me, promising to be careful with the crumbs.

'You can be certain Mr More will spot a crumb!' he retorted, 'He's very particular. Of course Mrs More is as well. Ooh! the slightest…' He chatted on and on.

I hung my head and concentrated on my sandwiches. I returned from my thoughts every now and then and pretended to listen to stories I didn't want to hear. Was he knocking them out hoping to find my reflex points. I coped quite well. But it seemed the most uncomfortable car in the world to me that afternoon.

'As I see it,' Kenny said, 'it's purely a practical problem and practical problems are there to be got round!'

A straight look from me, trying to show nothing. I dug my nails into the palms of my hands. 'If the estate agent wants seven hundred pounds for the lease,' he turned the page, 'that's not bad for nine years – then that must be my responsibility.'

I thought, hey, do I look cheap. 'Ooh, I don't know about that,' I quailed.

Kenny picked up the phone and asked for a line. 'Well I *do*… Call him and secure the flat, we want it.'

I moved swiftly from the chair and grabbed the receiver from his hand and thumped it back on the cradle saying, 'No, no, I must be independent!'

'Seven hundred pounds won't take your independence away from you, silly girl. You'll be paying the rent and running costs... Let me contribute, please.' I felt a pang. 'Darling, don't make things more difficult than they already are. Tell me, do you want to see me?' I looked at his face and my heart welled.

'Yes.'

'So.'

'So?' I blinked stupidly.

'So, we take the flat.'

'Okay.' My voice was simple relief. It all seemed suddenly right. He smiled one of his winning smiles; it was a smile I felt I knew, which I certainly did – as most of England did. Close to it was a stunner. Physical closeness was becoming all the more important.

I now had somewhere to live that was my own and the savings of a thousand pounds, my nest egg from *Cleopatra*, for my spree. Kenny had managed to come with me one afternoon, collecting me in his Mini from outside Madame Tussaud's, my arms overflowing with net curtains. As I bundled myself into the front seat I explained I'd just collected them from Marcel.

'You look like a bride,' he joked. That registered. He loved the flat, though he was unaccustomed to rooms that small. I'd wanted him to see it 'before and after'.

'Furniture, darling,' he said looking around him, 'you're going to need everything, aren't you?' He handed me an Agfa-Gevaert box containing the seven hundred pounds for the lease money and a note which said, 'An extra two hundred and fifty, towards the saucepans!'

I wanted everything to be perfect for him, clean, pretty and cosy. For a whole week I went out buying, returning at night to fill the flat with endless bags and boxes. A bed was ordered... Double or single...? Don't be silly. Chairs, a sofa, curtains, carpet, tables, dressing table. I knew the way I wanted it and I didn't have anyone to ask how they might like it. I didn't want to disappoint him. I wasn't prone to falling in love. My affairs with Mark and Chris, although lively at times, had been in a sense necessary, and lacking in rapture. Now, unexpectedly, exhilaratingly, I had lost my reason. I was so in love. Kenny said my eyes were a giveaway: 'They radiate the look every woman would recognise.' I was lightheaded with joy. I opened my mouth to talk and a laugh would come out. It was new territory for me. It was a gamble – a matter of chance. I had taken the plunge and to take half measures was not my way.

It was planned. It was simple. I wanted to be the perfect mistress. Kenny's perfect mistress. Love was in the air. I concentrated all my energies on him and if he wasn't aware of it, all the better. I meant him to believe that everything came naturally to me, that I actually was what I seemed to be, because being only what I truly was couldn't be enough for him – could it? I got to know the local shopkeepers, placing an order with the newsagents for '*all* the Sunday papers'. I must be well informed, clued in and up to the minute for my widely read and articulate lover. I emerged from W. H. Smith's armed with more books on the Second World War than I could ever hope to wade through without dropping off to sleep. I was certain he'd want to discuss the war with me at some point and if he didn't require my opinion on the latest films and plays, then surely he'll be craving food and I couldn't cook, so a large red copy of Constance Spry was added to my load. And supposing he wasn't too engrossed in talking to me or eating, then it was likely he'd want to be in bed with me, so off I trotted to Weiss in Shaftesbury Avenue for three sets (I couldn't afford more, I mean, *look* at that price tag!) of sexy and – I hoped – alluring underwear. Frilly and lacy, black, white and French navy to suit all moods. And some baby-doll nighties please, that one and *that* one. This twenty-one-year-old who felt she had nothing to offer, except youth, didn't use scent or lipstick now – you don't if your lover is a married man. He isn't mine. Any move I make might place our relationship at peril. And the thought of Kenny leaving me, of not seeing him again, made me feel so despairing that I knew I mustn't put a foot wrong. It must not be my fault, I would do all that I could.

It seems so implausible now, hard to believe. But then I thought I could see it all. I could see that Kenny's real life, his other life which didn't include me, was settled and secure. In real terms he was way out of reach – and I wasn't reaching. I could see I was in love with him, but was he really in love with me? He was his own man. I loved his ways. For a year, just one year. It was a fantasy I suppose. Unrealistic. But I'd thought it out on my own. I could see it only in terms of a year. I had no former mistakes to learn from. I was being reasonable, logical, wasn't I? But I wasn't allowing for my emotions. Whether through foolishness, or my old trait of living for dreams, and if it makes no sense at all now to love someone in terms of time, it was the only way I could cope with someone like Kenny coming into my life. It was so good. When we made love we knew it was right; but to survive, to stop me falling apart, I had to condition myself. It's a dream – only a dream. I was in love with a beautiful man and I must believe that he couldn't be mine.

I moved into the flat and Jill appeared on the second night with a bottle of champagne. My oldest and dearest friend, a friend I could trust. She was desperately in love with a married man. So she'd tell me about him and her and I'd tell her about Kenny and me. Perhaps speaking about our lovers aloud made them more tangible, more credible. I couldn't talk to anyone about Kenny except Jill.

'Will it last, Ange?' she asked.

'It's not intended to.'

'But you say you're in love?'

'We are.'

She shook her head and looked at me – 'You are going to get hurt.'

'Jilly, I'm not going to give him my heart *forever*. It's all so complicated,' I offered and broke off. 'Married men are bad news.'

'Are you telling me!' She picked up the bottle and refilled our glasses.

'One year, Jill, I'm only going to be frivolous with this one year... I'm not going to fritter away my twenties on someone who's married.'

She stared at me blankly. 'You're being unbelievably naive, Ange.' I didn't say anything. 'Do you really feel so in control?'

'Jill, I used to know a woman who'd been in love, having an affair with a married man for eleven years. Her youth gone – *Woosh!*' The tears started – 'That's *not* going to happen to *me*.' I was frightened and stifled the thought.

What would I have done without my friend Jill. She could grouse about love to me and I could grouse about love to her. We had some terrific evenings grousing with each other. Natternatternatter...

One evening that week Kenny was able to make it over to the flat. He'd been attending a big official dinner in the city and had managed to slip away early. He arrived at about eleven o'clock and I was watching from the window as he carefully parked his beautiful new Mercedes (another new car!) below my window. I knocked on the glass with excitement to attract his attention. He looked up, saw me and grinned, motioning for me to come down and let him in. Of course, how silly – I hadn't given him his key yet. I thought, as he came into the room, that I'd never seen anyone so handsome. I couldn't believe he was really here with me.

He looked around exclaiming, 'You've done wonders, clever girl. It's so *different*.'

He sat down in the velvet wing chair I'd bought specially for him.

'Let me take it all in.' His eyes settled on an old oil lamp. 'I like that, where did you find it? Harrods?'

I laughed. 'No, Portobello Market; this mirror came from there as well.'

He's pleased, I thought, and I basked in his approval. I gave him a whisky and stood in awe. I'd never before seen a man in white tie, tails and decorations, except on television. My Battle of Britain hero, I thought. 'This one,' I said, pointing gingerly to a medal on the end of the row, 'what did you get this one for?'

'That? Oh just for being there, darling, honestly, we all got one,' he said, looking at my eyes all the time. 'You're so enchanting, come here and kiss me,' he pulled me down and could he feel my heart thumping?

'It's so good to have you here,' I whispered.

'For me too. We'll have to be very discreet, careful, you understand, don't you? Darling, if circumstances were different, well I'd show you...'

I interrupted him. 'Shush, Kenny, I understand, I really do. No one must get hurt.'

'You wonderful thing! What the hell are we doing sitting in here?' We went into the bedroom. I didn't know until Kenny what love-making was about.

He sat on the edge of the bed and pulled a tiny box out of his pocket and opening it he said, 'I'm a sailor at heart... always will be... so that makes you a sailor's girl and I want you to have this.'

'Ooh Kenny,' I breathed.

'It's a replica of my naval cap badge.'

'Ooh Kenny, are they diamonds?'

'Well, they aren't marquesite!' he said smilingly. Reaching out to the corner of the mantelpiece he took down my old teddy bear and pinned this pretty thing on.

'Do you have to go?' I asked.

'Sooner or later.'

'Later?'

123

I curled up in my foetal position. I lay on my left side with my right hand on Kenny's pillow. He'd kissed me and said, 'I love you, that's all I know,' and he'd gone, clicking the front door quietly behind him. Loving was so easy. I could sleep and forget about everything.

I was determined to handle this love and not have my life turn topsy-turvy. But that's what love does, it alters everything. Would my life ever be the same? Did I want it to be? I wasn't torn. On one hand I didn't know much, but I knew my life couldn't depend on Kenny. My love, my first... My be-all and end-all... Yes. But he was only borrowed, and only for a year. On the other hand my work, now starting to get exciting: 'It's starting to go great,' said Joan. Everything coming my way at once. I was consumed by the thrill of it all. Don't let it rush to your head. I could cope, couldn't I? *Would* cope with both of these happenings. Taking chances. That's how it goes – take it where you find it, and give it everything.

I was happy. I felt I was now self-sufficient. I would mess about, quite content in my tiny little kitchen making my supper. I'd switch on my two-bar electric fire and stare into it. Did life change so swiftly, so entirely in just three months? This little bird was to learn it could change so swiftly and entirely in three seconds.

I'd spend my evenings swotting over my scripts, sitting up half the night stuffing my head with dialogue. I'd study my roles and probe for meanings that were not evident to me, and very likely not even there. That summer and into autumn I had almost no free days. No sooner had I finished one TV play than I was asked to do another. The phone would ring and I would jump to it. *Yes please. No thank you. Yes please.* Rehearsal time fixed, costume fittings, money settled. But it was not as simple as that. Finding myself playing leading roles, working with the finest actors, directors, and play writers was like a tormented fantasy. They must be mad – *I* must be mad. I can't learn all this... I'm out of my depth... why hadn't I settled for doing bits and pieces. I would sit there clutching my script and let the tremors take over. The flat was very quiet. My concentration would break and my eyes would go to the phone. I'd try not to phone-watch. But I longed to call Kenny, and say help me. Above all else, I longed for him to call me. Then more studying.

In the morning, half asleep, I'd step into the bathroom for a bath, into the kitchen for coffee, and hurry out of Cross Keys, through Marylebone High Street, meeting the swarm of glazed morning faces all surging like rabbits down the escalator at Bond Street tube station.

Looking back now, as it sometimes seems from another life, almost another world, I realise with gratitude how extraordinarily fortunate I was to be involved with such clever creative people, and despite my youth and relative ignorance, to be accepted as one of them.

London was exciting, humming. I felt stimulated. On the train I would sit, preferably in a corner, and watch the others chatter. A dull lot I thought, erased faces, toneless. With a firm grip on my handbag and script folder I'd look out of the window and feel that I was really living. Everybody's so nice to me I thought, and felt thrilled that my whole happiness was love. Kenny. And my work. My thoughts would rattle on.

Kenny had obviously worked it out in an organised way.

Darling little one,

I have told Bill that I shall be late home after golf on Sundays and also I want to have one night a week out with the boys. So that time will be ours. I'm sorry love, that it has to be so clandestine and that I'll never be able to take you out, but we have promised each other, haven't we, to be as discreet as possible. I know there will be times when you will feel terrible alone, and sexy. You are so very young. I'll have to go to France for the long family holiday, darling; if you meet a young man and let him make love to you, which would be perfectly understandable, *please* don't ever tell me. I know this happiness can't be permanent, will it all end in tears? Sometimes I'm miserable because I feel I'm being unfair to you and to Bill, but I can't be sensible all the time. I love you and want your little head on my shoulder. You sounded a bit depressed on the phone this morning, please don't be, even though I love your sad gentleness. I do know the ache of it all. I loved your card, it was kind and delicious.

Sunday's almost here, *goody, goody.*

Joe.

It was Sunday and by six o'clock the drinks were on our appropriate tray; by appropriate I mean not chipped or plastic, but polished mahogany. The ice bucket was ready, the record player grooving Sinatra, the table laid with a small bowl of red roses, and my two best glasses polished. And candles. The dinner cooling and warming at exactly the right temperature. It was a pretty room, looking down into the cobbled mews, and I wanted Kenny to feel at home and to be happy when he was with me. The flat, as much as he need see of it, was ready. My old shopping bag, tap shoes and wellington boots, and the plant from my bedroom which had begun to droop, had been hurriedly flung into the spare bedroom along with the growing mound of ironing. The room was now perfectly useless; we christened it the 'frightening' room: I could barely open the door for clutter. Kenny complained that he was not allowed to see into this room. He'd wander round the flat like someone at an art exhibition; he'd study the contents of my cupboards and drawers – 'What are you looking for?' I asked.

'I'm only getting to know you,' he answered.

'This pastry is wonderful, so light,' he'd enthuse, 'aren't I lucky… not only are you sexy and funny… but your pastry and chicken in a white sauce is the best I've ever tasted!' Praise indeed, but I flinched, thinking of the empty tins and frozen pastry wrappers hidden in next door's dustbin. I bullied myself into thinking that being a married man's love was a game of

126

illusion, and that included pretending I was a better cook than I was, better read than I was, always careful to shove the *Sunday Pictorial* under the bed, and leaving the *Telegraph* ostentatiously on the loo seat, the pages with the art sections folded neatly on the top. I kept a child's blackboard in the kitchen and I wrote memos and messages to myself, things to ask Kenny, things to show Kenny, things to tell Kenny. I wanted to fill my life with him, I wanted to do his laundry, buy his shaving cream, buy presents for him. Buy toys for Sarah. Tell lies for him, type his letters, manicure his nails. I longed for quiet domestic evenings with him. Him mending the hoover, him carving the joint. Me scrubbing his back in the bath, me making the cocoa. I wanted to dote on him, tell him how beautiful he was. I loved him, old enough to be my father, broad-shouldered and gentle and aware, in his neat cavalry twill trousers and scratchy sports jackets. Five feet nine and three quarter inches and yet to me he seemed to be as tall as a tree. To be with him would be the perfect life I thought. When our one year comes to its end, however, would I live without him? For the first time I was desperately in love.

I went into the bathroom to prepare myself, with the most acute focusing down to the last eyelash and toenail. I wanted to be feminine and sexy and pretty for him. Kenny must not feel disappointed with me. I was beginning to feel nervous. I hadn't seen him since Wednesday evening; the waiting had seemed an eternity. Scented and smooth, and tolerably happy with myself, I went into the bedroom which I made as pleasing as possible, switched on the electric blanket – a gift from my mother and the only heating in the room – slipped into my black see-through baby-doll nightie and into bed. I carefully arranged the pillows and propped myself up with one arm draped across the blanket, and the other rapidly getting pins and needles above my head. I arranged my hair so that it was half down across my eyes like a curtain. I lay there looking as limp as possible, my state of eighteen-carat sexuality all very carefully arranged. I lay there and all I could think about was

127

him. My arms started to go to sleep and feel uncomfortable, and I began to feel it was a sham; tears like glycerine started to run down from under my lashes; I mustn't cry, not *now*, my *mascara*. Staring at a spot on the ceiling, they ran back into my hair making my temples sticky and matting my hair. It's all hopeless I thought. Two thirds of me was love; one third fear. But I lay there heavily coated with an air of nonchalance and admitting that resting like this was a real effort. I heard the click of his key turning in the lock of the front door; the front door slamming. There was a whistle and the rushing sound of him bounding up the stairs two at a time. At this point his jacket would be dropped, tie thrown off; there was something endearing in the fact that he was so shamelessly eager. I gathered from the endless flow of information that streamed across the bedroom that golf had been good. 'Harry was in good form, so was I, kept my head down... I've been thinking about you all day. It's freezing in here... the traffic in Putney was awful... a solid jam.' I looked up at him, thrilled. His curling hair and the heightened colour of someone who had enjoyed an afternoon in the country air. Shoes, trousers off – the great laugh roared out. 'Ooh it's freezing, move over... have you got the blanket on?' I nodded. 'God bless your mother!'

He yawned an enormous yawn. 'All right for you, little one?'

'Yes, thank you.' Perfectly so. The pinging sound began and I leapt out of bed. 'That's the oven timer – dinner's ready.'

Rumpled and flushed we ate and drank some wine. We got through a bottle and we talked incessantly, our conversation like a game of ping pong.

'We've got the Nivens and Hawkins and Rex Harrison coming for dinner tomorrow,' he said through a mouthful.

'We', the unbearable, insufferable 'we'. I mustn't cry – that would be unforgivable.

'He was married to Kay Kendall, wasn't he?' I asked. 'What was she like?'

'Great fun, lovely girl. Before she knew Rex, we had a brief affair – the sex wasn't much good… we giggled too much.'

Another name on the list. My heart ached. I hadn't expected to hear that. I didn't want to hear that. I was jealous. It hurt. Change the subject, talk about something else quickly. Tell him about your job.

'Could you help me, I've got this big speech and I can't get it right.' Common ground. 'I want to try and do it on my own… but I don't find acting easy.'

He leant towards me very confidentially. 'Show me… what do you find difficult?'

I pushed the script into his hands. I felt shivery, and pulling my blue sweater around me, I went and sat by the electric fire; the red bulb under the imitation logs flickered.

'Who wrote this?' Deliberately he flipped to the front page. 'Alun Owen, he's good… and Ted Kotcheff directing.' He grinned suddenly, 'Colin Blakely and Frank Finlay, eh?' His eyebrows rose in a zigzag of surprise. The expression on his face was sweet, thoughtful and not without humour. 'Little one, I'd better watch out… you'll soon be catching me up!' Reaching forward he enveloped me in a huge bear hug and kissing me roughly on the back of my neck he said, 'Will I be able to say, I knew her when…!' He turned back to the script and commanded, 'Homework time.'

We started on my first scene. At the finish, after an hour and a half of suggestions, instructions, coaching, my head was swimming. 'I feel silly, standing here doing it in front of you… could you close your eyes and not watch me… I'd do it better then.'

He raised his eyebrows. 'I know that feeling… now have you got a copy of *Hamlet*… there's a speech I want to read to you… it's his speech to the players… it tells all the secrets.' I passed the book to him. 'Ah!' he cried, clasping it to him. 'Ah! marvellous Hamlet!' I stared at his crumpled face whispering, the strength of the words enveloping us like a vapour.

Confidence began to slip in; cautiously I began to feel maybe I'm not so bad.

'He's said it all hasn't he?' The small room was still, my face turned upwards towards him, an immobile beige mask. He took a sip of his wine and suddenly smiled at me. 'You know what, darling... I see myself in you all the time, I remember... you have all the enthusiasm that I had.' He fingered the corner of the book thoughtfully; his eyes looked sad for a moment. Then he slapped his thighs. 'Do it for me again, one more time.' He dug into his pocket for a tissue. 'That's right... take a pause there... titch longer... when you say... "Do you mean it..." look Colin right in the eyes... head still... keep your head *still...*' He looked at me steadily.

'I *can't*,' I sniffed.

'A bobbing head is distracting – stillness... that's the first bloody golden rule.'

'All right... I'll try... but everyone will notice I've got a big nose.'

'Big noses are interesting.'

'Not to girls who've got them.'

He was standing up. He was leaving. We kissed on the mouth, our eyes open, melting into each other's reflection; we held each other tightly. I was not unhappy: I felt almost light-headed, high with the fantasy of the evening. I waved him goodbye from the window and watched the tail-lights of his Mercedes disappear round the corner. I didn't start to clear away the dishes. I sat for a while in his chair, trying to preserve the illuminated feeling.

It was a see-saw of a life. It could have been thought a lonely life for a girl barely out of her teens, but my eyes had a sparkle. I didn't wish I was out partying, meeting people. Like Daddy I believed in miracles; I had to – only then would things get done. There was no doubt in my mind, none whatever, that if you believed you could do something, then quite simply you could. How could I fail? I turned myself over to learning everything I possibly could about the theatre. I would fly all over London on my borrowed bicycle to dance classes, standing in line with other girls in sweaty, darned leotards, stretching and straining in unison at the wooden practice barre to the rhythm of a clapped out piano; iron-willed and competitive youngsters with sore muscles, we devoted ourselves to endless afternoons of sweat and fatigue. I was thrilled to be one of them. I was beginning to feel not a baby any more. The teachers were demanding, severe, and their striving for perfection eventually got the better of me. Distressing as it was to admit, there really was no point in deceiving myself: I was not meant to be a dancer, my feet refused to turn out. I was awkward and heavy on my feet. As I sprained my ankle for the third time, I finally convinced myself that dancing had nothing to do with my dream, so I swiftly and without difficulty gave it up.

Voice lessons, Miss Iris Warren's classes, stand out vividly. She was the most wonderful teacher. A dignified, gentle woman with silver hair. She taught me the beginnings of projection, breathing. I'd stand in front of her, my hands on my rib-cage, breathing deeply, using my diaphragm, making the most absurd sound together with even more absurd face pulling. I'd feel a fool and giggle a lot, but I knew I'd have to forget my self-consciousness or I'd never achieve anything.

'We have a lot of work to do on your voice,' she said. 'The first thing we must do is to try and lower your register,' she smiled, 'and you're biting your bottom lip again... it looks unattractive, try not to, dear.'

'Sorry,' I muttered.

I loved her classes. She sat at her piano with a stately bearing that reminded me a little of the Queen Mother. She would tell me the secret of whispering a difficult speech to yourself ('If you whisper the words, you'll find the true reading'), of being aware of myself in a new way, of using every part of your being to express emotion. I hadn't realised all that was about being an actress. How had I done as well as I had so far, knowing so little? As she talked, her graceful hands soared through the air, her small diamond ring glinting, adding expression to her words. It was her enthusiasm addressing mine.

I stared at the gilt-edged invitation and my mouth went dry. Our film, *Some People*, was to have a Royal Premiere on July 17th. I couldn't believe I would actually be meeting the Duke of Edinburgh again – and Kenny's wife. Our worlds were so apart, it never occurred to me that our paths might cross socially and that we would come face to face. I started to shake.

My evening dress was ballerina-length oyster satin and lace. It had been made for Gina Lollobrigida. Her sister Fernanda had sold it to me when I'd been in Rome. I danced around in front of the mirror, flirted with myself. I rehearsed the yet-to-happen evening. I did it becomingly, so easy when you're playing all parts. Wasn't I cute? The dress would do it for me, I thought. Wouldn't I cope brilliantly with royalty and wives wearing something so stunning?

It was a star-studded evening. I saw my parents briefly in the throng, they looked so handsome. 'Hello,' I called and just had time to see their faces light up before I was whisked off to an enormous party at the Savoy Hotel. Stuart Lyons, Joan's boyfriend, was my escort. The women were all in glamorous dresses, prettied up even more with their best jewellery. I stayed close to Stuart and watched the famous faces – old, not so old, and nearly new. I saw Kenny; almost sauntering over, he asked me to dance.

'Hello, darling,' he whispered in my hair, 'you see the fun we can have... evenings like these... if we are careful.' He rattled on.

'I think it's time for me to leave,' I said as other dancers squeezed past us on their way round the floor.

'I'm sorry I can't take you home... I hate to see you go... I'm sorry,' he said again.

I was nervous and stunned enough to obey when he said, 'You'd better come over and say hello to Bill... she wants to meet you.' I was full of conflict as he steered me towards their table; her blonde smiling face swam into focus. I was so unnerved by the meeting, I could hardly say anything. She spoke in a bright voice.

'Kenny thinks you are so talented... he calls you his protégée... do come to tea and meet Sarah.' That was all I could take. I said something witty, like 'That would be nice'; my eyes bounced off her face on to his and I tried to smile as I headed towards the ladies' cloakroom. For a few seconds I stared in front of me and trembled. There was so much I didn't understand. I now had a face to put with the name. Did she love him? My every nerve jumped. Oh Kenny. Oh Kenny, damn you. The churning emotions came through my eyes, my clenched fingers and my trembling knees. The tears fell and I looked up and saw reflected in the mirror the face of a mascaraed baby.

There were things about being an actress I hadn't known about, but was starting to learn.

'Miss Douglas, my name is "Fred Smith" – it's good of you to come and see me. Won't you sit down? I saw you on television on Sunday evening... I thought you were good.'

'Thank you... did you really?' Imagine. 'Fred Smith' had just said he thought I was good. Famous name. Famous film producer. Wow! I looked at him surrounded by awards and silver cups, framed pictures of the Royal family, fancy recording equipment, and a pile of scripts. I saw an elegant man of obvious prosperity, straight back, a slight paunch, evasive brown eyes, but quite attractive.

'Angela,' he said, settling back into his huge chair, his pudgy fingers clasped round his cigar, 'I'm making a new picture and there's a part I think you'd be just right for.' Words one assumes every young actress aches to hear.

Perched on the edge of my chair, I piped, 'There is?'

He looked at me and nodded and pulled a script from the top of the pile. Talking quietly, looking at me across his large mahogany desk, he made me laugh, relax. When he stood up and approached the corner of his desk, I noticed he wiped perspiration from his top lip with a crisp white handkerchief. Sitting on the edge of the desk, his leg touching my knee, he reached forward and took my face in his hand and tilted my chin up towards him. 'You really do have baby-blue eyes, don't you?' I waited, wearing a saintly smile, shoving my feet firmly into my shoes, thinking, you can't run without your shoes on. 'My car's outside... shall we go for lunch... it would be nice to be in more relaxed surroundings.'

I'd never thought before in terms of casting couch. 'Mr Smith...' I began, hearing the echo of my own voice, 'I'm sorry, but I don't...' I tried to edge away. And then I sneezed.

'Bless you,' he said.

I sneezed again, 'Achewww!' in full cry, covering us both this time with spray.

I apologised and said how embarrassed I was as I sidestepped my way to the door. 'I'm sorry, Mr Smith.'

'When you realise how good the part is,' he said sourly, 'you will be.'

I left his office feeling sick. Morosely I walked to the bus stop. What did he think I was?

I can't stand the rain. I can't stand the rain, I thought as I hurried up Berners Street towards Sandersons determined to order my new bathroom wallpaper before catching a train to Manchester to rehearse a new television play for Granada. The rain, dropping from heavy dark clouds, had already drizzled through my jacket and I was trying to function on positive thought and control my dread of being cold and wet. I peered at people more sensible than I, sheltering in doorways, as the rain splashed against me. Time was important to me. And time was short. Hurry, hurry.

Suddenly, not more than ten feet from me, I felt a shadow; heard a whoosh, and looked up, and in the middle of my eyes I saw a brown billowing spread-eagled sack shape, with a distorted pale biscuit face of a man toppling towards me. What I was witnessing was staggering. I was being dive-bombed by a suicide attempt. Slowly, slowly he was descending on me. I stared, horrified, immobile, rigid in the grip of terror. My legs left me. I felt my muscles knot and my mind lost its consciousness. I remember that I lay, clutching the base of the lamp-post with my trembling hands, my legs shaking and feeble. I found I was looking at what was left of the face lying close by me, cracked and running with blood, smashed away by the pavement.

My stomach turned over in fierce nausea and my head pounded. I was terrified. I was conscious of a woman who was gently wiping some of the man's blood and my tears from my face. This poor man had killed himself. I had seen it happen in front of my eyes. For months to come I was to see it happen again and again. A policeman swam in and out of my consciousness and I heard him say, 'He's done it at last, has he?' More sound and as a man grabbed my arms and helped me, stumbling footsteps, into a waiting ambulance, I looked down at my torn tights and skirt filthy from blood and the gutter, and heard from somewhere beside me a voice say, 'Poor girl... she nearly copped it... she was calling a name... some bloke Kenny... to come and help her...' God, had I mentioned his name, out loud?

'No, no, I'll b-b-be a-all r-right,' I stammered, 'could y-you call m-my agent, Joan Gray... she'll look a-after me.' Waves of longing for Kenny swept over me. I'd known about being frightened before, but not about terror. So this was terror. And somewhere in the back of my mind, I heard the actress in me say, I'll know how to play this one. It was perhaps the first time I was conscious of feeling detached from reality – that I was an observer rather than a participant in my own life.

I was alone. It occurred to me that I could lie here in my bath in my jeans all day, all week, lolling like a corpse. There was no one to fuss me, worry about me. No one to say, get out of that bath dear, these are the best years of your life, a lie has no legs, but has wings. Peter, what are we going to do with Angela? Your jeans must be shrunk by now. Oh, Mummy, if this is love, why am I crying all the time? After about half an hour I pulled the plug out, stood up and struggled out of my jeans, emptied the basin of my marinating undies, picked up the wastepaper basket half full of crumpled sheets of writing paper, the rough copies of my letters to Kenny. Tidying up, I moved my books from outside the loo, my copy of Freud very much in evidence, remembering Kenny's comment when he saw it. 'Christ – I wish you'd stop reading this stuff, it has a very heavy effect on your chat!' I laughed, and then seeing myself in the mirror, I thought that being in love and being alone made me look a bit bleak, so I blew a raspberry at myself and went to answer the phone. There was a pause, then a click. Anonymous calls, dirty and to the point, or just breathless, were beginning to unnerve me, however much I tried to arm myself with self-assurance; they had become an intolerable intrusion. My fear of the unknown male caller was physical; I'd quiver with nerves.

My eyes had been wide with disbelief; sitting in Joan's office in Cork Street, she laughed. 'They must be mad... the BBC want you to review next weekend's programmes... an eight-minute live slot.' She pulled at her earrings and slipped them into her make-up purse and, as unthinkingly as ever, I said yes. Easy-peasy.

Television had discovered me. Flavour of the month perhaps. I had chosen to splash myself across the small screen; I'd sought the love and praise of people unknown to me. I wanted success and I wanted recognition. But could I bring it off? Now suddenly I had a little more money and I found that I was being stared at when I waited for a bus, watched while I chose a pair of shoes; people seemed to be interested in what I thought. I'd become a little somebody. It was a big surprise. I was young and not ready, but I have to admit it, I loved the novelty of it all. I wonder if I knew then how close to the wind I was sailing, how easily I could have bombed. I must have been hugging an invisible safeguarding cloak – called youth.

Slumped in the hard leather chairs of the make-up room at Lime Grove, I looked at Jill who'd come with me, and admitted that this time I'd surely gone too far: me, a critic? Could she tell the producer that I had malaria, and would they please get someone else. Jill's voice was calm and quite unworried. She turned towards me, her eyes smiling.

'Pretend Kenny's here watching you. Go on, Ange... show him what you can do.' I hugged her. I did like her. It seems you can sometimes make friends at a tender age, in whom you can effortlessly delight, for whom you feel a trueness. Jill was this sort of friend of mine.

Gripping my notes I felt a sudden surge of confidence. Yes, I'll show him... make him proud of me. Bless him... love him... oh, yes... all right.

The actress with the wild red hair and curvy figure took off her dark glasses and sat back lazily and beautifully in her make-up chair next to mine.

'You look sort of different today,' said her make-up artist, wrapping the blue nylon gown loosely around the gorgeous girl.

The actress expelled her breath. 'I should,' she said, and roared with laughter. 'Boy what a night... my boyfriend... all night... five times.' Her face looked almost mad with delight. She held up one hand and snapped at her cigarette lighter in one quick movement. I flinched at the tone of her voice. God, how common I thought, to talk about sex so blatantly; such a girl had to be a tart. I sat there in prissy silence, straining to hear more. I lolled back in my chair, eyes closed, ears wide open. Her conversation was exciting me against my will, making me feel distinctly lightheaded.

137

'No, he didn't... oooh, I've never done *that*... that's not possible,' said the make-up girl, giggling while she struggled with a pair of false eyelashes. The actress reached over and pulled her nearer, her voice went lower, quieter, and I strained to catch the whispering. I sat there astonished.

The actress stood up and pouted in the mirror. Stretching, she beamed her easy natural smile around the room. 'He thinks all I'm good for is spending his money and bed... all men think that though, don't they!' These sentiments made the others laugh, but my eyes had a frozen look. She'd used words like, freaked out, turned on, toys – I'd heard a new language. I couldn't take my eyes off her. I wondered if the girls Kenny had known before were anything like her. With a last look at her face, she clicked on her dark glasses, touched her hair deliberately, in an idle way, said goodbye in her soft voice and was gone.

The make-up girl turned her attention to me, bustling around. 'I'm too old for toys in the bedroom.' Somehow her voice held a note of regret. I wanted more than anything to dash after the actress. Tell me more, teach me.

Jill and I went down into the studios, but I remembered little about being on television that evening. I must have looked very bewildered – it didn't help that my mind was filled with visions of my teddy bear sitting in my bedroom.

My lover, sitting head in hands in our rumpled sheets, roared with kindly laughter. 'What are you *doing* with your teddy!'

It hadn't been a triumph. 'I heard that toys... when you make love... that, er... well... y-you'd be turned on.' He rolled over on the bed, taking Teddy away from me, kissing me, whispering, telling me the secrets of bedroom toys. 'Really – truly? I've seen one of those... I thought it was an old Indian musical instrument!'

'You are such an innocent. Hold on to that... it's precious... no one must rob you of it.' I'd grown up a little more.

We kissed the chocolate from around each other's mouths, his car keys already in his hand, as he opened the door, 'Got to go, little one.' I knew, of course, and nodded, couldn't say anything for fear of crying, so I nodded and smiled a little more. He was going to the South of France with his wife and Sarah for several weeks for their summer holiday. He was going in August and already it was almost the end of July. 'Love, love... kiss,' I said, my head on his shoulder. When we are seventy will we be together in a little house somewhere, and love each other till we die? I wanted to plead with him, *don't leave me, look after me.* But I stood there smiling, trying to please him. I wanted to be his sweet love. My life, my senses revolved around this man. And our relationship was utterly hopeless. My heart is yours, he said. I wanted more. I must try my hardest; I must pretend not to love him so much. It was tough going.

'Love you,' he said.

'Me you too.'

'All right?' he said.

'All right Kenny.' I'm all right Kenny.

It was almost impossible in the first moments after us being together to know what to feel. I went to the phone and called Jill.

'Kenny's going to France for weeks,' I wailed, my heart shrivelling at the words.

'Do you want to come over?' she asked.

'Yes.' I was depressed and terribly frightened. To know that he was going away was devastating to me. I must somehow find a way to live in the present, confine myself in a twenty-four-hour box. I must not let my emotions leak out.

Another letter from Kenny! Just seeing his handwriting gave me a thrill, it went through me like a bubble. There it was waiting for me, half out of the letter box. I pulled it out. Then, as always, I read it standing in the mews. I would have re-read it again by the time I got to the landing, and then on to our bed, to memorise each line and to kiss his name. He said:

Monte Carlo

Darling little one,

    I heard a song on the radio today. 'You're my first, you're my last, my everything,' which says it for me.

    You're hidden in my heart.

    Je t'adore.

    Joe

I answered c/o Barclays Bank, Monte Carlo:

Darling Joe,

    I could not love you, couldn't miss you more than I do.

    Endless love,

    In misery without you.

Darling little one,

    I love innocence and since you are… I'm like a fool, I keep hearing your little voice calling.

    Joe

Darling Joe,

    I have that beautiful picture of you, it is such a comfort, I kiss it all the time. All the love I have inside me is for you.

A letter a day, all on the same story line.

Three nights later I was standing starkers, in front of my mirror, thinking I was no glamour-puss. I couldn't claim not to see the dimples. Kenny had said, 'Your bottom will spread a bit when you're forty – but it won't be my problem.' I'd pretended not to hear him; I wanted to be his problem at forty, or, anyway, to be his at forty. Begone fat thighs, and I started to limber up. Early nights and exercise gave me a good feeling. I was becoming accustomed to being alone, but sometimes the silence was unnerving. Still I wouldn't have it any other way. Or would I?

The rapture of an occasional surprise phone call almost made up for everything, even the loneliness. Once he played Ray Charles's *I Can't Stop Loving You*, and sang along with it. 'You're being extravagant darling; this is long distance,' I said.

'Ah, I'm a lover,' he hummed. I was glued to the phone.

'Will you bring me back some sugared almonds?' I asked.

'Yes, yes, sunshine, I want to sleep with you too.' I began to laugh and have grave doubts about his hearing. I followed that call with a letter, posted the same evening.

There was one thing wrong with the way I was living: when I turned out the light at night, my dreams were of Kenny and he was married, and he was in France. If I could only sleep with him all night. Just once all night. How could I love him so much when he was seldom around?

Soon it would be his birthday. Birthdays were birthdays, and special. I *wished* I could be with him. I was jealous, green as a shamrock, as they say. But there was no use in crying. Oh dear, I wish I were rich, someone else. As a child I was always wishing. Mummy used to say, 'You'll wish your life away, child.' Nothing has changed, I'm still a wisher.

I went in search of little presents for him, past the brightly lit shop windows, the off-licence, the newsagent. My thoughts were busy, crossing at the lights, skipping past the cars... touch and go... brakes screeched... 'Bloody bird...!'

'Sorry!' I shouted out. Stopping at the greengrocers, my mind gave a little leap. I clapped my hands and said rather too shrilly, 'What beautiful carrots!' There they were, two intertwined, like lovers. Like us. Lovers' legs, I thought. The man with the short fat neck, who called himself Bruce and wore bright pink shirts, had a smile for me and asked if I were in love. My expression and my hands clasping these two precious carrots must have already confirmed that. Bruce, surprised and amused though he may have been, said nothing, just put them in a brown paper bag with twisted corners. 'That'll be thruppence, Angie.' As I went down the road I thought, sweet, sweet, he'll love them... they'll be his best present. Trailing around the shops I bought him a pair of shorts that had an Italian label on them, two paperbacks and a record, called *I'll remember you*, he will he will, won't he. And some aniseed balls and three cards. I posed for a picture in a booth and when I was wrapping my gifts, on a wild impulse, I slipped my picture and the carrots into a pair of my best white lace knickers. Parcelled up and posted, care of the bank, I regretted not being able to see his face, as he sat in the small Monte Carlo park in the shade of exotic palms and the Casino, reading my mail. He'd read it once, twice, then the evidence would be shredded up and left in the wastebins, along with the empty Ambre Solaire bottles. I bet he'll think they're the most beautiful and romantic presents, I bet he'll smile.

Apparently he didn't. He told me that he turned bright red and had stood there for a few moments wondering what to do after the bank clerk, a girl, pushed this package across the counter, string snapped and paper all torn. The clerk stepped away from him, her face turned, partially buried in her hand. 'Are these for you, Mr More?'

'Christ, nothing to do with me,' he said, slowly picking up the knickers and in that moment the carrots fell out. He stood stupidly staring, motionless. Jesus, I'm embarrassed, he thought, how am I going to carry this off? 'Listen, M'selle, please do something for me – lose these!'

'Yes, Mr More,' her eyes twinkling and looking a little past him. He didn't realise he could walk so fast until he reached the end of the avenue and leaned against the railing, out of breath and smiling now; Wow, that's my baby doll.

'Rex made my birthday for me... gave a small party for me on his yacht.' He'd missed me of course, but he'd had a good time. *Oh, Kenny, Kenny,* I wanted to say, *how could you have a good time without me?*

I read the telegram sitting up in bed. I placed it on the side table, astonished. I threw myself back on the pillow rigid with excitement.

> I AM IN ROME FOR FORTY-EIGHT HOURS DOING TESTS LOOKING FOR A NEW GIRL TO BE IN MY NEXT FILM. DARLING COULD YOU DROP EVERYTHING AND JOIN ME AT THE EXCELSIOR HOTEL. DON'T WORRY ABOUT THE AIR FARE I WILL REIMBURSE YOU LITTLE LOVE. JOE

Still undressed I yelled around the flat, '*Kenny! Kenny...! Kenny I love you!*'

Jill got me to Heathrow Airport early the next morning, October lst. Overnight I'd washed my best white jeans and they were still damp, no matter. I had an apple and Mars bar in my pocket and felt somehow so grown up, five feet four-and-a-half of impudence. I'd never felt so happy in my life. We'll be together, *all night.*

The entire party, about eight of us, went out to dinner that night. I felt conspicuous, it took courage for us to be with other people, we'd always been so solitary. Kenny, tanned, looked incredibly attractive; his manners were as polished and suave as only those of a film star in full flight. My eyes followed him around and I hardly ate a thing. I really didn't hear a word anyone said, except perhaps, pass the bread. As the wine flowed on far into the night, the guests lounged lazily back in their chairs, all except for me, who was busy trying to find Kenny's leg under the table to gently kick. We exchanged longing, baleful glances. When can we leave this lot and be alone, in bed?

Later that night, Kenny waited until the corridor was clear before he slipped quietly through my door, locking it behind him. Sitting on my bed, my arms circling my legs, which were

143

drawn up under me, I felt as though I'd been sitting there waiting for him for such a long time. He put his arms around me.

'I'm yours, little darling… just being together,' he said in a voice so gentle I could only just hear him.

Hug me, hold me, promise me… I was so content with our affection and closeness, I felt safe.

'I'd better slip back to my room,' he muttered. I lay there half asleep, hugged in his arms.

'Why?' I said, bewildered.

'It's against the law in Italy… to sleep together when you aren't married.'

'No… Kenny… *no*… you can't leave me… what are you saying…' Emotion spilling out, I couldn't keep it in check.

'I *must* darling… we daren't get caught.'

'You *mustn't*… I haven't seen you for weeks… I've flown here to be with you for just one night… and now you are going back to your own room?'

'Don't cry… don't be a baby… I love you… don't make it difficult for me… please… it's the law.' To hell with the law, to hell with convention. 'Darling, darling,' he whispered. I couldn't stop crying; he tilted my chin, kissed me and left me, burning with heartache, sickened with disappointment.

I sat on the edge of the bed; the anger and loneliness would not leave me alone. I thought of him sleeping, just three rooms away from mine, content and prepared to catch the first flight back to Nice in the morning. And the reality of the situation exploded in my heart. My brain began to work and the feeling began to creep over me that we couldn't continue. I wanted to tear our relationship apart. I had to protect myself. Hurting me like this definitely wasn't on. I rang down for coffee and sat at the desk in my room. I wrote and cried through the night. I loved him as I had never loved or ever would again… it had been a dream where we'd both found such happiness… I was prepared to tiptoe around London in the shadows, obey the rules of Kenny's double life... I sat grimly in a pool of light from the desk lamp, tears plopping on to the paper. If you want to live by rules, then what the hell am I doing in your life at all... leave me alone... I'll sell the flat and give you your money back... I won't be treated like this, so casually. I screamed it all on to the page. I can't take it... measure it... hold back... it's over. Seven months into my one-year plan, and a crack had appeared. I looked at my watch; the sounds of the lift told me the hotel was waking up. Beginning to quiver with exhaustion at the whole miserable night, I thought I'd have a bath and rest for a few minutes, slip my letter under Kenny's door and go for a long walk before making my way to the airport. My mind was full of images.

I pulled myself up on the pillows; it was ten-thirty and I woke in a panic. 'Baby,' I read, 'I crept in to say goodbye and you were still asleep. I wanted to kiss you. I'll be back in London in ten days, bear with me my little one, at times I must appear to be such a stuffy old bugger to you.' I read and re-read his note with speed. He was gone. Yes, I thought, you are a silly old bugger, but *I love you*, and I tore up my letter.

I went back to London with a head full of muddled sensations and a particularly brittle pain at our parting. When the taxi drew up outside my flat, there was a cellophane-wrapped bouquet of flowers on the doorstep. 'Darling, time for the dark clouds to move over and let the sunshine in... love you. Joe.' I turned the key in the lock and thought, hey diddle diddle, how lovely.

A few days later our reunion, in typical fashion, in bed. I kept on laughing as he'd emptied three packets of sugared almonds over me, and six lipsticks all the same colour, and a bottle of perfume, 'Je Reviens'. I still have the box. We settled down, like children, hand in hand, and ate toast and jam with enormous appetite, and slept a little. We had many lyrical afternoons when he didn't want to leave, staying later than he should. The mark of a married man is that he wears his watch in bed. Kenny's thin gold dial, strapped to his wrist by a black crocodile strap, sent a pang through me. He'd fold myself around him as he went to leave our warm disordered bed.

'You don't have to go, do you?'

He'd tap his watch, shrug and say, 'I do have to.' He'd sit on the small stool, dressing briskly: the room was so cold. Reaching over to kiss me, he'd pull the blankets up around my face, and do his best to jolly me up. But our goodbye kisses were swift; both of us afraid of my bursts of grief.

The weeks passed quickly. Happy indeed to be working again with Colin Blakely in a play called *The Slaughter Men*, directed by Christopher Morahan, then immediately into another TV play for him. It was called *Rosemary*, written by Elia Kazan's wife, Molly, set at the turn of the century. I played an American girl half of a vaudeville act. It was virtually a ninety-minute two-hander. Chris said, as he handed me the script, 'This is your Waterloo, Angela.' He was spot on. I loved every minute of working with him.

Straight after that I said 'yes' to doing a play with Alfie Lynch and John Thaw called *A Smashing Day* written by the talented Alan Plater. Work-wise everything was fantastic. Good scripts and actors, devoted directors. Professionally it was a challenging, demanding and exciting period. Mummy and Daddy said how proud and pleased they were. I went home a lot. There was a warm feeling for me there. They still weren't happy that their daughter had fallen for a married man, almost their age. But they were still protective, unjudging.

On the twenty-ninth of October, my twenty-second birthday, red roses were delivered to my flat. A card inside said:

Oct. 29th 1962

Happy Birthday my darling
    I will love you always
    Joe x

He took me to lunch at the Brompton Grill... the first time we were seen alone in public. He'd ordered a cake for me; he gave me a Victorian brooch, a delicate diamond and turquoise heart with pearls. He said he was sorry he couldn't be with me that evening. I said it was all right, knowing it wasn't. On the pavement we hugged and kissed quickly before I got into my taxi and he got into his. We pulled our windows down, reached out and held hands and hung on until we got to the lights and had to go our separate ways. I put my hand over my eyes to try and keep my tears a secret.

That night Jill and I sat in the Circle at the Haymarket Theatre and saw *The School for Scandal* with John Gielgud. I had my beautiful brooch pinned on my jacket collar, and my eyes went from John Gielgud to brooch, brooch to John Gielgud. Both sparklers.

One evening I heard him calling through my letter box, 'Darling, it's me... let me in... I've forgotten my key.' I went quickly to the window and watched him look up at me, unsteady on his feet, winking and grinning. I looked at my watch: eleven-thirty. I clenched my fists and shook them at him, stuck my tongue out, switched off all the lights and went into the bedroom and lay staring up at the darkness. How *dare* he roll up here drunk; and as I said it out loud, I started to listen to the clang-bang-crash of my dustbins. I raced downstairs shaking, and opened the door. There he was, red-faced and holding his sides: 'I was climbing your drainpipe... it gave way... the dustbins broke my fall... my ribs, darling... ooh... I've hurt something... it's agony,' he muttered. I was face to face with my lover lying amongst the contents of my dustbins and my drainpipe hanging off the wall. Somehow I got him to Jill's who got a doctor somebody and he said something or other about two cracked ribs. Jill and I took Kenny in a taxi to where he lived. I sat well back in my seat and watched him, hands in pockets, try and saunter past the porter's desk. It was almost impossible for me to see him go.

I kept everything in the flat spotless, except for the 'frightening' room, Mummy coming round occasionally to check that I was not forgetting the corners. What with being in love, working and attending my classes, the days passed agreeably. During the evenings I'd play my records or watch TV, and there were long telephone calls with Jill; otherwise my evenings were quiet. No parties, no other lovers, no lunches in smart restaurants with flowers and presents. I didn't think I was lonely, but Mummy once said, 'You sigh a lot, child.'

When Annika went to the Charing Cross Hospital to have her baby she said she wanted me with her. I'd seen her many times since *Some People*, and in the long hours of her labour we talked and talked. I rubbed her back and sponged her face. I suppose the experience is something that will always mean a lot to me; it did at the time, and still does. She talked in a rush in between contractions, disconnected and with humour. I remember we sang pop songs and couldn't eat anything, and I remember that, at a gut level, I could never define how very changed I felt by this experience. The baby, a girl, beat the air with her slippery little arms and legs, almost in protest against her new circumstances. Annika cradled her baby and said, 'Polly... does she look like a Polly... what do you think Ange?'

Runny-eyed, my mind whirled. 'She's very special... you'll never be alone now, Annika.' I said what I felt, but was I *supposed* to feel, *I want a baby too*?

The day was almost breaking when I finally left the hospital and made my way home. In addition to all my other confusions, I now started thinking about a baby. Kenny's baby. I thought a lot about that. I had dreamed of having a baby since childhood. More and more, I wanted the real thing, a real life.

Weeks passed and it was Christmas. Christmas Eve afternoon was to be our time together he said, and there was nothing he'd like better for lunch than eggs and bacon and champagne. I decorated the flat with pretty bunches of holly and ivy tied with red ribbon and fir cones I'd painted gold. I'd been busy for days. From Bruce the greengrocer in the high street I bought a huge spray of mistletoe, dividing it up into small sprigs which I pinned round my bed-head. Christmas cannot be complete without a tree. I chose a small one and pushed it in a plastic bucket normally used for washing my windows, now smartened up in red crepe paper. I hung yards of coloured lights and it looked brilliant and sparkling with the trinkets and sweets and bright objects I'd bought to decorate it. My fingers lovingly tied the strings and coloured paper round the lavish and silly Christmas things: a briefcase; a Big Ben car honker; leather shaving case with K.G.M. (smart!); indoor fireworks; a little felt pink elephant in white tie and tails; parcels and packets spilled from under the tree, and at about eleven-thirty I collapsed into the armchair exhausted, but delighted. My little sitting-room looked like the Fairy's Grotto. This was our first Christmas and I was determined that it would be an afternoon we would always remember. Kenny, typically, arrived in a hurry laden with presents – his spending had been extravagant. There was a nightdress with satin ribbons... a radio... a watch... an apron... a box of coloured Sobrani... a book – *Winnie the Pooh*... and he'd wrapped everything up in Christening paper. But he'd wrapped them himself, and that was important to me. We squealed, opening our stockings with the apple on the top and the orange in the toe, and a lucky sixpence somewhere in between. After lunch we didn't play Hunt the Slipper, or Blindman's Buff, but we laughed. I shake when I laugh, like a bowl of jelly, and he laughed when he saw me.

'Oh, darling… Happy Chrissymus… I'll call you tomorrow at your parents'… just before I have to do the carving… it's Chrissymus and I've got you… I'm so lucky.'

Before I could realise what he was doing, he was kissing me goodbye, whispering words of love. I saw tears in his eyes, but we smiled bravely. I crumpled down exhausted under the blankets to dwell on the excitements and delights of our stolen afternoon, and for the millionth time, listened to our favourite record, Sinatra singing *Close To You*. I refused to cry: no more tears, I'd had my share, more than. It had been wonderful, hadn't it. Sniffing the traces of his aftershave on the pillow, I fell asleep.

Jill did everything she could to distract me that New Year's Eve, cooked dinner for me, took me to a film, but really all I was good for was sitting in a lump by the phone waiting for Kenny to ring. He did, at about one-thirty in the morning. I'd fallen asleep. He was at Jack and Doreen Hawkins' lovely house in Roehampton – the Mores and the Hawkins were great friends. He was high. 'Hello baby… I've just told Noël Coward that if he was as pretty as my love Angela… then I'd give him a big kiss.'

'You *didn't*!'

'I *did*…! And he said that if my Angela was as pretty as him, then he'd be with her and not with him.'

Reason told me that if I loved him then I would be pleased to hear him chuckling so happily, but reason didn't enter into it. 'Stop laughing… how can you sound so happy without me…' I wailed miserably. Emotionally I was disappearing.

It was the beginning of January 1963 and I was filming at Shepperton Studios opposite Tommy Steele in a musical called *It's All Happening*. I'd get up at 5.30 a.m., so cold, the flat was freezing and so was London, we were all trudging around with snow up to our ankles. The minicab would crawl along the icy roads to the studio and I'd slink into Makeup and

Hairdressing, my eyes clogged with sleep and my mind filled with the day's work ahead. A cup of instant coffee would greet me – no sugar, no milk – and I'd cautiously eye the plate of freshly made bacon sandwiches, holding back with iron self-denial. On the set by 8.30 a.m., overanxious about the work, overanxious about everything, Tommy and I would rehearse, the crew bustling in the background. He was terrific, making me feel good, putting me at my ease. 'Silence on the set.' The bell rang. 'Quiet please, rolling,' said the first assistant. The work went well. They were a marvellous crew, fun and relaxed. One evening Tommy took me with him to the Abbey Road recording studios to sit in on a session. As we walked in, he smiled and said hello to everyone, calling them by first names. As I gazed around, a secretary poked her head through an adjoining door. 'The studio is ready for you, Tommy,' she said. On the way we passed another studio, the door open, and right in front of me were the Beatles. I could feel the adrenalin flooding through my body. *There they are*! I fled after Tommy. I couldn't wait to tell Daddy.

My school friend Gillian, still beautiful, was my stand-in. We'd lunch together and one day she told me, 'You'd better be careful, Ange... the word's getting around.' I'd said nothing to anyone, except Jill. But she said there had been a dig at me in one of the gossip columns. Kenny's Mercedes had been spotted outside my flat. Inclining to the simplest view, I panicked. 'He'll leave me if we get found out,' and I poured my heart out to her. I told her I hadn't set out to capture him... but he was a *fan-tas-tic* man and I desperately wanted him... I cry like a child when he leaves me... I'm so scared I'm too far gone and that I'll love him always and never have a real life. Gillian said, anyone with half an eye can see you're in love. But I can't go on like this... I'll be ill... I almost hope he'll leave me. *That's not true*. Or is it? I react instinctively before intelligently. I feel before I speak before I think. When you are full of insecurities and your head is in chaos, then your philosophy falls between the floorboards. My one-year plan had only two months to go.

The situation was undoubtedly awful. I was so chaotically in love that it was like a madness. I'd been in love with love to start with – and I'd been hit by it! And I didn't understand all of what I was feeling, part of which was a remote kind of wretchedness. I could keep going a little longer, but only a little. I wonder at what precise moment I had come to feel, if only I could find another man attractive; well, there were plenty around, I could try. I didn't like the idea: my mind ran on torrid scenes, and it seemed to me a shaming thing, it would not be easy. It was the second week of January and I was standing in the middle of a vast empty sound stage feeling disconsolate, the walls looming above me. An oddly detached voice called my name and I turned around recognising the familiar face of 'Famous Actor'. He talked to me and as he spoke his eyes never left me. I felt utterly strange. Next day he called me and asked me out to dinner. I thanked him and said yes please. Then just for a shadow of a second I admitted to myself what might happen. I read my horoscope in the *Daily Mail*: it didn't help much so I didn't dwell on it.

Dressing speedily I slipped on my new mohair coat, pulled up the collar and went out. It was a small restaurant that looked on to a square. We sat down; the circular table was covered in a heavy white cloth with stiff edges and there was a bowl of rose-coloured roses in the middle. The waiters hovered, bringing us plates of pasta, some chicken in wine and a small dish of chocolate ice cream. We ate quickly while we talked. We stood up and on the way out shook hands with Mario, thank you, thank you, he said meekly, too meekly I thought. I gave him one of my butter-wouldn't-melt-in-my-mouth smiles.

'What a gorgeous little flat,' he said as we went into the bedroom. He closed the door. I love Kenny I thought, as my date smiled and touched my neck with his hand. 'Can I kiss you?' he asked nicely, his eyes shining at me. Nodding, I shrugged my shoulders, took a deep breath and thought, I love my Kenny. I stood there, a little unsteady on my high heels. 'Sit down,' he said and began to stroke my hair. He kissed me again and again, and began to lift my jumper. 'I want you,' he said, kissing me behind my ear, making me shudder.

'Do you want some cocoa?' I asked.

'*Cocoa*?' he repeated, as if it were something only barbarians drank.

'I can't do it!' I said suddenly with vehemence. 'Leave me alone… I'm sorry… I've used you… it was an experiment… to see if I could be unfaithful to my boyfriend… he's married… I thought if I could go to bed with you… it would prove… mean I won't love him forever… I'm so scared that I'll never have a real life… a husband and babies…' I was getting nowhere. I suddenly remembered Mummy's words – 'Never lead a man on, dear, it gives them a pain.' Conscience-stricken – 'I'm not a tease you know… I'll go the whole way if I've hurt your feelings,' my voice was more glum than I meant it to be. I bent down to find my shoes and saw Kenny's slippers under the bed with the dust and fluff, and I felt miserable. He shook his head. I pulled at my skirt and the zip went. I tried to be funny but it didn't work. I started to chatter foolishly. He took his coat off the sofa. 'I'm sorry,' I whispered. 'Golly I'm embarrassed.'

'Oh for Christ's sake stop going on,' he said, 'everyone knows you're straight. I've always fancied you… you'd be great… come here,' the way he said that I felt like a pet. He kissed me again, hurting my tongue; he left me and he didn't say goodbye. My hanky was wet that night from crying. I kept blowing my nose, continuing to make little hiccupy sobs.

The following week was a glorious one, work-wise. I was surprised to see Joan waiting for me on my doorstep waving and smiling as though she hadn't seen me for a year. I soon realised why. A film was to be made of Douglas Livingstone's book *The Comedy Man* and the producer wanted me to play

Fay Trubshaw. Within an hour I was opening the book and reading it, not as a reader, but as an actress. A memory crossed my mind like a coil of shadow. I was a girl of twelve, dressing up in Mummy's clothes, pretending to be Debbie Reynolds, punching the jokes and being bubbly. I realised I'd been acting behind my back all my life. There was nothing to say, except wow-ee! And wait for the script. I looked at my watch; did I dare call Kenny at home to tell him my news. I didn't. It was one of our rules. I waited for him to call me in a torment. That night the phone rang. I jumped to it. A message from the studio: a conference the following week. *The Comedy Man* was to be shot at Shepperton starting immediately I'd finished *It's All Happening*.

England was still scowling with snow, the winter seemed eternal. Sitting before the fire I opened the evening paper and my eye caught a small caption: 'Kenneth More to star in *The Comedy Man*'. I felt inside me a string of tiny fireworks igniting and spluttering and the print went hazy. The flat was very quiet. I stared at the paper. What was going on… why hadn't he told me? Had he used his influence to get me the part? I put a record on and curled up under the blankets, clutching my flick rag, still in my clothes, for me a sure sign of turmoil.

I sank into a stupor, coming to with a start and looked at the clock, twenty minutes past ten; as I muttered it out loud, I heard a car. There was a loud swish and then it stopped, the car door banged shut. I heard a key in the lock downstairs, then footsteps solid and fast. I sat bolt upright so I'd look prettier, smoothing down my hair, and smiled a smile to welcome him. He was in the doorway, hands on his hips, grinning. It was nothing to do with him that I'd got the part, he'd known I was on the spot list and hadn't mentioned the film for fear of my being disappointed. He'd just heard the producers had chosen me… we'll be seeing each other every day for eight weeks… it'll be a wonderful little film… I said can you come to bed, a minute later with a thud of his shoes and a creak of bedsprings, he blinked round the room with a sigh, 'Can't stay long, little one', and turned out the light.

Sitting slumped in bed with our scripts, thumbing through them in a happily engaged state, secure in having the chance to make a film we both believed in with marvellous parts to play. It was a small budget film, Kenny taking a very reduced salary, agreeing his contract on the back of a cigarette packet, no matter, no complaints. And for me lovely weekly cheques, I could make plans, two films on the trot, suddenly I had 'capital'.

'Have you read this last scene between us?' he asked.

'No... I'm almost there.'

'Well, I have to say to you, "Goodbye... take care of yourself, little Shrimp."' He hugged me, he was sparkling. 'Shrimp... that's what you are... my little mother-of-pearl Shrimp.' We held each other gleefully, promising each other our love.

We stood together and looked across the Serpentine. It was cold, white, the ducks and swans clattering around on the ice. He put his arm around my shoulder and scuffed the January snow into a fluster. 'Don't be idiotic, darling, you haven't said no, have you?' We started walking towards 'sparrow flats west'. 'Isn't it funny, you suddenly being invited to all these big do's. You must accept this one... you can't let the fact that I'll be there with Bill stop you going... it's very important for you to meet people and to be seen.' He stopped and scrabbled about in the paper bag for some more bread for the birds, shaking it and screwing it up into his pocket. 'I don't like geese, they do such big poohs... isn't it silly? I'm grown up but I haven't changed much... I'd love to slide on trays in the snow with you. I look in the mirror and I can see I'm getting older... but will I ever be really grown up like real people, like our parents, do you suppose? You're the same... we are both Peter Pans. I don't know – does it matter, Shrimp?'

We reached the gate leading to Knightsbridge and his flat, which overlooked the park, the lights in the windows of his home glowing. 'Well...' he polished his glasses on his sleeve, 'it's ridiculous, I shouldn't be living like this... I have to pay the salary of seven staff to look after three of us... sometimes I feel as though I've lost the real me. I should be living in a little flat like the one I had in Eaton Terrace Mews, with two suitcases. This is all silly... not me.' He waved his arms wide.

I said, 'Don't be stupid, you are one of our leading actors, a star... people expect you to live in your kind of style. You are special.'

'Oh, phooey... I'm just a short-arsed nobody who got lucky.' He threw the paper bag into a bin and slid on the snow and wobbled. 'Two things I'm sure of... I'll love you till the cows come home... and we'll never grow up.' He ran his fingers lightly over my face. 'How have I been lucky enough to find you? You're so young I should leave you alone... are you going to leave me, with my life in ruins? I feel such a shit... it's no life for you.' I watched him thread his way carefully across the empty road; abruptly he turned and patted his breast pocket: 'You're in here... wherever I go.'

'And you're in mine, Joe.' He went on towards his home.

My invitation was to the Guild of Film Producers Annual Dinner. Perhaps I shouldn't have gone, but I did. I leaned against Stuart's shoulder, grateful for one less direction to fall down in. There was so much noise, so many people; I felt claustrophobic and couldn't see straight. I had survived the wild embraces at the entrance to the Savoy Hotel Ballroom. Each and everyone there seemed to be 'on'. Drawn into the large as life and twice as natural greetings of hugs and 'Daaahlingsss' and the awaited kiss on the cheek. Thinking pin-the-smile-on-the-face, we made our way to our table. Sounds of famous voices filtered through and I held my breath in an effort to pull myself together to greet them. Straight back, tummy held in, I looked down checking my dress for the hundredth time. I watched the women, flushed with excitement, whirling in splendid rich confusion, drawing back ever so little for fear a smear of lipstick might spoil their meticulous make-ups. Diamonds spilling from ears below coiffed backcombing. High heels clicking, skirts swishing. They seemed so confident, aware of how magnificent money makes you feel. I felt an outsider. The producers, directors, stars, wives of stars, husbands of stars in large doses. My stomach turned over as I caught Kenny's eye. His wife just following him. We blinked vacantly at each other, our expressions anything but relaxed. He almost quick-stepped over to me. 'Isn't it good, we're on the next table... are you all right, darling?' he hissed. 'We've just been to a party at St James's Palace with the Queen Mum.' He put his arm around me, and I tried to smile, but it was a very small smile. He *mustn't* acknowledge our relationship in any way in public. I was aghast when he kissed me on my shoulder.

'Kenny,' I hissed at him, 'are you sloshed?' He roared with laughter. But he was, by golly, he was. His voice was low and oddly sad.

'Shrimp, come and meet –'

'No Kenny!! Go back to your table!'

He caught my wrist. 'Don't be cross with me for Christ's sake.'

'Sit down darling, *please*.' I felt the blood rushing to my cheeks and made a last appeal, pushing him gently when he whispered, 'Can I see you tomorrow?'

'Maybe, maybe,' I breathed.

'Huh?' he said, '*Maybe*...? I didn't mean it as a *question*! Tomorrow?' he repeated. He kissed me again, this time on my mouth with his drink-tasting lips. I felt shocked and guilty. It was a nightmare of an evening. He sent dear old Tom O'Brian over to me; he was also well away, telling me how long they'd known each other and the fun they'd had, when Kenny came over, his linen napkin tied round his head like a scarf and said, 'Tom, I said five minutes with her, not five fucking hours!' He barracked all through the after-dinner speeches, and I saw Bill snap, with restraint, 'Sit down, Kenny, sit *down*...!' Like a small boy he looked over to me, his eyes seeking reassurance, he was too far gone to reason with. I feigned interest in my dinner companions, but I was fidgety and nervous, my smile frozen. I tried not to glance at Kenny's wife, ironically sitting directly in my eyeline. I saw her nervously touch up her make-up, her compact held high. She could have been anybody or nobody. But that wasn't true. She was Kenny's wife and for the first time my heart knew how cruel I was being. I wanted to surrender. I felt empty and hollow and when the speeches were finished I retreated as quickly as possible, threading my way through the tables towards the door.

'Shrimp! Don't go without saying goodnight!' It sounded like a cry for help. Sweat trickled down my legs and I couldn't move, as Kenny roared across the room towards me. His grip was strong on my arms and I longed to hold him. People around us exchanged private looks, nervous shifting smiles. Our secret was out. I collapsed into the back of my waiting car. Stuart just looked at me and said, 'It can't go on, Angela.'

Stuart stayed talking to me until 4 a.m. He was a nice honest man, and I deserved all he gave me: 'Kenny's behaviour this evening was insane. Get on with your life... you are a very good actress... happiness doesn't come at the expense of other people...', but it needed a bit of taking.

'Thank you Stu,' I said, realising that he hadn't asked me the burning question but answered it.

In bed I reflected pain and pleasure, reflected the fine line that separates intense emotional stimulation. What feels wonderful and makes you want more and what makes you feel awful and perished. My heart was pounding and I felt full of stress and pain. Pain was for wicked people. *Me. Me*. Tears filled my eyes and ran down the sides of my face rolling into my ears. They came and came. The morning was full of silence until the phone went.

'Are you okay, darling? How are you feeling...? Oh, God I feel *dreadful*... *nobody* has ever had a hangover like this. Did I behave badly? Oh God, I'm sure I did.'

I couldn't trust myself to say anything.

'Are you okay?' he tried again.

I tried to say something; instead, an anguished sob tumbled out.

'Tell me, tell me, Shrimp,' he said soothingly.

I let my tears fall and I told him. 'Last night... it was awful... you were so drunk... I looked at your wife... I can't take any more, Kenny... I'm so unhappy...' There was silence on the other end of the line. Seconds seemed to pass. It took all my resolution. 'It's over darling... I'm leaving you,' I said, trying to sound calmer. 'I mean, you're sitting pretty aren't you.'

'Sitting lonely,' he said.

I went home to Mummy and spent the day doing her ironing, zombie fashion. I took four white Valium tablets from her bedside table and back in my flat I slipped the phone off the hook, swallowing the Valium, I thought if I can just live through this hour and this hour... I am certain the pain will go away. Somewhere inside me was my baby self, so uncontrollable. Very near to the surface now – begging, look after me someone. *I want my Daddy.*

It's the next afternoon. I lay in bed trying to work out a rough plan. What of the flat? Sell up, give Kenny back his money and go home to Mummy and Daddy? I needed them and missed the warm comfort of my family acutely. Burn my boats? Certainly they had been leaking. Come in number twenty-two your time is up; *was* our time up? Love is a miserable business; for the first time in my life I felt old.

I stopped rolling these thoughts around my mind when the doorbell rang. I sat stiffly on the edge of the bed and squashed my feet into my slippers, replaced the telephone receiver and went downstairs. The bell kept on ringing, a constant clamour, long and loud. God, I'm not deaf. On the stairs I remembered how often I'd heard Kenny race up them. A key was rammed into the lock, and there he was opening the door. He sprang forward and tried to put his arms around me, but they were holding a large bunch of flowers. As he lurched through the doorway, I stumbled and half fell behind the door. He was supporting me as I slumped into his arms.

I heard his voice suddenly trembling behind my ear. 'Haven't I suffered enough?' He put his cold hand with its responsive fingers over mine as I waited like a child having a tantrum and clung to his shoulder. Like a baby I wanted to be held and hear soft words. He kissed me gently on my cheek, my neck, whichever was accessible. We sat on the stairs and he told me he wanted me, needed me... did he know what a potent word need is? How could I hold back or deny my urge to cherish. An urge so deep-rooted in me that it naturally over-ruled my every decision and doubt. We talked about the night which had brought things to a head. We talked about how many Valium I'd taken, about us parting, about he and his wife parting, and the possible effect on Sarah. How I couldn't take it – the loneliness, the rushed comings and goings – perhaps, I said love is letting go and not hanging on. Our words ran together. We had a lot to talk about. We were both crying. We kissed, wiping our eyes on our sleeves. Then we went upstairs and made love. I was willing to love if I was loved. Could I learn to want less and give more? We didn't allow our thoughts to creep deeper. Agreeing not to make any decisions about anything until we'd completed *The Comedy Man*. Our next two months were planned.

Friday, February 1st 1963. I sat on the carpet in front of the fire, put a record on – one of the old records, *I Wish You Love* – and lay back closing my eyes and drifted into the words. 'I wish your heart a song to sing, but most of all when snowflakes fall, I wish you love,' I sang out. Feeling daring I looked at the telephone and was tempted to call him at home: he'd said I could as long as I was careful. Until now I had resisted. I rang him.

'Uh... could I – er – speak to Mr More, please?'

'Who wants him?' I guessed it was the Nanny.

'It's Mrs Lyons calling,' I blurted.

'I'll get him for you.' When her answer came, I realised I was being silly, after all I only wanted to say hello. Silence. After what seemed a lifetime, I heard an intake of breath: 'Shrimp?'

'It's me, darling,' I whispered.

'I can't talk now, love... I'm in the middle of telling Bill about you and me.'

He had spoken so quickly I could hardly understand him.

'Will you be at your flat this afternoon?' he continued.

'Yes, Kenny... do you feel sick?' I stammered, my own stomach heaving with nerves; I found I could only manage a whisper.

'Yes I do... can I see you there at four o'clock?'

'Yes, yes,' I felt meek and nodded dumbly like a child.

'Goodbye love,' and he hung up. I stared at the phone in shame. I'm hot. I'm cold. I'm winded. I had my foot in the world of scandal.

Waiting for him to arrive I was jumpy enough to pace up and down the flat. I felt queasy and searched my conscience. Homebreaker? At twenty-two? To be called that would offend me. But did I have the right to be offended?

By four o'clock he was sitting in his chair with me squatting at his feet. He'd greeted me with a hug and asked me to marry him.

'Are you sure, Kenny?'

He murmured at once, warmly, carefully, 'You can't see any doubt in my eyes, can you?'

For a moment I could say nothing. I scrambled on to his lap wiping my lip gloss smear from his face. 'And Sarah...?' I asked.

He caught his breath in anguish, paused, then with desperation edging his voice, he spoke for several minutes about his concern and his love for her. I will skim over the details. He shook his head in a slow, positive way, and lay his manicured fingers on my hand, squeezing down on my knuckles like a child clinging to Mummy. We went over the options. We weren't lost for words, but there were no options.

'Will you wait two years for me? Until Sarah is twelve and can go to boarding school? It will be easier for her to cope with then...'

Strangely perhaps, I was not totally shattered at this suggestion. I was too young, I thought, and too ignorant to make the jump with smooth continuity between being just me and the woman in his life.

'I'll learn to cook for you and to type your letters, and I'll take French lessons,' I said, 'for when we go to France. I'll wait for you forever as long as I have hope that we'll be together.'

'We're in love with each other, we *have* to be together,' he responded. I was absorbed in his words and as I gazed at him I was totally mystified, free of delusions as to why this beautiful man, with his wonderful smile, loved me. We were silent for a moment. I went into the kitchen for a bottle of wine and Kenny filled our glasses. I saw that my hand was quivering and I saw him glance at me, then raise his glass, as I then did.

'To this wonderful love we've found,' he said and reached forward lightly kissing me. A chill went through me and my heart began to thump clumsily. I hid my eyes behind my fingers and thought – out with it. I told him, trying not to sound too intense, that we had to start with a clean slate and there were two things he ought to know about me. Maybe I was making a horrible mistake in telling him, and I hadn't rehearsed all this, but I had to confess that I almost went to bed with someone, someone you *know*, this winter, it was a charade, a failed charade... and my pastry is frozen. I don't make it myself, *can't* make it, I have to buy it and I'm sorry I lied to you. *There*, I'd done it. My heartbeat was wild and

162

violent, but I was quite pleased that my voice hadn't gone squeaky and shrill and that I hadn't cried.

'What do you mean?' he said, his voice close to a wail.

'I swear…'

He cut me off with a small groan. 'Oh, my God… I knew it was too good to be true… you told me,' he said in a subdued voice, 'that your pastry was homemade… that *you'd* made it… I *believed* you! I've told my chums that not only are you terrific in bed, but you are the most marvellous pastry cook!'

Oddly he'd ignored what I'd feared most. I reached out for his hand and tried to soothe him, 'Come darling… don't worry… I'll learn to make wonderful pastry for you.' But I had little faith in my words.

'I'm being silly, aren't I… any silly old bag can make pastry… oh, you're a little doll, you are,' he said quietly. And that was all. Lucky me.

I shall never forget the moment when it became clear to me that the love I felt for Kenny was real. I'd given him a whisky, three fingers, which helped enable him to tell me about his marriage to Bill before I came on the scene. All of which I consider unnecessary and unfair to recount here. Despite my badgering questions, it was difficult for me to gain a complete picture of his life, though some things became quite clear. In the small hours, after his long soliloquy, Kenny was helping me get ready for bed; I was exhausted and slithered between the sheets. He stood above me and I watched him struggle into his jacket. Just then, with a sudden change of mood, he said, 'Shrimp' and I saw that he was smiling at me a little, his eyes shining and he said, 'Shrimp, will you love me for ever?' and I said, 'Yes, Kenny,' and it happened, this sharp stab of love. *God*, I said to myself, *I really love him.* Total and for ever? Wasn't that the name of an old song? The words ran round and round in my brain, that was the only way I'd want it, for ever.

Sometime late next morning, not long after finishing my washing, I was squatting on the floor brooding glumly over the complex workings of the Hoover plug, when I heard Kenny's footsteps on the stairs followed by the sound of his voice calling my name. 'Shrimp,' he shouted, 'I've got to talk to you!'

My heart faltered, then sped on: 'What's happened?'

Apparently he'd had a meeting early that morning with the director, Ted Kotcheff, to discuss the casting of a new TV play they were going to do together, and in their search for a girl to play opposite him, Ted had mentioned my name. 'She could make it,' he'd said, 'she could be a star.'

'She doesn't *want* to",' Kenny had blurted out. Later, with me, he was anguished. 'Tell me you don't want to be an actress,' he said. 'I hate ambition in a woman, I find it unattractive.'

I laughed at him and asked him why with a man it's called a job, and with a woman it's ambition. He just shrugged slightly and struggled to explain. He was sitting in a slump and looked bewildered and I loved him so much that I put my arms around his neck, and made him a promise that to be with him was enough for me, all I could ever wish for. And I believed that.

So lost was I in my relationship with him and in preparation for *The Comedy Man* that I took very little notice of what was going on in the world. I was sealed off, self-absorbed. I had a lot to think about. One of the things you have to do before starting work on a film is to have a medical test, enabling the film company to get cover for you from an insurance company. I had begun to fret on the short walk to the doctor's surgery. My period was five days late; would he be able to tell if I was pregnant? I was dogged by Catholic concern and the question was troubling me as the doctor stood up to greet me. Later that afternoon, sitting in bed, our tea tray balanced on our laps, I told Kenny all this. 'I was terrified... you see, darling, the doctor asked me for a urine sample, and he sent me into the loo with a jug... and I thought, Oh my

God... if they find out I'm pregnant... they'll know I've been sleeping with my boyfriend... and I'll lose my part in the film... and I was so frightened that I tipped half of my pee-pee sample down the loo, hoping that if I only left half in the jug – well – maybe the laboratory wouldn't quite be able to tell... and that they'd think perhaps I was only half pregnant!'

This exploded him into helpless laughter. 'I've heard of the split atom, but that's ridiculous! It's the most back-to-front Irish thing I've ever heard of. You are a joy... Christ, look at the time! I've got to go.' His sense of duty prevailed. Still chuckling, he kissed me goodbye – the gentlest of men.

The following day I discovered, much to my relief, that I wasn't pregnant, and slid the quinine bottle back in the bathroom cupboard.

The film didn't begin until the following week, and I had lots to do to fill my days. Throughout this period I kept telling myself it would all be all right for Kenny and me. He told me that he'd put a lot into life, and now he wanted to take a little happiness out of the kitty. 'I don't want the world, I just want things to be right for me, because the wrong thing's bloody murder. And at my age if you're sure of something you grab at it.'

We started shooting, and we both played it very cool on the set, very correct, very professional. He called me that night, just to hear my voice, he said. He was depressed. He hadn't enjoyed seeing me working: 'You became just another little actress.' I took that on the chin and told him that I'd found it difficult too. I want to show the feelings I have for you, Kenny, not hide them.

The Comedy Man was the happiest film I'd ever worked on and not just because I was with Kenny every day. Almost every actor in London was in it, or wanted to be. It was a marvellous cast, we all liked one another. The story was about a middle-aged actor and his struggle to make it. A path Kenny had taken twenty years earlier. The film was filled with colourful characters, I suppose we were quite a handful, but Alvin

Rakoff, the director, would never make a fuss, he just gently controlled us all. One day I was with Kenny in his dressing room when the door opened and a bespectacled man came in; before he could utter, Kenny said, 'We'll be on the set in a minute, thanks for coming to get us.' And the man just walked out and silently closed the door.

I stood there aghast. 'Kenny, that was Peter Sellers!' I told him.

'Blimey O'Reilly, I thought it was the call boy!' He kept saying 'Blimey O'Reilly' to himself on his way downstairs.

About three weeks into the picture it was our first anniversary. It fell on a Sunday and he said he'd take me out to lunch. 'As we are one today, we'll go back to near where we were born… Would you like that – lunch at The Bull near Gerrard's Cross?' He stood in the bedroom doorway and watched me get ready, and he told me that the two-year plan wouldn't work, it was too tough on Bill. When we finished the picture, we could start looking for a house. He was leaving. He'd told her he'd fallen in love with me, that he respected her and appreciated all she'd done for him, but that until now he hadn't thought that love like this existed. He was worried that I'd be cited in the divorce, that he couldn't protect me from the press – they'd drag me through the mud. Did I love him enough to be able to cope? How did I feel? he asked. He suggested we go to Cyprus for June to get away from it. I was mesmerised with his plans for us. What was going to happen, was going to happen and I had no intention of running away. We were going to be together because we had to be.

Things were said about us in the press during those few weeks, that Kenny, twice married, loved me. How he'd fallen for the other woman, and at twenty-two could I possibly love him, old enough to be my father? They made me want to die, I was so upset by them, as were my parents. Daddy was livid: 'What's he got for you?'

Unnerved, I couldn't begin to put my real feelings into words, so I came out with 'He'll make a wonderful husband and father, Daddy.'

'He's already been that, *twice!*' I tried to defend him, but they loved me as only parents can, and perhaps they saw unhappiness ahead and were afraid for me. But they were supportive and loving and gave us strength in the early difficult days. They grew to love him, but I was their daughter and as such their primary concern was for my happiness. I was a growing woman. I knew what I was doing, I knew what I wanted, and they knew what he meant to me. They understood.

'I love him Daddy.'

'Didn't I know it, darling,' and he came across to me and hugged me.

I wanted to tell my parents I thought them wonderful – but that's always difficult.

Kenny's personal anguish was only for me to see. With his love for me splashed across the daily papers, it was humiliating for us, misery for his wife. He was ripping his life apart at the seams and I didn't understand all the implications of that. I do now. For me then, it seemed straightforward, simple.

I went shopping for my bikinis and dresses and sun hats with Jill; we chose to start in Bond Street. Mummy was horrified, exclaiming at the wild price tags. We bought everything I needed in one day, Jill sitting in a chair, me putting on, taking off, preening and twirling in front of the mirrors. For the first time I could afford to buy some really lovely things; I couldn't go mad, I had to be a bit careful, but compared to a year or two before, I felt like Jackie Kennedy. For my dashing, beautiful man, I wanted to be everything he'd ever wanted.

Kenny bought the air tickets for Cyprus. We were to fly off on June 4th, all arrangements were made; it was really happening.

He was leaving to be with me. I was so happy. Mummy came to the flat the night before we were due to fly off, to spend the night, and to do my packing. Her mother, a lady's maid, had handed down her talents. Somehow I got through the night. Excited, monosyllabic – I couldn't stop thinking of him. I kept hugging my teddy and looking at Kenny's photographs which I had all over the flat, on every surface. I couldn't take being separated from him. I couldn't get any happiness from anything away from him.

He called me just before going to bed and said, 'See you in the sunshine, darling.' I hardly slept that night.

Mummy watched me from the waiting car, running out of Vidal Sassoon's hair salon in Bond Street. 'Hurry, Angela.' I was, I was. I scrambled in quickly. We had suddenly decided, independent of each other, that I was going to be late for the flight.

'Better move, driver.' My voice was too sharp and I didn't mean it to be, this day of all days. Mummy handed me my ticket folder and I went to put it in my bag: *panic*.

'What is it, Angela? she asked. I groaned and felt quickly all around me on the seat. 'Have you forgotten anything?' She means my *bag*, my *bag*!

'Yes, God, *everything's* in it!' Halfway by now to the airport, we had to turn the car around and go back for the precious handbag. 'I've missed the flight,' I fretted.

'Well, never mind, there's one other to Nicosia today isn't there?' As if that ended the matter.

'Yes, but Kenny's on that!'

'You can go with him then.'

'Mummy, it isn't that simple We're dodging the press… being discreet… and he's going first class. He'll be cross and think I've missed the plane on purpose…' I was really suffering and felt irritable, helpless. My mind was soaring ahead; I was already thinking about Kenny's carefully laid plans being disrupted – so much depended on this holiday. 'Please

TOP LEFT Mummy and Daddy on their forty-eight-hour honeymoon in Brighton, 1936
TOP RIGHT Mummy and my first smile for the camera!
BOTTOM Elaine, me and baby brother John

TOP LEFT Wide-eyed sixteen-year-old
TOP RIGHT Sweet seventeen
BOTTOM The look of love: on set together in *The Comedy Man*

TOP LEFT With Kenneth Williams in *Follow That Camel* Photo © Rex Features
TOP RIGHT As Princess Jelhi in *Carry On Up The Khyber* Photo © Rex Features
BOTTOM Mr and Mrs More – at last! Kenny said, 'Good luck to us, darling'

TOP Fun together in St Tropez with M'Lord, 1969
BOTTOM LEFT A weekend in the country
BOTTOM RIGHT Starting out again, aged 30

TOP Shrimp with her borrowed babies – nephews Joe and James
BOTTOM LEFT Me and my best pal Timmy at Bute House
BOTTOM RIGHT 1974: making a guest appearance in Kenny's TV series *Father Brown*

TOP Script reading in the garden at Bute House
BOTTOM LEFT On tour in Hong Kong, 1978
BOTTOM RIGHT Settled in for Christmas, 1979

TOP In St Thomas's Hospital with loving daughters Jane and Sarah
BOTTOM LEFT Kenny's last birthday party – 'Let's make it the best one ever, Shrimp'
BOTTOM RIGHT What now?

Just my Bill and me

driver... don't stop at the crossings. I've got to catch that plane.' We were on the dual carriageway to the airport now; I could hardly breathe with exasperation. I looked at my watch: *too* late, I'd missed it. The car came to a halt on a 'No Waiting' sign. I hugged Mummy.

'Have you got your toilet bag?'

'Oh, yes.'

'Tickets?'

'*Yes*, Mummy.' By this time I wanted to scream, my nerves fractured.

'We haven't forgotten anything?'

She meant had *I* forgotten anything.

'No darling.' Another hug, 'Thank you Mummy... and Daddy... oooh, I'm going to cry' – she offered her cheek and I kissed it.

'Off you go... relax... I hope you're happy... don't lie in the sun too much... you'll regret it... dreadfully ageing for the skin,' that was Mummy talking.

I ran into the airport, the two women behind the desk were friendly and did their best to calm me down, giving me a seat on the next flight. Kenny's.

I got through Passport Control and walked quickly into the Departure Lounge, my hands full of holdall, *handbag*, boarding card and wig box (long, black and silky, another fantasy). I didn't see Kenny at first, because he was half buried behind large dark glasses and a copy of *The Times*. Oh, my God, I thought, there he is. Oh, he doesn't look very well, his face the colour of ash. I wondered how it had gone when he left home that morning.

'Hello,' I said quickly, standing to the side of him.

And he just stared at me in hostile horror and muttered, '*Christ*, what are you doing here?' My sudden appearance didn't go down too well. His face stayed shut as I gabbled an explanation. He just nodded and said, 'Okay, love, it doesn't matter as long as you make yourself scarce... two of Bill's best friends are sitting over there. Don't look so stricken, love. The flight will be called... I'll see you on the plane. Buzz off, Shrimp... have you got enough money for coffee?'

'Yes, darling,' and I turned and walked towards the other side of the Departure Lounge. I looked at the clock: it was just gone eleven-thirty... and at three-fifteen I was still sitting there! Blanked off with nerves, and probably I was foolish anyway, certainly not used to travelling, I had missed that flight as well. The check-in girls hadn't told me the new flight would have a new number and I'd been listening out for the number of my original flight. I'd stayed out of the way, hidden behind the magazine counter, congratulating myself on how wonderfully discreet I was being – how proud Kenny must be of me. My control suddenly went.

The man at the information desk, his mouth full of biscuit, just stared at me. 'Not you again Miss Douglas? You missed the *second* flight? He asked me to sit down and offered me a coffee. His voice had sounded very loud and people seemed to be staring at me. They put me in a car, clutching a new ticket, to spend the night with Mummy and Daddy.

Kenny, meanwhile, sitting up front in the first-class cabin, ordered a bottle of champagne and asked the steward to bring me forward: 'She's blonde, blue-eyed... you can't miss her. I'll pay the difference in the fare. She missed her flight... what a joke!' Apparently on being told that no one fitting that description was on board, he said, '*What*?' and he fumbled and groped his way down the aircraft aisle, peering into the faces of the other passengers, in a quick flush of panic; he said he felt an absolute bloody fool, making an exhibition of himself in this way. After all, he'd just left home, hadn't he, for a girl who could miss two flights in one day?

At home that evening, feeling dispirited, I did all the ironing for my bemused mother and sent Kenny a telegram: 'Darling Joe, one broken-hearted dizzy blonde will be flying out to you on the same flight tomorrow.'

Next morning my mother delivered me, safe and sound this time, into the hands of a steward. 'Ah, Miss Douglas, we won't lose you this time. *Wait* here... go there... here is your boarding card... Okay... is this your hand luggage?' They turned me around and walked me on to the plane; I had been taken care of, organised. The awful feeling that I might have missed this flight too, was too much for me and I thought, I'm twenty-two, I've got to learn to cope better than this if I want to be a traveller. I mustn't panic. This is an adventure. The man nodded and, I thought, sighed, 'All right now, Angela?' as he strapped me in my seat. He turned around at the door as people began to crush against him. I smiled and waved my thank you. 'Goodbye Angela, good luck!' And he was gone.

I leaned back and held on to the arms of my seat as the plane lifted up and over the heavy smog of London. I looked out of the window and the lurching view made me think better of it. I had the shakes, for pity's sake. What a coward. I swallowed and hung on to my nose to lessen the strain on my eardrums, and then the stewardess was there with a glass of orange juice, and that tasted good – I finished it in one long gulp. I looked around the cabin and saw a grey-haired man looking at me and thought, *Oh no.* I closed my eyes to block him out and waited to land in Nicosia.

I was thinking about it all, about Kenny, when a steward said, 'Fasten your seat belts please,' and he bent down and adjusted mine. 'All right, Madam? We'll be landing in a minute.' Madam! He called me *Madam*! This was the way to live. The VIP treatment, and met at the airport by the man I love. All the waiting months worthwhile. A thrill of anticipation, almost sexual, ran through me. I peered out of the window into the eye-catching sunshine of Cyprus, I got to my feet, the first to do so, and hurried down the aisle ahead of the other passengers and off the airplane. This was the moment. Could I see him at the barrier? No. Yes. No. My eyes searched for him frantically, my pace quickened. The crowd of people from the plane hurried by. In all the bustle and chattering there was no sign of Kenny. Everything depended on this greeting. I waited for ten minutes, it felt like hours, where was he? I wanted to hug him, hold him tight, tell him I loved him more than words could say, like they do in the movies. I wondered if he was waiting outside somewhere. I stood in the shimmering heat, and as far as I could see he wasn't. I was upset and trying not to be frightened when a porter, wearing droopy brown trousers and browner teeth, started to hurry me into a taxi. The feeling of apprehension that had been with me the previous day came flowing back, thicker than before. What are you doing? Wait! He waited, looking at my legs quite openly. Had I got it wrong? Was I meant to go directly to Kyrenia and meet Kenny there, I wondered, telling myself not to panic. Did I have tip money for the porter… a quick search in my purse… no, I didn't… would he settle for just looking at my legs. 'Kyrenia, please porter,' I smiled at him and he smiled back. 'I'm sorry I haven't any money to give you,' and shook my head. He looked suitably glum and shook his head. I checked once more with the information desk, no message, then my porter found me a taxi, which looked to be on its last legs, and I settled back into my seat, the springs pressing into my bottom, and stared curiously at the brown fields and soft olive trees of the countryside on my way over the mountains to the coast.

There was no message for me at the Dome Hotel, and no Kenny either. The desk said he had left there hours earlier to drive to the airport. That threw me. How had we come to miss each other? Had our cars passed en route? I was shown to my room, cool and large. It was on the first floor and had a beautiful view over the bay. I kicked off my shoes as the phone rang.

'You poor girl!' Kenny cried down the phone, 'your plane was early. Our cars must have passed on the mountain road. Just stay put, I don't want to lose you again tonight!' I padded around the room in my bare feet and ran a bath and wallowed in it, I soaped myself and thought about what to put on. I got out of the bath and dressed myself in a white cotton dress with small mother-of-pearl buttons and a delicate broderie anglaise collar, very pretty, very French and very expensive. Soon he would be here, and all would be well. I gazed at myself in the mirror, spraying some scent on my arms; my eyes didn't look tired, no lines yet, nothing to worry about there. I pulled up my skirt, not much waffle on my legs, and thought I was okay really, as long as I held my tummy in. I was hungry and it was getting dark; I looked at my watch and it said seven-thirty. I put on the lamps and lay down on top of the bed on the coverlet, careful to arrange my dress so that my legs looked long and provocative. I pulled myself this way and that, placing my arms languidly over my head. This is it I thought, this is the moment. I needed now to be adorable. He had to feel, when he saw me, that all the misery he had gone through was worthwhile. And so he did. We had fairy cakes and instant coffee for supper, all the little cafe on the quay could produce. The soft warm night air fanned our faces, and we relaxed.

When I woke, our bedroom was warm and light. I could hear rain. *Rain*? That was odd I thought for Cyprus, in June. Kenny had said it rarely rained. I looked at my watch and it showed five o'clock.

'Kenny! Kenny!' I cried and prodded his shoulder, 'wake up… it's five o'clock! We've missed a whole day of our holiday… and it's pouring with rain!'

What I thought was the noise of rain actually turned out to be the sound of the sea crashing against the hotel's walls, and it *was* five o'clock, but in the morning.

'Great… wonderful… I've got a girl who misses two planes in a day, thinks she hears rain and can't sleep at night… what have I taken on?' I didn't feel at risk; his quick smile was effortless, and the tone of his voice loving. That day we were on the beach by 7.15 a.m. – but we never were again.

Our days simply blended one into another – the scorching heat of the beach, the warmth and softness of the sea. We swam and slept and made love, and felt marvellous, and swam and slept and made love again. The physical attraction was so

173

strong; but it wasn't just that, it was our hearts, our thoughts, everything. We'd sleep in a tangle, our sheets creased and twisted. The hotel put in a wider bed for us, and that kept us laughing; however, Kenny couldn't ever quite meet the manager's openly twinkling eye. The sun was real, the sea was real, and Kenny was real. We were so happy, no more having to say goodbye all the time. We'd rub oil on our bodies and sunbathe and then swim to cool down, catnapping after lunch in the shade of the trees. The days went by and we were light-headed with love, and at peace. The far away smoky city life, with all its own problems, seemed unreal, as did the life we had lived there. All our secrets were out, we told each other everything – why our past relationships hadn't lasted.

We hired a little car and drove around the island, through the villages and into the mountains, the villas flecked white against the wonderful calm of the mountains, past the high, sparse vineyards with the occasional peasant and his herd of goats. I'd squeal with delight, 'Joe, Joe just look!' pointing at the trees laden with lemons, or my first sight of jasmine, growing wild. And I thought: if this is not happiness...

We made plans for our future. He told me he'd talked it out with Bill, told her he was definitely leaving. He'd felt they'd left each other years before, but he'd tried to be a good husband and he thought she'd got a great deal from the marriage, though perhaps not what she'd hoped for.

'We'll marry,' he told me, 'on our next anniversary... you'll be twenty-three by then, it'll be almost decent!' He talked about getting a divorce, no problem, he assured me, they'd agreed before their marriage to give each other a divorce if either one fell in love – 'She won't hang on to me.' He seemed sure. He supposed everything was against us and he feared his friends' loyalty would be divided and he was sorry for that. But he felt they knew the score, and if they loved him they'd want him to be happy. He expressed regret that his adored Ronnie Squire could never meet me – 'How he would have loved you.' He'd make a property settlement on Sarah, and also buy us a house, not a flat – a real home, he felt, had to have log fires and a staircase. The economics, the figures he mentioned seemed to me to be telephone numbers. He'd worked hard, and in the early days it had been a real struggle: he'd gone hungry to accumulate what seemed to me to be a great deal of money. He reckoned the divorce and buying two houses would just about halve his investments; I nodded a lot and said I understood, but I didn't really. I didn't have anything to divide up, and friends to involve, a small daughter to hurt.

'We'll be starting from scratch,' he said uneasily. 'I can have my desk and chair, but everything else we'll have to buy.'

As the prospect of drinking out of her favourite glass, while sitting on her favourite sofa, under her favourite picture, didn't fill me with ecstasy, I *wanted* to start from scratch.

'Will you have to discuss it with her again?'

'No, she'll be in the South of France when we get back… it's over, we both know it… anything we have to talk about can be done by letters.'

'Solicitors?'

'That's right.'

Months later I told Kenny how I'd been thrown when he'd asked if I wanted a cook and a maid; as I'd never envisaged a life with servants as such, I couldn't cope, I thought, I wouldn't know how to deal with them. No, I wanted to cook and care for us and was determined to learn fast.

'You'll need pocket money,' he said fondly. I'd never taken money from a man, it's childish I thought to get upset but I didn't like the idea. I murmured about wanting to contribute, perhaps pay a couple of the smaller bills?

'You are my financial responsibility,' he told me firmly.

What about my independence? But I had to accept that he saw things in a different way from me, he saw lots of things in a different way, that was inevitable, wasn't it, our age difference being what it was. I discovered that his generosity was overwhelming, he was always dipping his hand in his pocket, and I felt he gave me much too much. He said it made him happy. Our life on a domestic level had been decided.

We sat, Kenny and I, in the shade of the trees at a small iron table; he drained his glass and held it out to be refreshed. I wondered if it was decent to feel so wonderfully content. I sipped some more of the alcoholic liquid and thought it quite lethal. The sun was still hot but there were shadows, like pieces of a jigsaw, across the square as the sun fell behind the hills.

'Kenny?' I almost purred.

He looked at me: 'Ummm…?'

'That girl over there… poor thing, she's all on her own… Would it be nice, do you think, to ask her to join us for a drink?' A girl of about twenty-five sat there. Very attractive, I thought. She nodded politely and seemed cool but accepted my offer and sat down next to Kenny. He smiled one of his engaging smiles at her, asking her questions and the time passed easily; Kenny refilled our glasses as we began to like her. I wondered if the girl had ever been desperately in love, like me. It seemed possible. Kenny stretched and put his arm around me. 'What do you – er – do for, er… a living, young lady?' he asked.

'Oh – er – I'm… sorry to have to say this… but I'm a journalist… a reporter for *The People*.'

Kenny forced a smile in reply and then said, 'Oh that's nice for you… dreadful for us though.' He shrugged his shoulders and looked back at her levelly. I picked up some nuts from the bowl and crunched down on them, smiling civilly and thinking, God, of all the luck… how come I hadn't seen the I-know-who-you-are look in her eyes. Why doesn't she blush or grope for words. How stupid we are to put ourselves in this position. Kenny said, almost offhand, 'Oh well, Shrimp, we've done our best… all we can, if we've been discovered…' he threw open his hands, 'so be it.'

We sat in a very long silence. The girl said nothing and pink patches had appeared on her cheeks. Instead she looked at us with intense sympathy. It did not help. Our eyes followed her as she walked away.

'Bitch,' I said, snooping on us!' If only we'd known that incredibly she'd keep our secret, I wouldn't have said that and I wouldn't have lain awake half the night.

On the last night of our holiday, after we had made love, Kenny was lying back drowsily when he told me, 'I thought love was an illusion. I didn't believe in it, a dream for kids. If I'd known then what I know now, little Shrimp.'

He lifted his head up and kissed me. 'Don't be frightened of going home... I know now that what we have, works... we can face the music.'

I understood what he meant. 'Don't be frightened,' he said again. Then we fell asleep.

Now, as close to each other as any couple could be, we flew home, changing aircraft at Rome to arrive separately in London. He planned to make a formal statement to the press the following week, which he did. He'd left his wife, yes, he was entirely in the wrong and he wanted to marry me. He had exposed himself emotionally and was as vulnerable as anyone in love could be. He was hypersensitive and full of anxieties during this period, the press outside our flat night and day, it was all so new to me and made me very nervous to go out. We were walking a tightrope. It must have been as painful for Bill as it was difficult for us. I can understand it now, so much better than I did then. Finally, after a distressing few weeks, Kenny tiptoed out of it all, never looking back, and she left for the South of France, saying that she didn't want a divorce. Kenny was stunned and I was scared, hardly able to believe it. Living together, unmarried, in the early sixties was far less prevalent than it is now, and inevitably we wondered about our future and were filled with despair. During what were often difficult days, we set about finding a house and were delighted to discover an enchanting mews cottage in

Bayswater. Impatient for us to be together, Kenny wrote out a cheque there and then, no subject to contract or searches. 'How quickly can we move in?' he asked the owners, and four weeks later he carried me over the threshold, across his shoulders like a sack of coal, a duster hanging out of his trouser pocket, and a screwdriver clamped between his teeth. I said goodbye to my flat; I'd been longer alone there than ever before. I sold it well, getting more for it than Kenny had paid. I gave him the money, and he gave it straight to my mother – 'She can use it, can't she?'

Harmony and happiness seemed to be just over the horizon. But there were no clear blue skies for us, only shadows. Leaving Bill and seeking a divorce had been a devastating public admission of failure, and few wished us well or congratulated us on our love.

Just before Kenny arrived to meet my parents for the first time, there was the most awful scene. John lounged in a chair, his legs sprawling, and refused my pleas to comb his hair, with a smart 'piss off!' Mummy went *mad* – nobody ever swore at home. Filled with tension I fluttered around nervously tucking things behind cushions and into drawers, and felt ill with a migraine when I saw that Mummy had overdone the roast beef, and the mustard was instant – Mummy it should be *fresh* for him, he can tell the difference. Daddy, have you opened the wine? Anyone could see I was a nervous wreck. The great man arrived – polite smiles all round, when Lady, the family poodle, decided to join in the excitement, jumping up on to his lap and yapping. After a few minutes of this and as the yapping continued, he turned to my mother, nudged her in the ribs and with perfect enunciation he said breezily, 'Do you know what I'd do if this was my dog – I'd kick it out of the fucking window!' John visibly brightened up. So did Daddy. Mummy didn't have much to say, she damn near fainted as she fled to the kitchen. Also that was the evening he thanked my mother for bringing me up so well – 'She's so wonderfully *clean*,

Marjorie – thank you.' We've laughed many times talking of that evening. We all remembered it very well.

'Brother' Cyril (Kenny's brother-in-law) and his wife Pat were early and understanding listeners and we were able to confide in Laurie and Mary Evans (his agent and his wife), old friends Harry and Nellie Bryan, Frank Lawton and Evelyn Laye, Lloyd and Mell Nolan, Leslie Dawson, Maxwell Croft, Carl and Eve Foreman – Jill, Joan and Stuart Lyons, who unlike the others hadn't known Kenny before. It was soon clearly apparent that others of their joint friends sided with Bill. At times the mental stress seemed to permeate our every hour, and in addition to all our other worries, the possibility that Kenny might lose contact with Sarah because of me was intensely painful. I loved him: by that I mean I felt a commitment with caring – when something happened to him it affected me as deeply as if it had happened to me. The gossips started in on me; the bitches with their 'sweetie' voices didn't bother to go into corners. *Look at her, look at that.* I'm not a category, I ached to answer, I am me. *She doesn't drink, doesn't smoke – but we all know what she does do.* The innuendos were unsubtle, but I was learning about life just by unscrambling the sickening shadowy meanings that packed their gossip. I was comparatively unknown, an enigma. What they didn't know about me, they made up. Kenny said there's nothing so sincere as a woman telling a lie. I was held up to ridicule, and it's a difficult bag to get out of. All of a sudden I had to care what everyone thought of me – a continuous screech of gossip. They stripped me; I was too vulnerable and too much in love. It was a lot for a twenty-two-year-old to handle, and I couldn't. It never occurred to me that eighteen years later I would still, at times, feel socially ill at ease, the scars from that unhappy period.

One never-to-be-forgotten evening was the premiere of *Dr. Strangelove*; it was to be our first public appearance together and I'd spent three hours at Vidal's, John combing my hair this way and that. I felt buoyant, hopeful that I looked okay, all done up in my fine new feathers, as clutching Kenny's hand we stepped out of our car in front of the Columbia Cinema in Shaftesbury Avenue. Cameras were whipped out, we were photographed from all angles. My knees were knocking and my smile twitchy, as Kenny guided me into the foyer. There we saw actors, with their wives, actresses, writers and directors, people that Kenny had known for years. As we approached them they literally drew away from us. Close friends of his some of them, not even turning to smile. It was as though we were naked and covered in leprosy sores. It was such a shock, a slap in the face in front of so many people. I spent the evening trying not to cry and holding Kenny's hand, which was icy cold with nerves. We were going for dinner to Les Ambassadeurs, a wonderful restaurant near Park Lane. Still holding hands we walked into the bar and sat at a table. Kenny ordered dinner, we felt sick, we couldn't eat – impossible. Our nerves were shot. The beautiful room, full of people, full of laughter, they looked at us with interest and looked away whispering. Kenny was attentive, I was over receptive. Couldn't they see we were mad about each other, that it would *last*? We knew that when you want a new life, it costs. But not that much – were there to be many nights like this? No – after this public humiliation we couldn't endure to be seen in public if we could possibly avoid it. No one asked us out to lunch or to their houses. We were ostracised. We kept together; we had us.

I knew where I stood with Kenny. He made it very clear that it was out of the question he'd start a life with me if I was uncertain as to what was important – him or my work. I could keep my career going in second gear. I turned down work: a TV series, a film with eight weeks' location in Paris. It wasn't terrific work, but work nevertheless. Joan and my parents were distressed, said I was being foolish to step back into Kenny's shadow. But I wasn't frustrated, I was thrilled. I tried to reason with them: 'Look what he's been through for me – he left home for me.'

'He left home *for him* – not for you. I hope it's worth what it's costing you,' I was told.

He warned me that if I went into the theatre, 'I won't stay home every night like you do... I'll be off in the nightclubs getting into trouble.' Jill said that sounded like blackmail. If it was, I bought it. He wanted his whisky ready, his slippers by the fire and me waiting for him when he came home. He had the right girl for that; I was eager to be what he wanted. It was going to get better and better. I didn't want to waste another day. I wanted to learn more about him – we wanted to learn more about each other.

I learned that he bathed in the morning and dined at night, that he pinched all the coconut ones out of the liquorice allsorts, that he was resolute about paying bills immediately they arrived and that he sometimes cried in his sleep with fearful nightmares. I had to move his bedside table away from the bed in case he hurt himself when he lashed out. He *hated* using the telephone, didn't believe in anyone dropping in, close friends even. His rule was positive. Call first and see if it's convenient, or wait to be invited. He felt a little family went a long way. Only once did Daddy arrive unexpectedly and he chose a glorious moment. Just for fun, Kenny was lounging back in his chair and allowing me to play around with some make-up. I put bright lipstick and false eyelashes on him – mauve eye-shadow and rouge, and I topped the look off with a velvet bow in the front of his hair – he looked revolting! Daddy arrived – 'Hello, Kenny,' 'Hello, Peter... would you like a drink?' and they sat and talked and drank whisky together all evening – I couldn't believe it – but neither of them referred to Kenny's ridiculous appearance – no questions from Daddy, no explanations from Kenny. Extraordinary. His need for privacy had to be respected and to that extent our homes were like castles – inasmuch as they looked inwards. And I learned that he was obsessively tidy – even with his emotions.

The next few weeks were consumed with settling into our new home. I loved playing house, wanted everything shining. We found a 'treasure', Adela, a petite Spanish woman who never complained. She only wanted to please; she'd gaze at Kenny star-struck, and we adored her. Kenny took me shopping for our furniture to splendid antique shops. 'Do you love it?' he'd ask, and I'd throw my arms around him and say, of course. Our china and silver we chose at Aspreys; and, after a long lunch at the Caprice with Laurie and Mary, we went to Harrods to buy our linen. I blushed purple when our assistant murmured audibly, 'They've asked for double sheets, but are they married?' Loving junk shops and markets as I do, Kenny would stare amazed and laugh in a hooting way at the boxes I'd bring home. 'That's clutter, Shrimp! – look, that jug has been repaired – that cup *hasn't*!' But I hung on to my finds, exclaiming that a chipped cup here and there was what was needed to make our home look as though we'd been together for twenty years, which was what I needed. For us it was heaven. Kenny's greetings were so joyous. I remember him coming home and walking smiling into the kitchen: he hugged me and kissed me, saying it was a wonderful feeling having a home of his own where he paid for everything, and that everything he really wanted was right here.

I was living with a man who knew what he wanted, what he would put up with, what he wouldn't. Letters were still going back and forth between lawyers. Our adviser, Bill Wallace, an avuncular Liverpudlian, came to see us at home. I liked him; we hugged, then small talk – I can't remember what was said – and we went into the study. Sitting on the sofa next to Kenny, he said simply, 'I think you should forget about a divorce.' We discussed the matter for some time and finally agreed to put the divorce out of our minds. We arranged with him to have my name changed to More by deed poll. On August 6th 1964 I sent a telegram: 'Angela More. She loves you, yeah, yeah, yeah.' And we got on with our lives.

Kenny was in a mood for burning boats, for erasing the memory of the past; deciding to sell his Rolls and Mercedes, he came home laughing excitedly driving a Mini. He wanted to part with his cars and all they represented. 'I've bought you a present too, darling,' he said and handed me a large box, insisting I open it there and then. As if I could wait! I couldn't imagine what was in it. I tore at the box, pulling at the string – I gasped – it was a mink coat. He'd bought it from Maxwell Croft and embroidered inside were my new initials in a small heart. I put it on and hugged him, telling him it was beautiful and I'd treasure it always.

I couldn't remember ever having been so happy. It didn't bother me that we weren't married. My name was the same as his and that was enough for me. He took me to Paris to buy me a wedding ring, and I still remember the astonishment of the jeweller who served us. Kenny crashed his hand down on the counter and told him, 'My little wife wants a wedding ring!'

From Paris we headed south for Monte Carlo; he wanted to show me his apartment there. He told me it overlooked the bay and he loved it. 'It's a beautiful holiday home – would you like to try and make it ours, or would you feel uncomfortable there?' I replied that I didn't think there would be any problem and readily gave the proposal my enthusiastic approval.

There was a silence as I stood by the drawing room door, as Kenny walked slowly round the room, plucking at the curtains, wearing an expression of astonishment which slowly gave way to extreme anger. He made his fists into balls and banged them down on the back of a sofa. I wanted to say something, but he put up his hands to fend me off.

'We can't live here, Shrimp. Let's sell the place… I never want to see it again!' he said in a voice strong enough to drown out any contribution I might have made. He was so vehement I knew there was no space for my argument.

Kenny had started rehearsing *Out of the Crocodile*, a new play by Giles Cooper, and he looked forward to working with Celia Johnson and Hugh Williams. It was Kenny's first play in eleven years and this fact drew some publicity before the play opened. He was apprehensive, frightened he'd lost his nerve; he was so professional, didn't want to let anybody down. He understood why his film career was in a state of limbo.

'I've had a bloody good innings… eleven years at the top… it's time I went down the other side. I can't play ageing juveniles for ever!'

Unfortunately, in the second week of rehearsal Hugh lost his voice. Cancer of the throat was diagnosed. Kenny was very distressed – everyone was. Hugh was an old friend of his, 'a gentleman'. The part was then offered to Cyril Raymond. Kenny had doubts about the second act, but he felt confident that with a rewrite here, extra rehearsals there, and with such an experienced cast, they could make a go of it, with a little bit of luck. But luck just then was elsewhere for all of them… but especially for Kenny.

Kenny, as the leading man, planned to give a party in his dressing room after the opening night. It's a tradition in the London theatre. We went to Searcy's the caterers and ordered the canapés and smoked salmon, the cases of champagne and a butler and waitress, because Kenny really wanted this to be a night to remember. 'I'll show you a first night, darling,' he'd said, 'so thrilling!' The audience applauded enthusiastically when the final curtain came down and, my heart pounding with excitement, I ran round to his dressing room to congratulate him. He'd hurriedly removed his make-up and with the waitress we made sure everything was ready for our guests. Laurie and Mary arrived. We waited, full of anticipation. Five minutes passed. Then ten. Then fifteen. We were in a state of shock.

'Shall I open the champagne now?' the butler asked.

'No, wait a minute longer.'

Five more minutes. Ten. Still no one arrived.

'A bottle now, sir?'

We tried to laugh it off. But we were so hurt and embarrassed. It was a cruel blow that friends of a lifetime could treat him like this. No good luck telegrams, or flowers. No warm hugs. And in the background, like a long-playing record, the butler kept asking, 'Shall I open the champagne now, sir?'

We went for dinner at the Caprice in St James's. Holding hands we walked into the bar, and there they were, Kenny and Bill's circle of friends. They didn't speak a word to us, they looked in our direction but looked straight through us as though our chairs were empty. They didn't even acknowledge our existence. Our humiliation was indescribable. There was no way we could understand such behaviour – or handle it. Was this cloud we were under permanent? We were on the defensive, our sense of humour had deserted us. I was shaking as we drove home in a stunned silence.

The following day, after reading the notices, we realised that the play wouldn't run. Kenny told me that he felt there was something wrong with the construction. There had been no fault to find with his performance – or anybody else's – but the show would close. He knew that if it had been a hit, likely to run for months, all his so-called friends would have been only too eager to congratulate him. And if they hadn't then, it wouldn't have mattered so much. But because the play was not going to run and because he had been ostracised socially, his mood was gloomy.

As I look at it now, it seems unbelievable that the reaction to us was what it was. Did people think by making everything so difficult for us that he would go back to her? Perhaps the wives of other actors of Kenny's age and standing, with whom he'd been friendly for years, thought that falling in love was contagious and their husbands could become infected by the wish to do likewise. At that impressionable age I thought – friends? Who needs them if they turn on you and squash you when you're down? I didn't feel bitter – I just didn't see the value of friendship. All you need to get through, I thought, is your man, one close girlfriend and your parents.

I was becoming aware of his nerves. We'd noticed a small red patch on one of his legs; then one patch increased to several, and the irritation drove him crazy. We went to see our marvellous doctor, 'Mac', and he told him in layman's language that it was a form of eczema, the result of all the stress he'd been under for the past year – years. His nerves were worn out. He'd need tranquillisers and vitamin injections; and Mac gave us some awful sticky cream to smear on his legs, and that stuck to the sheets which worried him to death. So we made a game of sticking pieces of Kleenex on all the patches; we laughed and said that in a stiff breeze he could take off!

There were many changes in those first few months, so much adjusting to do. From the time I fell in love with Kenny, I hadn't exactly zeroed in on my work, but I still went to my classes without let-up, trying to rise above a lifetime of self-consciousness and nerves. I had to work overtime on my voice and with every class I felt I was improving. My admiration for Iris Warren never lessened.

One afternoon before dashing home, I went into a shop to buy a pair of boots.

'Could I try on the black boots with the small strap... in the side window,' my voice boomed out. It works, I thought. I really sound terrific.

'In't you Angela Douglas?' squeaked the assistant.

'Yes, actually.' I *was*, I really felt I *was*!

'I fought it was you... I was at school wiv you... I recognised your voice.' I laughed and fluttered my eyelashes a lot and thought – oh, hell – all this work and I still sound just like *me*.

I still hadn't learned to cook. You have to earn your stripes somewhere: I got mine in the kitchen. I wanted to cook dinner, I wanted to cook it well. Having enrolled at the Cordon Bleu Cookery School – I never worked so hard in my *life* – I'd curl up in bed beside Kenny, reading cookery books as though they were novels. I don't do anything by halves – when I plunge I stay plunged. I was full of enthusiasm and raring to go. There was almost nothing I enjoyed as much as fidgeting in the kitchen, which was just as well. Kenny was a gourmet and there was to be an awful lot of food in our marriage. It was fun, it was new. I'd dote on him and tell him how lovely he looked and I'd sit and watch him eat as though he were an Eastern potentate.

It's hard to imagine the difficulty of learning to be what you're not, from scratch. I started with the blank belief that I couldn't cook or do anything right for anyone, except Kenny. I was a nervous hostess, I could only relax when I cooked for him, going through recipes used by my mother and grandmother. In the kitchen he sat down at the table and drank the coffee I put in front of him. His fingers made little dives in and out of the bowl of icing – pretending to lick and pull away.

'Take your fingers out of that!'

'Who's it for, Shrimp?'

'*You* silly – it's your birthday cake – it's meant to be a surprise.' He watched me for a few seconds and as the 'Happy Birthday, darling' written in chocolate icing started to run down the sides of the cake and slipped all over the plate, I know I'll always remember our laughter – it was so special, how could I forget?

Through all this time I kept myself busy, mostly TV work. I recorded a play with Michael Caine, playing his wife. He didn't make a pretence of remembering me. He was more attractive than ever, a wonderful actor and a pleasure to work with. He seemed to be his own man now, extremely confident. And I was delighted to feel we worked well together.

For Kenny it could have been a forlorn time, familiar faces sliding away; but if it was, he never said so to me. And Christmas was coming. We decided to do our best to obliterate at least some of the misery of the previous weeks. Mistletoe, holly, a giant tree, presents galore. It was a splendid effort. Wendy Toye, of whom Kenny was especially fond, popped in for a drink. Jill, ever loyal, came for dinner, which Kenny cooked, wearing the tea cosy as his chef's hat. 'Howzat?' he said triumphantly producing the sizzling turkey with a flourish. At the end of our meal he proposed the loyal toast and, chucking another log on to the dying embers of the fire, he eyed the five Christmas cards on the mantelpiece, raising his glass towards me.

'Out of all the friends I thought I had, perhaps I have six that are true... best that we should know, Shrimp... but bloody painful to discover.'

Kenny was no fool. None of it, he'd told me, would be plain sailing. Everything he warned me about came to pass. So, to be fair, I had almost expected all this to happen; but when it did, it was the most unpleasant experience.

One bitter sparse Sunday morning there was a gentle knocking at our front door. Two smiling faces, Mummy and Daddy. Eager eyes, brimming with confidence. For a few moments I stared helplessly before me and then took the small white puppy from Mummy's arms. Daddy suddenly took my face and kissed me: 'It's your Christmas present, darling... his name is Timmy.'

I was beside myself with joy, slapping my knees, banging the door with the flat of my hand. Brushing the tears of excitement from my eyes, I rushed upstairs to where Kenny was bathing.

'Ah!' I cried, hugging the little dog. 'Ah! darling, look...! look what Mummy and Daddy have given us!'

There was a dreadful silence, so silent I could hear the tap dripping, and then he looked at me with a slight smile and deliberately patted my arm. 'We're actors, love, we can't be tied down... I'm sorry... we can't have a dog...' We battled for almost ten minutes and finally, reluctantly, I capitulated. 'Take him away... I'm sure he's enchanting... don't let me look... I might get to like him,' he commanded and turned back to his shaving.

It was distressing to tell my parents, they looked so crumpled. Daddy looked at me with a weary eye. 'Did you hear that, Mammy...? Actors can't have dogs,' I heard him say as I closed the door.

When I think back to those early days, it's as though the incidents I remember happened to someone else.

Did I actually throw a turkey with all its trimmings at him during a jealous rage?

Would I stand on a table in a Yugoslavian restaurant and send plates flying through the air towards a group of excitable Italians, as I ducked the ones they hurled at me? – the floor was white with broken china, and Kenny sat looking stunned – I thought it a wonderful game.

Was it me who climbed through the dining-room hatch clutching the roast pork on a dish with an orange in my mouth...? Taking him at his word when he'd suggested that at a smart dinner party, food should be served through the hatch. I wanted to make him laugh. He did, long and loud, incapable of speech.

Could I really have been discovered by Kenny and our guests, coming home early from the theatre after the show, for our first dinner party, standing in the middle of the drawing room wearing nothing but my false eyelashes, black stockings and suspenders, naked from the waist upwards, except for bits of cotton wool, soaked in a special sticky bust-developing lotion I'd got from Paris. 'Wait till you see my bird!' I heard him announce breathlessly as he thrust the front door open. I could see his appalled expression, we both froze, stuck to the spot, staring at each other in horror.

'Kenny,' I began in a very small voice. I'd desperately wanted to make a good impression; I was heartbroken, standing there in utter bewilderment holding my bosoms. I wanted to make a dash for it, but didn't dare. The hush only lasted for a second, then he laughed, 'Well, you've all seen her now!'

Was that really me? It seems so remote now, it could almost have happened in another life; and in a sense it did.

We would drive to Woodstock, an enchantingly pretty village in the Cotswolds, and then on to the Thatched House, 'Brother' Cyril and Pat's lovely home. The house, set in glorious gardens, was even prettier than Kenny had described to me. Filled with wonderful country antiques, dogs, thundering log fires and glistening copper bowls filled with flowers from the garden. My eyes were out on stalks. I was agog. Cyril and Pat, larger than life personalities, took me in as their own. Pat, disarming with her soft Irish accent, taught me a lot about keeping house – laying a table, caring for silver, arranging flowers, dinner parties at home, and lots more. Leslie and Maxwell were often there – friends of Kenny's, slowly becoming friends of ours. Kenny had so obviously been born with a gift of giving happiness and receiving it, and I wanted to join in, wanted everyone to like me, do everything right. Willing to please, I wanted to be part of their mutual delight.

It was against this background that I was introduced to what was for me a world of heavy drinking. My sweet-natured Kenny, never passionately angry, was, I discovered, quite a famous drinker. Not at home, however; he never drank there. But socially Kenny's definition of a good evening out was when he came home with an empty wallet and a hangover. He tried to teach me to drink and I once asked in a pub if I could try a rum and blackcurrant – 'Not with *me* you can't,' and he hurried me out laughing. I didn't drink, I couldn't. I did try but after two I was sick. So I stopped. The parties we were asked to were foreign territory for me. No music, no dancing. Just people standing around drinking drinks with cherries in. I tried to find something in common with someone, but I just wasn't chameleon enough to become part of the cocktail party generation. The women with their green eye-shadow and no mascara all seemed alike. Saying nothing and talking out loud, they took their voices and manners from each other.

I met some unforgettable characters at this time. I was still a curiosity; the husbands seemed happy to see me, the wives less so. They all seemed to laugh a lot, their hands never without a glass. Horribly sober, I'd laugh too – but I'd really want to go to bed.

'Aren't we having a lovely time!' Kenny would enthuse. He would want to stay up, and much as I would long to go to sleep, I wanted to be with him, and I was determined to enjoy everything he enjoyed. And Heaven knows I tried. The plain fact was, I was out of my depth, and in spite of my tender age I simply couldn't keep up with him. As the evenings wore on, the drinking would continue, the conversation would get muddled, the jokes repetitive. I became anxious when Kenny drank a lot; I'd continue to talk to him as if he were sober, reason with him, plead with him at least not to mix his drinks. I was lucky that even when he was drinking he was still (to me) enchanting. His pleasure was almost childlike, his face alive and full of fun as he gleefully mixed martinis with wine, wine with whisky, whisky with brandy – deadly. And he positively enjoyed his hangovers, felt he'd earned them and well worth it for a 'wonderful evening'! His inebriation went into four stages – charming, intelligent, invisible and bulletproof. I tried being furious, tried the tears, telling him it was lonely for me going out with him, but after more tears I'd pull myself together, realising I'd get no sympathy. 'You come from a family that only drinks at Christmas!'

My feelings about his drinking were based on emotion; partly due to my insecurities, that overworked word, and partly due to the fact that he was an outrageous flirt. I was convinced he'd leave me. I so adored him, thought him so stunning, I was sure every other woman would – and some did. I was wildly jealous and showed it. I love you, did she say it like that? – did she say it better? – I didn't feel a thrill in competing. And however much he reassured me I wasn't – I felt I was. Kenny was aware, he couldn't fail to be, of my sudden plunges into despair. I felt inadequate, uncertain; I'd been brought up a Catholic, made to feel inferior to God, to everyone, and I realise now that I spent the first thirty-five years of my life walking around on my knees. When he entered a crowded room, people would shift and stir, and, as if by magic, a way would clear for him, then the ranks would close and I'd be left on the outside, feeling, *talk to me someone*. I would listen to the women, sigh almost to be in his company. He had the gift of making any woman from seventeen to seventy feel as though she was the only woman in the room. He was attentive and gay. So was I struggling to be, but no one took me seriously when he was around, and if they did notice me, their gaze would wander away. When the man you love is a celebrity, someone who generates so much interest and impact, socially you are on your own. You never enter a room on equal terms. Everyone wanted a slice of him. It meant not having him at my elbow, steering me through a crowd, or simply to turn and smile at. He was a piece of public property.

Going out was seldom a pleasure, it became part of the job. Was I envious? Would I have liked to have been the centre of attraction? Everyone telling me I was wonderful, witty, attractive? Very probably. But most of all I envied his precious energy. I would watch him pumping it out in all directions – and *I* wanted it. More than I felt I got. I could see quite clearly that this was how it was going to be, the pattern of our social life. I'd have to suppress my neurotic feelings. Years later when I talked to Doreen Hawkins and Elizabeth Harrison, told them how it had been for me, I was staggered to find that they had similar stories. I needn't have taken it all so personally.

It was a shock for him (and for me too) to discover I was so excruciatingly jealous. And also that I refused to do the washing-up at night. Kenny, with his Navy training, hated that; there was no excuse: 'It takes two minutes.' He bought me a stunning double row of pearls with a diamond clasp the size of a boiled sweet, his form of persuasion. However, after three weeks of him inspecting the kitchen, asking, 'Is it A1, Shrimp?' I offered them back and continued to loathe washing-up.

'You're behaving like an adolescent,' he said once.

'I almost am.' I suppose I was quite often a pain in the neck.

Kenny More, who wrote me loving notes when he lunched at the Garrick Club, knowing I enjoyed receiving letters and seldom did. Kenny More, who hated being so obsessively tidy and threw his clothes all over the dressing room floor one night, sneaking out of bed at three in the morning to hang everything up. 'I can't sleep, darling... my lovely things... all in a heap!' I thought him crazy then – but in that way I grew like him. Kenny More who was big enough to laugh and say, 'Now you know why I love her' to Noël Coward when I'd told the Master in all seriousness that Kenny had been asked to appear in Chekhov's *Three Seagulls*.

Kenny More. I was certain he was the last man in my life. Every part of my day was designed to one end; the comfort, benefit and pleasure of Kenny More.

We were at Brother Cyril's, in bed in the early hours of April 1st 1964, when the telephone rang. Joan said that she had agreed terms with 20th Century Fox for me to go to Hollywood and appear with Shirley MacLaine in the film *John Goldfarb, Please Come Home*. I told her, 'Oh, yes, – very funny, haha – a happy April Fool's Day to you too!' And we went back to sleep. About four hours later the telephone rang again. It was Joan, extremely irate, telling me I had to collect my visa and be over there in thirty-six hours. So much for an April Fool's Day prank.

'It's true, Kenny! It's really *true*!' I found myself gabbling and couldn't stop. Kenny said nothing, just sipped his tea. But I could feel his dismay. He didn't ask any questions. I recognised the resentment and felt the old stab of guilt as I watched him shake his head. He's unhappy and it's all my fault. There was a very long silence.

'What about *me*? – you haven't given me a thought.' The words were out.

Poor darling, I said, I love you. I know I'm awful to be so excited – *please* come with me – it's only for three weeks. I'm a bitch, bitch – but I've got to go.

'I can't follow you around when you work.' I didn't answer. 'You've broken your promise, you damned actresses are all the same!' I felt dismayed and low. His way of handling this had been the English way, controlled. My way was to toss a bowl of pot-pourri over him while he lay in the bath. Infuriatingly he hardly reacted – merely raised his hands and said, 'Pax.' And I then crumpled in a gale of tears. I was still shaking with sobs as he tenderly strapped me into my seat on the aircraft. He simply shook his head and said, 'No more tears, Shrimp.' I thought I mustn't lose control now and say – don't let me go Kenny – come with me Kenny – hold me tight Kenny – *I don't want to be alone* – but I did, and he held me tight. After a moment he freed himself and he walked away down the plane, his head droopy like a flower on a stem.

There was a bunch of flowers waiting for me at the Beverly Wilshire Hotel. The card read, 'I managed to dry these out for luck – Ophelia – I love you little one – Joe'. My room on the ninth floor was light and spacious, filled with cellophane-wrapped bowls of fruit, rubber plants and Monet reproductions. A doll with blue nylon hair sat on top of the fridge which was filled with everything from orange juice to champagne. In his book *More or Less* Kenny said he was jealous – but if he was, it didn't show. He had visions of me being leapt upon by every male actor. He needn't have worried. Los Angeles, then, seemed to be full of men on the couch or coke – or both. They had fixed noses, capped teeth and sun tans, and seemed to move around in slow motion wearing large sunglasses, as they discussed dollars and deals. Sunshine filtered through the smog and my eyes stung as I squinted at this land of make-believe, driven around Beverly Hills by a representative of 20th Century Fox in a black stretch-limo Cadillac. I gazed at this fairyland with its palm-lined boulevards, the houses approached through U-shaped drives, nestled into the lush hilltops. The sound of juggled gin and tonics and Sinatra carried on soft breezes as slender, incredibly beautiful women in scanty bikinis lazed in the cool comfort of their gardens, where they might occasionally stir to dip their toes in the shimmering turquoise of their swimming pools.

Three days before I was to start filming I was driven to 20th Century Fox studios, along Sunset Boulevard, Sunset and Vine, the Strip, names from all the old songs – thrilling new territory for me. Through the high metal gates of the studio and into make-up and wardrobe for tests. Huge buildings which turned out to be sound stages, executive offices, cutting rooms, dressing rooms. I was led through a vast hanger full of clothes, rail upon rail. My head swivelled – these were the clothes worn by Judy Garland, Rita Hayworth, Ava Gardner, Clark Gable, *Errol Flynn*. The labels went on and on.

I sat in the make-up chair – 'Hi Angela, how are you, my name is Jackie' – and she did me over. Julie Andrews, fixing her lipstick in the chair beside me, said how good it was to hear another English accent when I said, 'Good morning.' I went on to the set and the English director, J. Lee Thompson, an old friend of Kenny's – he'd directed *North West Frontier*, the film Kenny had made in India with Lauren Bacall – sat me down and examined my face; pushing my hair back he muttered, 'Urrhhumm' – nervously twisting a piece of paper between his fingers as he introduced me to Shirley MacLaine, Peter Ustinov and Wilfred Hyde White. Could they know how frightened I was? Would they like me – was I good enough? (I wasn't. I was awful – the film wasn't terrific either and it hardly saw the light of day, thank God. But I'm jumping ahead of my story.)

I was then taken to the commissary for lunch. It was bustling. Tables full of actors, extras and crews. The walls were hung with large photographs of stars – ancient and modern. There was so much to take in – *Hey look at me*, I wanted to shriek. *I'm where movies are made*! And just *look*! – isn't that *Joan Crawford*! Every man I saw, just for a moment, had Kenny's face. And I longed to share all this excitement with him.

I thanked everyone and was driven back to my hotel, completely exhausted with the thrill of it all. It was hard not to feel isolated as I got into my nightie and ready for bed. The telephone rang and it was an English friend – I hadn't even known he was in Hollywood. He said that I must be feeling lonely and 8.15 was a ridiculous time for a twenty-three-year-old to be going to bed. How about a movie and dinner? Goody, I thought, quickly pulling my hair into a ponytail, then into my jeans and a T-shirt and I was ready. Sitting next to him in the cinema he handed me a carton of popcorn and told me he'd known 'darling Kenny' for years. I felt grateful for his company and afterwards he took me to a Japanese restaurant up in the hills. We started to talk about the film. He spoke softly – I hung on his every word. I can't really remember how he began talking about Kenny, but almost out of the blue he said that everyone was watching us with interest, knowing that we wouldn't last and what a pity he was drinking himself to death, and wasn't it sad that his career was finished. That he and Bill had been a wonderfully devoted couple, and that I was being a fool, should think of myself. Right in the teeth, cutting me to the core, right through my defensiveness, and I felt lacerated, but I wasn't going to let him see me break. How could he say such things to me? – Kenny drinking too much? He and Bill *devoted*? I got out of the car in a very grim mood and said a quick 'Goodnight'.

I got to my room, closed the door and started to cry. The television set flickered in the corner – I went over and turned the sound down before I reached for the phone. I had to call Kenny. I'd wake him if need be – after all I was awake and was upset. I was crying and talking – he waited for me to finish, he'd heard what I said, but he didn't accept it. He wasn't upset or angry. I was being silly he said, can't you see it's a pass, darling – he's trying to get you into bed. The only thing to do, he thought, was to come over and join me, let everyone see he wasn't drinking himself to death – and that if he was devoted to anyone, it was to me.

I could hardly speak with excitement – gone suddenly were my fears. He talked quickly, telling me to book him a room and to expect him in forty-eight hours. 'I love you,' he breathed. 'Me too' – and the line went dead. I walked into the bathroom kicking off my shoes. The whole day had been a brave attempt at normality, and I was exhausted. Rubbing my eye make-up off I told myself I must be quite crazy. How old are you? – twenty-three? And you still don't recognise a pass? Pulling on my nightie I felt a welling of confidence; it seemed all right suddenly and I fell asleep with the thought: Kenny.

I'd heard rumours that in some States there was a law that forbade unmarried people to occupy the same bedroom. I didn't want any embarrassment when he arrived, so I went up to the reception desk and asked if this was true. 'You see we don't want to be arrested – we can't afford that sort of publicity.'

The assistant manager looked at me in amazement and assured me there wasn't a law to this effect in California. A stranger stared at me while I spoke quietly to the manager and

I overheard a snatch of her conversation: 'Is she under age, do you suppose?'

My grandmother always told us, 'No matter what situation you find yourself in – you must always act like a lady.' Would sloshing her with my shoulder-bag be acting like a lady? Perhaps not.

It was soon all over the hotel that my boyfriend was arriving – *same room* – *not married*. I was embarrassed and talked to dear old Willie Hyde White who suggested I rent an apartment, and he found one for us next door to him and his wife, Ethel. I moved into Fireside Manor the next evening; wanting everything to be perfect for him I shopped at Farmers Market, so big and abundant for our food. Champagne in the fridge – clothes in cupboards and drawers. Red roses *everywhere*. The apartment had its own pool – I was very excited. Everything was clean and bright sunshine crept from every corner. My chauffeur-driven limousine, provided by the company, cruised smoothly to the airport. Clutching a single red rose I settled back enjoying the luxury, my sense of reality abandoning me. I felt we were starting a lifetime holiday. Fantas–tic.

At the airport when I saw him I cried out, '*Kenny!*' rushing into his arms – we hugged and squeezed. How I had missed him. Life wasn't any good without him – I had so much to tell, but just for that moment we didn't utter – just stood there glued to the spot holding each other. We headed for our new apartment, with me pointing out places of interest on our way. 'Oranges and lemons grow from trees out here, darling – wait till you see' – I rattled on. He laughed, he was happy. We both were. I led him up to our love-nest – he breathed in, making a 'how wonderful' gasp. We had so much to catch up on.

It was glorious being away from London, from being outcasts. The wire-tense atmosphere was gone. We flew down to Cheyenne, Wyoming to spend a weekend with my sister and her family – Kenny was excited to be in cowboy country, and walked around hitching up his trousers and saying 'Yep'.

Our life in Los Angeles expanded and opened up. We were there for the excitement of the Oscars. There was Disneyland, Malibu, weekends in San Francisco and Palm Springs, and we met some friendly and generous people who welcomed us with open hearts. It was like a good film, with a star-studded cast – but without cameras and crews. It was all real. There I was, sitting between Vincente Minnelli and Kirk Douglas – he peeled my fruit – at a birthday party for Peter Ustinov. I looked over at Kenny, getting a kick out of talking with the mischievous William Wyler. My letters home were full of detail. I namedropped like mad, such a show-off. *Sinatra*, Daddy! – I knew it would thrill him!

Mike Frankovich, who was running Columbia Studios, asked us to have dinner one evening with his wife Binne. William Wyler was there too; he was making *The Collector* with Terence Stamp and Samantha Eggar. This told the story of a young man who kidnapped a girl (Samantha) and kept her his prisoner. Now the collector (Terry) had a confidant, an older man, known as J. B., and Willie was very anxious that Kenny should play this character. He made it clear that he had some doubts whether the character J. B. would fit as well into the screenplay as it had done in the original book, and that there was the possibility the part might have to be edited out of the completed film. Would Kenny take a chance? You bet he would. Kenny was very flattered to be asked, Willie being one of Hollywood's great directors, whose career had spanned more than forty years. The next few weeks were some of the happiest in my life – we really were on cloud seven. When all you dream of comes true, it's magic.

Our films finished, we decided to island-hop it down to Tobago. Vivien Leigh had told Kenny years before about a very special hotel, Amos Vale, on the paradise island of Tobago. There is no way to describe the impact of a totally different world. I couldn't have imagined it more beautiful than it was. I'd write to my mother long letters, pouring out joy and love and the excitement of it all. Now, when I think of happiness, I think of then.

After a month we flew home via New York – home to what? More ostracism, more evenings and weekends in our home alone, waiting for telephone calls that never came? More pretence that we didn't care?

Some good news awaited Kenny. Bernard Delfont approached him to play Crichton in a musical version of *The Admirable Crichton*, to be called *Our Man Crichton*. In the late fifties Kenny had starred in the film, one of his less successful. His first reaction to the offer was that he couldn't sing. B. D. talked him into it. Then he went to his agent, Laurie, and asked his opinion. 'I've got you £1,000 a week,' he told him.

'But I can't sing,' Kenny protested.

'Well,' Laurie replied, 'for that money anybody can!'

Determined to do the best he could, he became consumed by the work. He'd taken an enormous chance. He took voice lessons, worked out in a gymnasium. He stayed out of the crowded, noisy bar at his beloved Garrick Club, saving his energy for the show. On a daily basis it was hard concentrated work. He was filled with anticipation, and by the time the show opened in Manchester, his legs were once again covered in eczema. He didn't want me to be out front on opening night, he was nervous enough. I left for London on the 4.30 train. He put me in my seat, blowing kisses and waving me goodbye. I didn't want to miss any of it, so at the first stop I got off and caught the next train back, changing into my new velvet suit in the ladies' cloakroom. And by seven-thirty I was sitting in my seat in the stalls, clutching nervously on to Laurie's arm. I was expending so much nervous energy; hearing the score with the orchestra for the first time was a special thrill. The audience readily responded and I thought it had to be a hit, but I was so involved how could I be objective? His dressing room was filling up when I walked in. He looked so happy. 'She *stayed*... my baby... she *stayed*!'

After a short tour, the show opened at the Shaftesbury Theatre, but it only ran for six months. Noël Coward came round to see him after one performance. He shook his head slowly from side to side, and waggling his finger he gravely said, 'Dear boy... that was absolutely terrible. Don't *ever* do it again.' Kenny took Noël's advice, and never did.

Another trauma for him. He was hanging a picture in his study one day when the telephone rang. Willie Wyler was on the line from Hollywood. I was bubbly talking to him and handed the phone over. Kenny was excited too. We'd seen the rushes and felt that this had been some of his best work on film, it was a perfect part for him. And surely Willie was calling to congratulate him on his performance. But he wasn't. He was heartbroken, he told us, but he'd had to cut Kenny out of the picture. The part hadn't worked. It had in the book, but for the film he wanted to have all the action with the collector and the girl in the cellar.

'You played it beautifully, Kenny, but it doesn't work.'

They'd remove his name from the bill – Willie made all the right noises.

'Thank you for telling me, Willie, difficult for you,' was all he said. Our hearts turned to jelly at such a bitter disappointment, we both felt sick. Kenny looked at me and only said, 'It's a cruel blow, Shrimp... the buzz in the profession will be that I gave a bad performance. They won't want to believe the real reason... I suppose I was short-sighted taking such a risk.' And he went back to hanging his picture. Not another word of complaint or bitterness. He was starting to teach me, by example, how to turn the other cheek. Take life on the chin.

The strange part was that his contract stipulated that if he appeared in the film, he had to have equal billing with Terence Stamp and Samantha Eggar, because on paper at least he was still a star. Laurie, therefore, insisted quite rightly that they remove every trace of him from the film. If they showed one shot where he could he recognised, they would be liable for heavy damages, having removed his name. They cut him out completely, except for one scene where the cameras held a close-up of Sam Eggar in an English pub and Kenny, for a split second, was seen in the background. The scene was essential for the action of the film, and they must have forgotten that he had appeared in it. He could have taken the film company for thousands of dollars, but Kenny didn't have the heart to do anything about it.

'Willie's such a lovely man,' he told his lawyers.

Another blow he'd had to bear; he was so dignified and simply accepted his misfortune in silence. He had such beautiful manners in business, as in everything else.

It amazes me to realise that I am only six years younger now than he was then. He seemed to have a greater understanding than I have now. He was astute – it could be exasperating at times to live with someone who seemed to know all the answers. He wanted to teach me, and – because of my inexperience and youth – protect me.

'Tell me a story, Kenny… a true one this time.'

'True ones aren't so much fun!'

He educated me about life, and the first and second world wars, Mozart, Leonardo, and his passion: the history of the Roman Empire. Hidden behind that swift laugh and flippant, hail-fellow-well-met exterior was a very good brain. He had the answers to my questions at his finger tips, and if he wasn't a hundred per cent sure, then he'd refer to his beloved encyclopaedias. I told him he'd have made a wonderful teacher. He'd laugh it off and say, 'I only got minus two for maths at school – I was a duffer! I only know the answers because I've lived so long!'

But that wasn't true; he had an enquiring mind, was well read and I'd simply delight in curling up next to him to listen. I was so content. Tell me this, tell me that, teach me Daddy. He was my safe place and I loved him with all the love I had to give. My life entirely revolved around him. I worked a little to keep my hand in and my bank balance sweet. But there was no doubt that our life together was my priority. He gave me guidance and security. With his self-confidence he seemed to be everything I wasn't. Now, after three years, I was more in love with him than ever. And heartbreakingly in need of his love, I craved his attention. He was strong and affectionate. He was in control.

Things weren't precisely as I'd imagined they would be. Malcolm Muggeridge once said something along the lines of, 'Marriage transcends everything else, with sex and marriage tearing off in opposite directions.' I'd curl up in bed with my head on his chest and I'd say, 'Kenny, I love you.' He needed to hear that, I know. But he also had a need to hear, 'Kenny, I want you' more often than he did. I let him down there. But we never discussed it. I was afraid to tell him that when we made love, I felt the most intense pain, and I wanted to cry out, 'It's hurting me!' Instead, stupid girl that I was, I made excuses. I was frightened to go to the doctor, fearful of what he might discover. But reluctantly I eventually made an appointment to see our GP and, trailing into his surgery, I sat there undoing my skirt. He asked questions and probed, 'Breathe in, Angela... another deep breath', and he arranged for me to have X-rays. Yes, they found a little problem here, a little problem there. My appendix needed to come out, I had a cyst or two on an ovary and my womb was sort of back to front. I practically skipped home – there *was* something wrong! I was impressed with my list of symptoms. It wasn't my imagination. I would desire him again as passionately and with as much urgency as before.

I was booked into a private room in St George's Hospital, Hyde Park Corner, and when I awoke in the recovery room, my gynaecologist was bending over me calling my name. I squinted at him, trying to focus one eye at a time.

'It's all over,' he told me. 'It went very well, you've nothing to worry about.'

I was hurting and felt sick, and just nodded my thanks. I wanted to feel my tummy, to feel what he'd done to me. Was I still the same shape? I struggled to ask the all-important question, pushing the words out. 'How long until... we can make love again?'

The gynaecologist, his face close to mine, said quietly, 'Six weeks – best to wait six weeks.'

Kenny would have to be patient with me for a lot longer than that. A long time. Almost a year. For many months sex had, for me, equalled pain.

'It's all in her mind,' our GP told Kenny. Don't say it's all in my mind when it still *hurts* me! But it was a mental block. He was patient, undemanding. Too much so perhaps. We tried to reassure each other that it would be all right, that we would love each other like that again. We wanted to so much. There was a lot I had to learn – I really still knew so little of men, or the importance of sex within a relationship. If I saw the danger signals at all, then I closed my eyes to them. They went ignored. After all we loved each other. What could possibly go wrong for us? I knew better than anyone. And we never really admitted there might be a problem. Yet it was at the core of every trouble between us.

1966 began Kenny's connection with John Galsworthy's *The Forsyte Saga* which Donald Wilson of the BBC intended to dramatise for television in twenty-six parts. It would take a year out of his life, maybe longer. He was asked to play young Jolyon, a key figure: the whole series to be seen through his eyes. Kenny was to appear in fifteen episodes, from a young man until his death on the screen. He was asked to head the cast and was assured that a deal could be worked out to give him enough money so that he wouldn't mind turning down any film offers. Donald let him know that he needed Kenny's name to get the series off the ground. I remember Kenny telling Donald that his career was at a low ebb and he doubted he was much of a pull these days.

'Don't be silly, Kenny,' Donald told him, 'you are at the crossroads – but that doesn't stop you being a marvellous actor.' He wasn't alone in thinking that. A poll had recently been printed in the *Evening Standard*, choosing him as the film star most people would like to see in a war film. He was just behind Charlton Heston, Richard Burton and Elizabeth Taylor as their choice for an epic. And the *Sunday Times* had just published another chart in which he was listed as one of the twenty most exciting men of the twentieth century – in Britain, of course!

He sat at home in the study and he read the first two scripts. He felt Donald had written them from the heart. To produce this series had been a consuming ambition for years. Kenny could not afford to ignore its importance. He says in his book that at fifty he had come to terms with himself, look back on what he had done and what he could hope to do. Equate practicalities with dreams. Socially and professionally he felt he was being passed by and he couldn't see how to fight back. Worse, the will to fight back was itself diminishing. He felt he'd taken the popular image of Kenneth More, the extrovert, the perennial beer drinker and good fellow, as far as it could go. He was tired of playing Peter Pan. He wasn't seeking to build a reputation, only to hold on to what he had already achieved and, if possible, to consolidate his gains. He needed a role which would be a shop window for his talents. So that people could see what he could do, that he wasn't limited by a laugh or a sports jacket, or by the confines of a uniform. Jolyon was this role. It would give him the chance of ageing from early thirties to mid-seventies. This was a challenge he knew he must accept. In a sense he was being offered the longest audition in the world, to an audience of tens and finally hundreds of millions. He said, 'The chips are down'; and this was his chance – his last – to pick them up and play on. He was guaranteed about £16,000 for six months' work, with a share in any world sales that might materialise later. This wasn't movie money, but fair payment. But by then he was so enthusiastic, money was of secondary consequence.

I don't know why we select to remember the things we do; the antennae, after all, are always out. My life hasn't progressed evenly from day to day, tidily condensed into months and years. Remote days when I cried at losing my cat, or further still, hearing peace declared on a blaring radio at school, as I pulled a tooth out with a piece of string on a door handle, remain sharp in my mind. But what did I do last weekend? It's a great gaping hole. Entire chunks of my life are missing. The events of the years between '66 and '69 are dim in my memory, except for my overriding need to conceive a baby. Almost everything else is dim, lost in the hazy shadows of my memory. I wanted a baby, our baby. I loved him so much and wanted to reproduce him.

I had a real maternal instinct and I didn't want to waste that. We felt we could give a child a wonderful life. I was in awe of the family unit, and wanted one of my own. Our baby we felt would be a symbol of our love; it seemed an intolerable waste not to have a lasting, precious souvenir.

'He might not be a terrific looker,' he said, 'but what a personality he'll have!' Our baby was always a boy baby when we had our prolonged discussions. Kenny, the only son of an only son of an only son, wanted a son. He wanted me to have a baby, he told Jill, because if he denied me that, 'something in her that I love will die.' It's just as well he had that attitude, because I would have fought him tooth and nail. I felt so definitely about it. I was bent on motherhood. I wanted to be a young mother, and as I was twenty-six I felt time wasn't on my side. We weren't married, but that wasn't our choice. We didn't delight in flouting convention, but it seemed unlikely that he would ever get a divorce. If we waited to be married to have a baby, then I could grow old waiting.

'He will be a love child... we'll call him Bertie after my father... and we must put him down for Bradfield, his old school.' He took me there, we walked through the marvellous grounds and he showed me the lovely mellow buildings. Oh, we could just see it! Wouldn't it be wonderful, our little son, the image of his father, running excitedly towards us, socks down, tie all skew-whiff, calling 'Mummy! Daddy!' The picture was complete. I was acting my version of 'The Mores' family life'. I wanted to have nursery teas – fill my freezer – make baby clothes. I wanted to stay home and mix up the Ostermilk. I saw it all in images. My imagination ran riot.

Making love against the calendar was a sad mistake. My mistake. 'We can't... not until next Thursday... that's the right time.' I was so insensitive and unsubtle. My longing for a baby almost destroyed the joyful spontaneity of making love. You can't be passionate to a timetable.

I walked up and down Harley Street, seeing doctor after doctor. Naturally they all insisted on doing their own tests. I was examined, probed and prodded, X-rayed. 'Calm down,' they all said, 'there's nothing wrong with you.' But I was upset a lot, it was difficult for me when my friends became pregnant. It was such a powerful biological urge, not an emotion I could control on an intellectual level, and to have it thwarted was very cruel.

We didn't blame each other, but soon the whispers began – ooh, can't they have a baby? Is it *her* or *him*? I wanted to become pregnant and not being able to became an obsession. I once put the evidence of what I thought might be an early miscarriage in my deep freeze, before rushing it round to my doctor to have it tested. I thought about it all the time, turning down offers of work, not buying new clothes, because what was the point? After all, I'd be pregnant next month. Everything on television seemed to be about babies, every woman in the street seemed to have one, every woman in the world did, except me. When my period came on I'd weep into the pillow. *My turn*, when is it going to be *my turn*?

At this point in my life Kenny was engrossed with rehearsals and recordings for *The Forsyte Saga*, and although I was content to stay at home plumping the cushions on the sofa, my finances were at a low ebb. I hadn't worked for almost a year. Through all my life with him money was always there, more than enough. I never had to think about it. He over-indulged me, told me I could have anything I wanted, and I like to think I never took advantage of his outstanding kindness of heart. Well, not often. I loved to spend, on my family, on him – and I preferred to spend my own money. Some of my happiest moments have been spent shopping. So I had to keep my career going.

Out of nowhere 'Binkie' Beaumont called: he wanted to come over and talk to me about his new play. He arrived at about six-thirty. I liked him enormously and it was always good to see him. He said he wanted me, was certain I would be perfect for the part. I remember sitting next to him thinking, why is he directing his conversation towards Kenny, when he says it's *me* he wants. I won't offer it to her unless it's all right with you; it was happening again. More and more producers and directors sought Kenny's permission before offering me work. I was angry inside. I loved him, I wouldn't leave him every evening to appear in a play. But it was *my* choice, *my* decision. So ask *me* – not Kenny. My self-confidence had taken a heavy battering over the past four or five years. I was beginning to feel squashed.

Quite soon after that I did go to work again, on a film made on location in Morocco called *Maroc 7*. Gene Barry and Cyd Charisse were going to be in it. The producers wanted me for six weeks – Kenny told them if they could shoot my scenes in three, then he'd let me go. They must have really wanted me, because they rescheduled my scenes.

'I've got to let you go, haven't I?' he muttered. 'I gave them my word.' And off I flew. I was apprehensive, but tried to make it appear I could cope, travelling so far without him. But he knew I hated leaving him and reassuringly he promised he'd fly over and join me for a long weekend. He chose to come the weekend of England v. West Germany in the World Cup Final. A screen was rigged up in a tent way out in the desert and, naturally, all work with the unit came to a grinding halt. We howled and screamed and jumped up and down like a bunch of lunatics. *We've* won! *We've won*! It was World War Two all over again. My voice was hoarse throughout my next scene.

As a film *Maroc 7* was not particularly noteworthy, but lots of fun. For half the time we were shooting out in the desert, a four-hour drive from anywhere, so some of us chose to camp out in a large disused cowshed. About twenty-two of us: actors, actresses, the crew, a stunt man and a journalist, sleeping on rickety old beds, on an earth floor, our only light coming from kerosene lamps. The rocks were our loo – we would trudge out, two at a time, standing guard for each other. We must have looked hysterically funny, walking off into the sunset clutching a box of matches and some Kleenex. Our shower consisted of old tin barrels filled with water and balanced on a wall. When you pulled the corks out of the holes in the barrels – that was your shower! We didn't sleep much at night: it was hot and noisy and a lot of fun. I was dismayed to find myself looking at a talldarkhandsome man on the unit and thinking *that's nice*. I looked at him and looked away.

While the rest of the cast had several more months of work ahead of them, after recording episode fifteen of the *Saga* Kenny was free. Our finances were sweet, no problems there, but we had no idea how the series would go, and anyway it wouldn't be shown for some months. He lowered his professional sights and made a couple of pretty awful films. One of them was *The Mercenaries* with Rod Taylor and James Brown, a once-famous American football player. Kenny read the script, calling it 'a nothing part', playing a drunken doctor. He said anyone who could remember lines and pretend to be drunk could play it. But he hadn't been offered anything else, so he signed up for it. It was one of his least enjoyable experiences as an actor. He was being paid, it was a job. He said he had to accept that the wheel of fortune turns and he'd been lucky to have been at the top for so long, and now he was underneath, he had to hang on and make the best of it. He was depressed but determined. He would wake up, dreading each day, and yet he forced himself to go on. I was aware that he wasn't only acting in front of the cameras, he was acting all the time, displaying a confidence he didn't feel.

The climates on film locations are always either too hot, or too wet, and the work is slow. There was little for me to do except play earth-mother and try and make the hotel rooms feel like home, as near as possible. I'd read, write letters home, eat and sleep – and be there waiting for him. I'd go crazy trying to invent things to do. I'd start playing patience at seven in the morning, and that got boring when I started cheating on myself! I once devised a game counting the buttons on the air conditioning system. *Desperate* boredom.

It was while we were in Jamaica that we heard via a correspondent for the *Daily Mail* about the enormous success of *The Forsyte Saga*. Apparently the effect on the country had been fantastic. It was to prove to be the most successful series ever shown. 'It's going to be sold worldwide, Mr More... you are very big... bigger than you've ever been in films.' We were a very happy and excited pair. The wheel was turning. He was on his way back.

Metaphorically he could raise two fingers at anyone who had belittled him. He had gone down into that valley and now at last was out in the sunshine.

After Jamaica we went to New York for a week, booking into a suite at the Plaza Hotel. We adored it all. Everything was so new to me. Kenny took me to the famous '21' restaurant and to Sardies. He wanted me to meet some of his friends – people he hadn't been able to see since he'd left his wife. He took me backstage to see Lauren Bacall. I was nervous about meeting her – 'She's a friend of Bill's!'

'Fuck it, she's a friend of *mine*! Don't worry, she's a nice woman... and I want her to meet you and see how smashing you are!' I had heard so many stories about her from Kenny, of the fun they'd had together while filming in India. I found her so attractive and friendly. He was right – I needn't have worried.

One of my big events was a trip to Tiffany's where he bought me a beautiful black pearl ring set in diamonds. I loved presents. We always bought each other lots. Mother's Day – Father's Day – St Valentine's Day – we only needed half an excuse. We walked up Fifth Avenue and down again, lit candles in St Patrick's Cathedral, and saw the big hit show *Cabaret* – it was a wonderful trip. And I was crazy about him.

We arrived at London Airport to a cohort of reporters waiting to interview him. The excitement about the series was extraordinary to witness. Kenny, Eric Porter, Nyree Dawn Porter and Susan Hampshire were household names all over Britain. And quite soon they would be household names all over the world.

Kenny tells in his book just one story, out of several, to show how extraordinarily popular the series was, not only in this country, but everywhere.

Two or three years later, Kenny and I decided we would spend Christmas in Madrid. Our flight was delayed, and we arrived at the hotel at about half past nine in the evening, and checked in at the desk. Because we were tired, we decided to have a light meal in the hotel instead of going out to a restaurant. As we passed through the main lounge to the lift, we saw a large TV screen had been set up, with a number of people watching it. About fifty men and women in armchairs, eyes on the screen. The women wore diamonds and furs, and many of the men had grey hair and seemed the type who pass in advertisements as men of distinction. They were a pretty wealthy audience and all absolutely absorbed by the action on the screen.

I looked at the set to see what was holding their interest so closely. There was Kenny, as Jolyon, speaking the most superb Spanish. He was grasping the curtains in Jolyon's fatal heart attack and died in front of an audience of fifty Spaniards in a Spanish hotel. A woman in one of the front seats, a middle-aged, dark-haired, diamond-earringed and fox-furred lady, was practically having hysterics.

'*Es muerto…! Es muerto…!*' she cried in anguish. A friend in the next seat to her was fanning her and held smelling salts under her nose, and all because Kenny had died on the screen. It was an extraordinary sensation for us both. I had not realised the impact of *The Forsyte Saga* in Spain; and remember, this was the second showing. We both exchanged glances.

'This is too good to miss,' Kenny said. 'I'm going to tap her on the shoulder to prove I am still alive.'

'Go on,' I said. 'Give her a laugh. She won't believe it.'

On the screen Kenny's eyes were closed for the last scene, as he began to pick his way through the chairs.

'*Es muerto…!*' cried the woman again.

Kenny tapped her on her shoulder gently and said, 'No, madam. He's not. He's *here*.'

Pandemonium! The woman screamed and leaped out of her chair. The smelling salts were spilled and the glass bottle smashed. Everyone shouted in amazement.

Until then Kenny had not realised that we were the toast of Spain. Now, he was not allowed to forget it. Magazines displayed his pictures on their covers. The hotel proprietor insisted that everything we wanted must be on the house, and during our stay, when we went out to dine in a restaurant, someone at another table would invariably recognise us and insist on paying our bills. Whenever we waited for a taxi at a taxi-stand, we were immediately passed up to the front of the queue. Kenny would protest, 'No, *please*.' But a Spaniard would reply in perfect English, with a smile: 'No. No. Senor, please. After all, dead men do not argue.' The whole experience was extraordinary, like a royal progress.

On Christmas Day, we decided to attend Mass in the oldest and most famous church in Madrid. We deliberately arrived slightly late because Kenny did not want to be noticed. We crept up a side aisle to one of the small chapels, because I wanted to light a candle to St Teresa. No one saw us. Everyone was looking at the priest. Then a woman from the main body of the church turned and saw Kenny. I thought, Please, God, not here! St Teresa, please. Not *here*. The woman immediately nudged someone next to her, who also turned to look at us.

'Jolyon Forsyte. Jolyon Forsyte,' she whispered. Within seconds, the nudging went around the whole congregation and a kind of sigh ascended to the roof of the cathedral: 'Jolyon Forsyte. Jolyson Forsyte…'

The old priest was about to chant when he saw Kenny and went, 'Ahhh!' The whole service stopped. People now began to call from the back of the cathedral: 'Jolyon! Jolyon!' Kenny panicked. There could be no Mass for us that morning. We literally ran out of the cathedral, and we did not stop running until we reached the seclusion of our hotel.

The whole experience was exciting and I must admit I liked it. It wasn't anything to do with me, but that didn't stop me enjoying it. It was a lot of fun.

Now he was a household name again, we found that many of the people who had run away from him were slowly drifting back. They would ring and say, 'How are you, Kenny? Come to dinner… we're longing to meet your Angela. Congratulations on your success.' But the rejection had been so protracted, complete and very hurtful. He felt he had little in common any more with most of them, except a link with the past – a past he didn't choose to embrace. He accepted their calls graciously, but didn't return many of them.

The appeal of the series was truly international. Harold Wilson was Prime Minister then, and when he held a reception for a Yugoslav trade delegation at No. 10, he decided to invite the cast. Naturally, not being a member of the cast, I wasn't invited, and as the reception started quite late in the evening, I thought it a good idea to get ready for bed before driving Kenny to Downing Street. As we drove up I saw to my dismay about twenty members of the press waiting, cameras loaded, to catch the celebration. I saw women in diamonds and furs posing brightly. I pulled the car to a halt outside No. 10 and prayed, Please, God, don't let them see me. Suddenly one of them spotted me, doing a double-take. He nudged the man next to him and the camera bulbs flashed while I desperately tried to hide behind the driving wheel. I have somewhere the most ridiculous photograph of us – Kenny looking gorgeous in white tie, tails and decorations, and me, shiny face and striped pyjamas, outside the famous door of No. 10.

Our home was humming with activity, the telephone ringing, letters and telegrams of congratulations arriving with every post. A friend gave a large party for us at the Dorchester Hotel. It was a happy time. My sister came home for a visit bringing Lynette and Allison with her – Daddy and Mummy were ecstatic. My birthday wasn't far off and the night before, Kenny had gone to a dinner for young Guards Officers at the Savoy Hotel, a stag do, and he arrived home in the early hours bringing with him twenty-two of the Blues and Royals. My birthday surprise. They all stood there in our small drawing room, these young six-footers, and my five-foot-nine love, raising their glasses and wishing me a Happy Birthday. Kenny, leaning against the door, grinned wickedly and asked, 'Do you love me, Shrimpy?' How could I not?

It was around this time that the newspapers were full of the new Divorce Reform Bill. We read and re-read them. It seemed Kenny would be able to seek a divorce himself, as he and his wife had now been separated for six years. It was at this time that she finally agreed to divorce him.

We had hit calm waters at last. We were free to marry.

Part Three
Girl

To have married in a hurry would have smacked of a sense of desperation we didn't feel. He talked about how he felt he'd been married for *ever* and how he wanted to be a bachelor for a while; but really we wished to wait for our next anniversary, St Patrick's Day, eager for that special day to be our wedding day. Having waited six years – what were another few months? And we had plans to make.

Whatever he said I took as gospel, his rich voice filling my senses, he had the answers I longed to hear. His pauses were long enough for me to deliver yet another volley of questions which he'd answer, his face a completely grooved and wrinkly smile.

'I just want to get married in a church,' I said, as matter-of-factly as I could, knowing it was a difficult dream. He'll throw a fit, I thought, say it's an impossibility for a twice-divorced man. But his large and optimistic heart swept away practical considerations. We had love and courage on our side and we were good Christian people, he'd find a priest or vicar somewhere who'd hear us out. So determined: 'This is an arranged marriage – and I'm doing the arranging.'

'That sounds like a prepared speech for the press,' I teased, but he had the authority to talk that way. I couldn't manage to bite back the cheer of excitement that was tickling in my throat, trying to get out.

Wonderful things do happen and we live most of our lives in hope of them. Our wedding day was wonderful. The big day began with 'Wake up, Kenny! We're getting married today!' I

216

woke up ecstatic – completely awake by dawn. He got our breakfast – washed his hair – I laid out our pressed clothes in the bedroom. Kenny had everything new. My 'something old' was the pearl and diamond bracelet and earrings he'd given me; something new, my simple pale pink wild silk dress; something borrowed and blue, a small handkerchief from Jill. The happy home was alive with activity: telegrams and presents arriving; the telephone never stopped ringing with messages of goodwill. I loved all the fuss, feeling that if wedding days were so magical, I'd like one every year – with the same groom.

The house was glowing, the silver polished, tables waxed and spring flowers *everywhere*; even Pansy, our hamster, had a white bow on her cage. Such excitement. All was going smoothly – until my flowers arrived, then I got tearful because the posy was too large, not what I'd designed and there was no time to do anything about them. But I was only unhappy for a moment – nothing was to mar my joy. All my wishes and dreams were to be realised – nothing could go wrong for us.

I took a bath – my hairdresser arrived and combed my hair, pinning in fresh little snowdrop heads and white hyacinth flowers. I was getting nervous. Daddy arrived, he was nervous too. Kenny gave him a nip of brandy and they waited downstairs while I put my make-up on and finally finished dressing. I heard Daddy say, 'You'll be all right with her, Kenny... as long as you never let her have her own way.'

'I love her, Peter. I know she's not easy... but I treasure her, she's a child of nature – a total innocent.' Oh, *goody*, I thought, he's going to treasure me – I've fallen in love with this man and I'll never get over it.

I kept running to the loo. Roger Moore (Kenny's best man) arrived – we all kissed and hugged. And then suddenly, all at once, Kenny and Roger were leaving. I began to shake. Have you got the rings? – don't go yet – I'm not nearly ready! – do you love me? – Oh, darling! – see you at the church. We held each other tight, he opened the door and was gone. My knees were knocking so – and yet another dash to the loo – Daddy was tapping on my door. 'Are you ready, darling?'

If I wasn't now, then I never would be.

On March 17th 1968, Kenneth Gilbert More, aged 53, married Angela Josephine More – twenty-six years younger – in a beautifully simple service in the Kensington Congregational Chapel, conducted by the understanding Rev. Micklem. I promised to obey. No substitute word for me. It was Kenny's idea to make it a double ring ceremony, though he assured me this was very non-U for a Garrick Club member and he probably wouldn't wear it often. My ring was my grandmother's wedding ring: he had it inscribed, 'I love you Shrimp'. Kenny standing there at the altar waiting for me, looking his most serious, like a grown-up small boy on his best behaviour. So defenceless – and so handsome. When I reached him he held my hand and put his arm around my waist – I was shaking so, and had to feel his support. Later Joan told me that my 'I will' was the most determined response she'd heard – it came out of me in a voice I didn't recognise. My vow meant, I'll prove it to you, Kenny, how much I love you – I'll prove it to everyone.

Daddy bent down and gently kissed me on my cheek before stepping down from the altar. This unexpected gesture of tenderness moved me and the tears started to spill. I watched Kenny's face as he slipped my ring on – his 'I will' was firm and clear. I thought, he's so beautiful – I mustn't cry too much and make a fool of myself. Man and wife. We stood and hugged – gently rocking for a moment – 'Good luck to us, darling' he whispered. I saw tears streaming down his face – and more from me.

Outside the church our friends showered us with confetti and rice – the press were out in force and we were delighted to smile for their cameras.

Home for champagne, our family and close friends all together. I wouldn't toss my bouquet – I wanted to keep it.

The day continued through to the next – on a high. Carl and Eve Foreman threw an enormous party for us, taking the entire penthouse floor of the Royal Garden Hotel in Kensington. Our guests were asked to wear something green, however small, as a salute to St Patrick. It was candlelight, champagne and violins all the way – did all brides feel this way? Never have I felt as I did then. When we looked at each other rockets went off. We really loved. We had every emotion there was to have, they all ran together. So the newlyweds stayed home in Bayswater for their honeymoon – Mr and Mrs at last – secure in the knowledge we'd live happily ever after.

At last I would be able to meet Kenny's daughter, Sarah. She was now fifteen years old and I already loved her, but despite assurances from Kenny, I was apprehensive. As usual, arrangements were made by letter; we were allowed to collect her after school and take her to tea at Fortnum and Mason. I knew what she looked like, I had some photographs, she bore a strong resemblance to her father. What I didn't know was that she was totally sweet and unresentful in her attitude towards us; my fears were unfounded. I suppose I expected her to be spoilt because of the many privileges of her upbringing. I couldn't have been more wrong. I spent most of the time listening – not really at ease. Her eyes shone when she looked at her father – she hung on his every word. What was in her head? I guiltily wondered if I was looking at a vulnerable young girl who'd had a big piece of her heart cut away.

Our small mews home was bursting at the seams and we were in agreement that it was time to move house. We needed privacy and a garden. I wanted to plant flowers and watch them grow – I wanted to be settled and ready in what we felt was a suitable home for that longed-for baby. Until that very day I would compartmentalise. I'd try and put it out of my mind and get on with other things. With our friend and estate agent, Bernard Walsh, we went house-hunting. We found and fell in love with a fifteen-room double-fronted Georgian house, in an advanced state of dilapidation. There were basins in almost every room, boilers on all floors, dry rot, rising damp, it really was a nightmare, I suppose. It needed *everything* doing to it. But I didn't see the horrors straight away: I ooohed and ahhhed over the cornices, wonderful original staircase, and marvellous fireplaces. What really sold it to us was the large and wonderfully wild country garden – one of the largest private gardens in central London. So much room, so many trees, so secluded – so expensive! But I could talk of nothing else, my heart was set on it. Bill Wallace said we could afford it, but said we were crazy to think of living so near Notting Hill Gate; he was worried that the price of the property might not appreciate. Kenny pooh-poohed talk like that – 'We're actors, not businessmen' – he let Bill do the worrying about the money, and bought it for me, for us both. We decided that such an impressive house ought to have a name, and called it Bute House, after Kenny's childhood home, Bute Lodge in Richmond.

Given Kenny's loathing of having builders in the house, or disruption of any kind, everything had to be perfect before we could move. I set to work with almost manic energy. An obsessive drive. I dug the huge garden from top to bottom, it had been so neglected. I was literally ankle-deep in weeds. I cleared them and hundreds of black tulip bulbs, I thought they'd be very depressing in the spring. I hacked away at the tangled undergrowth and when my garden book said, sieve your soil, that's precisely what I did. I bought a sieve and religiously sieved the garden foot after foot. I had never had such backache, but then I'd never had a garden. I knew so little. I was upset one day to find a snail who'd lost his shell – how could he live? I covered him with leaves and waited to ask Kenny – I worried all day.

'I don't believe it,' he roared, 'don't you know a snail from a slug?' *That* was how little I knew.

I know more now, but not a lot. Kenny came with me one Sunday afternoon, I'd needed to take some bags of top soil. I remember so clearly him sitting on an old chair under the weeping willow tree, his mop of curly hair quite grey now; he looked up and said, 'I want to grow old here, Shrimp.' He didn't set foot in the house again once the builders started work. Don't ask me to come, he pleaded, throwing up his hands in horror at the muck and dust. I loved it all, every bit of the process of seeing a house take shape. But it made him really miserable, he hated the disorder. 'I'll sign the cheques, Shrimp – that's my contribution.' You see I knew where I stood.

Before he started rehearsals for his next play, we flew off to the South of France for our month's holiday. As we had done for the past five summers, we stayed at the glorious La Pinade Hotel, which was on the beach just outside St Tropez. Our holidays were wonderful. Easy, sunshine-filled days of love and laughter – and food. Our days were spent on the beach, either anticipating our next four-course meal or recovering from our last. We had holidays all over the world, looking at sunsets and sunrises with appropriate rapture, but France was special. Why do we bother to go anywhere else? he'd say, poring over the Michelin Guide, planning a visit to yet another two- or three-star restaurant – and he had the audacity to ask me why I got fat in France!

We didn't go on holiday to have 'fun' – we had all of that we needed in London. Our holidays were a marital safety valve – we were relaxed and quiet. No pressures. We would catch up, enjoy each other. I never wanted to come home. I felt I lost him in London. Most of his time belonged to his professional life there, and so much of that, because of the demands made on anyone who is at the top of their profession, was away from the home. Our time together on holiday was extra precious, we would talk and talk. And I would shop and shop. He was happy to give me everything I wanted, within reason. I would leave him seated at a cafe table in the old part enjoying a cognac, and head for the boutiques. He loathed coming into the shops, so when something pretty caught my eye, I'd take dresses or whatever out on their hangers and hold them up for his approval, 'What do you think? – the pink or blue one?' I'd bubble away.

'Ooh! Lovely… pretty as paint… do they take the card…? another cognac, waiter, when you have a minute.' With my every purchase, he'd order another drink. We'd laugh and hug. Great game.

'You spoil her, Mr More,' amused onlookers would remark.

'Ah! – she's my joy,' he'd reply, his right hand on his heart. The good times we shared were *fantastically* good.

Kenny was going into rehearsal for a new play *The Secretary Bird* by William Douglas-Home. It was about a man who had lost the affection of his wife. She admits to having an affair with another man, and he tries to win her back by inviting his glamorous secretary down for the weekend, claiming he is having an affair with her. It was simple, straightforward and had some witty dialogue. Kenny was a stunningly skilful stage actor, he didn't seem to do anything – he just *was*. Noël Coward wrote after seeing his performance, 'Kenny More is a lovely, deft comedian in the proper Hawtrey–Du Maurier–Coward tradition! In fact he doesn't apparently make any effort to get his effects and manages to get every one. No asking for laughs or begging for attention. Very satisfactory.' It turned out to be the biggest stage success of his career. After the first night, we went with our party to the Savoy Grill and as we entered the dining room, almost everyone stood up and applauded him. I almost burst with happiness for him, I remember a tear going clonk on to my cheek. He was excited too, talking overloud, couldn't eat, couldn't sleep. We made do with a few hours and were up early to scan the newspapers for the reviews. His personal notices must have been among the best recorded to any light comedian this century. Harold Hobson wrote in *The Sunday Times* the week after the opening, 'Mr More's performance is not only irresistibly amusing, it is morally beautiful... all his jokes succeed. He is the delight of the entire theatre.' Wonderful for him. It made us both very happy.

However, since living with Kenny I'd found it difficult to be unaware of constantly being observed. It wasn't easy for me to adjust to the fact that privacy seemed to be a thing of the past. He often told me he longed for his anonymity again – 'I'd give all I have' – and I was hanging on to mine. 'Sit me where I can watch the Mores eat,' we heard a woman demand of a startled head waiter. And I *minded*. The public had put him there, kept him there, given us all the good things in life, but my problem was I wanted us to live a normal life, as I'd known it. I longed for us to be able to do our Christmas shopping together, or relax on a beach without attracting a crowd and feeling like Exhibit 'A'.

I wanted to build a shell to protect us. The most amiable strangers irritated me because they simply stared at us, or came over to talk. I'd be very cool, I'd hardly smile, and I always felt so ashamed of myself when I got home. I suppose some people reading this might feel critical of me and we realised that it was unreasonable perhaps to resent the attention of members of the public, when Kenny in particular had struggled and worked so hard for the recognition and success he'd achieved. We had wanted to be somebody. How then could we complain about the encroachment on our privacy? In his heart he wanted to be wanted, but once outside our home we were almost constantly aware of being observed, and it's a very real strain.

Once in a public lavatory in Chelsea he was accosted by the attendant, a total stranger. 'I know you, don't I?' came the familiar approach. As Kenny hurriedly adjusted his dress and tried to slink away, the man took hold of his arm and, swinging him around and peering into his face, said, 'It's Kenneth More, isn't it... you've been here before. I've told my wife you use my urinal.'

On my own I was still tolerably free of it, but even so some of my private moments got whittled away. Often I couldn't do the simplest things without someone pointing me out and then poking his neighbour, and I'd be forced into my performance: my Kenny More's publicist routine. Yes, he was working – a film – a play – oh, you preferred *Genevieve*? Yes, he was wonderful. Yes, wasn't I a lucky girl? I remember being excited on a hot sunny day in '76 to see a man standing outside the stage door of the Theatre Royal in Bath waving an autograph book in my direction. I'd done two shows that day and felt tired – 'Could I have your autograph, Miss Douglas?' he asked. 'I've seen you on television lots of times… er… I can't think of his name… but… umm… oh, it's on the tip of my tongue… aren't you Mrs… er… somebody famous?'

I'm not so insensitive that I don't realise that feelings can be easily hurt, but I felt my smile waning. I was silent for a long moment. 'What would you like me to put?'

'Ooh! Would you say, "Best wishes Roy"… and would you sign his name? I've seen all his films… isn't he a wonderful actor?' Yes, he was. The British public, famed for its loyalty, loved my husband and so did I, but I hated vicarious living, and some people say it's awful of me to admit it, as though you lose your civil rights when you live with a man! But when we were together I became an appendage. Acutely aware of my shortcomings, I was afraid that I might not be what people expected. And I resented having to be so aware of *me*.

I often acted out this scene, but it didn't happen the way I had always dreamed it would. I liked to take advantage of Kenny's morning bathing ritual, to sit on the floor by the shower and talk. About anything – post-mortems on the night before – what movie we hoped to see next – gossip – or what did he want for dinner. 'Shall we have sausage and mash and onion gravy this evening, Shrimp?' My body gave a heave and I reached forward and leaned over the loo with my hot hands on the cool porcelain of the old-fashioned round-edge rim.

Whatever in the world? I thought to myself, gulping and swallowing hard – *I'm being sick* I wailed, as I went on losing my harmless breakfast. I'm sorry – I'm sorry Kenny, I said over and over again, feeling waves of nausea and shame. He held me from behind and pulled me upright, sitting me on the chair as he wiped my mouth with a towel. The room swam and I lost focus as he put my head down between my knees. He crouched beside me, holding me. 'Well, I'm blowed! I think my little one's pregnant,' he said quietly, patting my back. I gave a sort of foolish gulp. We blinked at each other for a moment. *I was*? *I was*!

'Congratulations, Kenny, you've done it,' said the doctor, walking out of our bedroom, confirming the marvellous news. He'd asked me when I'd last had a period; I checked the dates in my diary and was astonished, speechless, to realise that it had been three months since I'd had a proper one; I told him my underwear had shown evidence of dark violet brown blobs. I hadn't given it a thought – my energies were all directed into rebuilding of Bute House. I hadn't given any part of me recently to temperature charts and babies. It's quite unbelievable, but I hadn't noticed that for the first time in my life I had the most beautiful big bosoms.

Why was I spotting? What was the matter with me? What was the matter with our *baby*? The doctor prescribed Valium and told me to stay in bed. I did, for ten days. But the spotting got heavier. Had I lugged too many bags of soil? Would this be happening if I hadn't dug the garden? Was it my fault... *my fault*. Exposing my anxieties – I *needed* his reassurance.

He took off his stethoscope, twisting it around his hand before stuffing it into his case. Kenny was on the bed beside me and we gazed at the doctor waiting for our answers. He did his best to alleviate my guilt, telling me if heavy gardening caused miscarriages, then abortionists would soon be out of business. But it's difficult to tell what doctors think in private, and I wasn't convinced. He wanted me to go into Westminster Hospital, 'The Sister there is wonderful – she'll look after you.'

The ambulance men fluttered around me like butterflies.

'Are you in pain?'

'No.'

'Are you bleeding?'

'Yes, a little.'

Tucking my nightie between my knees, and feeling self-conscious, I gave them a good line in small talk, wisecracking my way into the wheelchair. I felt guilty at not offering them tea and cake. They chatted away, I tried to seem interested. 'I'm not frightened, Kenny,' I said in a tiny voice. *Please come with me*, I wanted to howl. But he had two shows, he couldn't have, could he? Be a pro, Shrimp, I told myself. Be a big girl. Do what Daddy tells you.

In a moment I was out of the front door and into the mews. Smiling, I tried to look jaunty at my neighbours as they clucked and nodded away to each other, titillated by the drama. The ambulance attendants pushed the wheelchair with me in it, clutching at my stomach, over the courtyard. *Bump – thud – stay baby stay* I pleaded into my pelvis. Please boys, not so fast, I squawked. I couldn't see behind me, couldn't see Kenny at the front door, but I put on my bright smile and fluttered my fingers at him anyway.

They drove me to the Westminster Hospital as though this were the emergency call of their lives. We raced across town, sirens wailing, tyres sizzling. Crossing my arms over my tummy I held on, bracing my feet against the rails, but still I got tossed around. The doctor had said it would be better for the baby if I went by ambulance, a smoother ride. 'Slow down, *please*!' I hollered. It didn't help. We continued to swerve and dive all over the streets of the West End of London.

This all happened in June. By the beginning of July I was still in hospital, gently sedated, not allowed to put so much as my big toe on the floor. Lying there with the sheets thrown off in the enervating summer heat, drowsily excited by the experience of being pregnant, I was getting a round ripe tummy and felt more like a woman. I had a medical journal by my bed and read all I could about having a baby; it wasn't very technical, anyone could follow it. The doctor had been right, there was something infinitely reassuring about Sister and her team. They were all doing their best for me, but I was still lightly spotting. Before my pregnancy I'd been heavily into health food – our fridge and our larder crammed with marvellously fresh organically grown fruit and vegetables, free-range eggs, and home-made brown bread. I couldn't be faulted in my devotion to nutrition. But now, when more than ever I needed to eat well, all I could face were the tins of cocktail cheese biscuits and gooey meringues and cream that Kenny bought for me every day. An average expectant mother.

We were only too aware that a child might come between us – after seven years we were used to being first with each other. Would a baby affect the incredible closeness we knew at home? A new life. We knew how Kenny was as a father, but I was an unknown quantity – would I go overboard as a mother? Would he lose me? Apprehension mingled with joy.

I wasn't allowed visitors except family. Daddy and Mummy were thrilled at the prospect of having a grandchild in England. People were being so kind, flowers poured in – I was overwhelmed. Kenny brought his camera and photographed me sitting up in bed wearing the new nightie he'd bought me. I wore a grin from ear to ear; with all those glorious flowers I felt like a pampered film star. He'd wander around the room watering and tending them, and every now and then he'd ask, 'I'm a bit fed up with all this... when are you coming home, Shrimp?'

The blinds are discreetly tilted, cooling the room, not a sound from the street outside. My whole team of eager doctors and nurses are in the room. Kenny standing at the bottom of my bed, his hand on the bed-rail. We are both wearing what we intend to be suitably good patient expressions. The medics seem to feel awkward, standing around with hands plunged into pockets, feet shuffling as they chorused their good-afternoons. A small black box, trailing wires, is placed on my bed beside me. Leads are put on my tummy, knobs twiddled – a long second passes and the doctor, bending over the machine, nods to a colleague. Kenny and I hold our look – tight. The doctor appears about to say something, but doesn't, just opens and closes his mouth – then suddenly – thrillingly – the woosh-woosh-wooshing sound they've been listening for fills the room. I am caught off guard, it seems to bounce off the walls – what is it? What am I listening to?

'That's it, darling!' Kenny says, coming towards me. 'It's the baby – the *heartbeat*!'

'Oooh – Oh… aagh!' I sigh, hanging on to his hand. Usually so good at hiding his emotions in front of strangers, his tears just run down his cheeks – now more from me in response to his; he's given me all this happiness.

'You keep her here for as long as you have to,' he tells the doctors, 'we want this baby.' Kissing me tenderly he shakes free from me and then he is gone.

At about six in the morning I woke with a start, hearing the babies in the nursery along the corridor. The crying came at me from all sides. It would be all right, everyone told me so. I lay back on my pillows, stroking my tummy in circular movements, praying, stay baby, please stay. Clean dressings for three consecutive days meant all was well and I could go home. Sister had promised me. There was nothing for me to do but lie there and wait for the trickle of blood to stem. I was sedated enough not to be driven crazy, the three weeks were tolerable.

On Saturday morning, Kenny strode into my room. I greeted him joyfully, waving my clean dressing in the air like a flag.

'Two days, Kenny…! No bleeding… look, isn't it wonderful… we're winning!' Despite the Valium I bubbled away and reached forward to hug him. He was already next to me holding me when something terrible happened; a rush of warm blood from between my legs and over my thighs, and I felt my first contraction. And at that moment I felt paralysed with distress. I couldn't do anything but cling on to him helplessly – terrified. '*Kenny!*' a voice that didn't sound like mine screamed out.

He was sounding panic-stricken too. 'Oh my God...! Oh my God!' Peeling my arms from around his waist, he spun round and rang the bell. 'Sister... we're in trouble!' My room was suddenly full of people and the little black box was fetched, the plugs and wires were attached to my stomach and we all listened to the horrifying silence. No fluttering heartbeat. The doctor drew back from my bed.

'I'm sorry,' I heard him say, 'the baby's dead.'

I was so devastated I couldn't breathe. Kenny took me in his arms whispering over and over, 'I'll be your baby, Shrimp, I'll be your baby... you can baby me.' I clung on to him wanting to tell him everything was all right as long as I had him, nothing else really mattered. I tried to tell him, but racking sobs poured out of me instead of words. My eyes brimmed with heavy tears that ran down my cheeks into my hair and over his shirt. They kept coming. I'd never cried tears quite like that before.

That was July 12th. The rest of the day was a blur of anxiety and grogginess before they gave me a D&C. Jill had said there was nothing to it and she was right. There wasn't any pain.

'Was it a wonky baby?' we asked. They couldn't tell us very much, except that the placenta had been a peculiar shape and that it had been a male foetus. I was desolate. Empty. Utterly wiped out. I wasn't the first woman to lose a baby son. But I was married to a man who had everything else. It took all my resolution to be fatalistic. But we were told I'd be pregnant again by Christmas. They were sweepingly wrong. I was never pregnant again. I never felt a kick inside, I never went to Mothercare.

During the next few months I filled my time with the rebuilding of Bute House. It was taking far longer than we had expected. Man had just landed on the moon, we stayed up all night watching it on TV, and it was hard to believe that building a home could be so *difficult*. Many unforeseen problems. Kenny had made a film called *The Battle of Britain* the year before and they asked him to publicise it. We went to Brussels and Amsterdam and Oslo – all expenses paid. We spent three or four days in each city, enough time to see the art galleries and museums and to discover the best restaurants. In Amsterdam at the premiere Kenny presented a model Spitfire to Prince Bernhard who had been a Spitfire pilot. It was relaxed – Queen Juliana took a shine to me. She chatted away telling me some of the horrors of the Occupation years. She made me feel like a daughter almost. We went twice to the Rijksmuseum to see the collection of Rembrandts. It was the tricentenary of the artist's death, and the museum had managed to get paintings from behind the Iron Curtain, New York, Paris, London – all under one roof. We just sat there – moved to tears almost. Quite stunning.

Our final promotional trip was to Oslo for the Royal Premiere. We were booked to fly out on the Wednesday morning, attend the premiere that night, spend Thursday and Friday sightseeing and giving interviews on TV and to the press and then return. I packed our luggage with evening clothes, all I thought we'd need – and we travelled, as we always did, casually dressed. It was a good flight, first class, champagne all the way and we looked forward to meeting the King and Queen of Norway. Halfway through our journey, the cabin steward approached.

'Mr More,' he began awkwardly, 'I have a message for you from the Captain that has just come through on the radio telephone. There has been a mistake – your luggage has been sent to Rome.'

'What?' we cried in horror and disbelief.

'Yes, sir. Your luggage has been sent in error to Rome. The girl on the checking-in desk made a mistake. We thought we should tell you, in case you might need something for tonight.'

'*Might need something*?' Kenny repeated. 'We're meeting the King and Queen tonight as guests at the premiere of *The Battle of Britain* – I've nothing to wear except this pair of flannels and sports jacket – and my wife is in jeans! How can we possibly go like this?'

'We'll do what we can, sir,' the steward assured him, 'but I'm sure we can't get your luggage back from Rome in time. What time is the premiere?'

'Seven o'clock.'

The steward scuttled off to see the Captain, who came back to explain that he'd spoken by radio to his colleagues in Oslo – an airline executive would meet us and take us to the best shops for a new dinner suit and a dress, anything I needed. And of course British Airways would foot the bill.

We landed in Oslo with only three hours before the premiere. The British Airways representative was waiting and whisked us to one store after another. The clothes were *awful*. I was offered lamé in dreadful colours. I finally chose one – short – gold and azure blue – it was frightful – but better than my old jeans. Kenny had trouble finding a suit – the jackets looked as though the hangers had been left in – the trousers were too wide and too long. He took the one that was the least bad fit, the manager promising that a tailor would alter the trousers immediately and bring them to the hotel. But when the suit arrived, the trousers hadn't been altered at all – so we had to leave for the film with trousers three inches too long. They slipped under the heels of his shoes with every step.

Because of our frantic search for clothes, we were late – an appalling social gaffe: we should have been there first to receive all the guests. The Royal party had already established themselves in their seats when we arrived, and, by etiquette, they should be the last to arrive. The Royal anthem was being played and the lights were about to dim when we came pounding through the doors. We had to pass the King and Queen in their box and prayed they wouldn't notice us. No such luck. As we tiptoed in front of the Royal Box, Kenny's ridiculous trousers caught under one heel and he went flat on his face. The King roared with laughter – and so did the audience. Then they all began to applaud. Kenny was embarrassed. 'They'll think I was drunk.' Afterwards we were presented to the King and Queen and we were able to explain the reason for our lateness. They thought the whole story highly amusing. For about ten minutes there was a panic – the King was missing! Eventually they thought to look for him in the gentlemen's lavatory – he and Kenny were in there together talking. He'd wanted to know how Kenny had overcome the difficulties of playing Douglas Bader in *Reach for the Sky*.

'Tell me, Mr More, how did you play a man with no legs so convincingly? Apparently, Kenny tried to show him, locking his knees rigid to reproduce Bader's walk – the well-known rolling gait. The King strutted around the gentlemen's cloak-room behind Kenny, trying to copy him.

'No, no, Sir – like *this* – lock your knees, Sir – now roll a bit like an old-time sailor.'

The King didn't pass his audition.

We threw a party for Kenny's birthday in the shell of Bute House. There was scaffolding up – floorboards missing and only a naked light bulb here and there. The name 'Bertie' was scrawled across the walls of the would-be nursery. We asked about a hundred people, wanting them to see it – before and after. Daddy got the jitters. Walking from room to room saying, 'Mammy, she'll ruin him – she's got such nerve – is everything paid for?' We tried to reassure him – but he wasn't convinced. But apart from Daddy's anxieties – it was a really good party. Voted a great success.

232

I didn't meet anyone else who might have been a threat to our relationship – there were no dates on the side. I didn't have a need for anyone other than him. I'd built my life around him, couldn't bear for us to be apart. I still felt passionately committed to him, but I was gradually becoming more aware that he was passionately committed to him too! He had survived his own slump. He was now once again much in demand. Highly acclaimed and highly paid and the pressures and demands were enormous. His public affairs began to take precedence over our private ones. Publicly he was living his life, as they say, in the fast lane. On the run. Rehearsals, performances, committee meetings, golf, long lunches at the Garrick Club, the Beefsteak Club. Business lunches that were none of my business. His life was very full and there were large areas that I was closed out of. I wasn't aware, but I was getting left behind. However, our time together at home or on holiday was precious, and almost always completely harmonious. Alone, we knew true contentment.

I've always disliked New Year's Eve, hated seeing people get drunk and behaving in a way they'd surely regret next morning. I'd always ask to stay home, on our own, or with friends – but Kenny loved seeing the New Year in with lots of razzmatazz, so we took Michael and Carol Havers to dinner at Les Ambassadeurs. I remember everything about that evening. At midnight Kenny slipped a folded piece of paper across the table towards me. It was a letter from No. 10 Downing Street asking him if he'd accept a CBE in the New Year's Honours List. There were lots of friends in the restaurant that evening, warm and welcoming. They hugged and kissed him. This was Kenny's night. Later, as we went to sleep, he held my hand and told me, 'It's all for you... I do it all for you... for your love, Shrimp'; and he wished, as he did every New Year's Eve, for 'one more year together, just like the last one.'

I was very theatre-oriented, feeling, if I couldn't be up there doing it, as sometimes I longed to, then I'd go and see everything I could, either on my own, or with Jill. I'd come home, starry-eyed and plead with Kenny to come with me, telling him, this production is special, or that performance is sensational. But he'd shake his head and ask me not to make him.

'My enjoyment is seeing your excitement when you come home... it isn't the same thrill for me... I've been around too long – I know all the tricks.'

There were times I really missed being a competitive actress. Often I'd go into a quiet decline on hearing Kenny praise a contemporary of mine he was working with. 'She has good timing... great stillness... very real,' and I'd feel a 'very real' stirring of envy. It seemed that in some ways loving him had stopped my life. He required that I stay the same.

'What have you done today, darling?' he'd ask.

'Oh nothing... I'm boring, I've only got the new saucepans to talk about.'

'I want to hear about your saucepans. I don't want clever conversation from you... I get all I need at the Garrick or at rehearsals. I want you the way you are... you are enough for me.' But to feel dull and ordinary *wasn't* enough for me. I felt I was just taking up the slack. I wanted more, but I didn't know what more there was.

Around the middle of February Daddy went into the Royal Free Hospital for tests; stomach ulcers were suspected. He'd been hospitalised for this before over the years. He was very thin and his colour waxen, but once there he seemed to pick up and put on a little weight, and we were less anxious. The doctors told us that as a result of the tests, they had decided to operate, taking most of his stomach away to prevent any possible recurrence of ulcers. It seemed so drastic and we were frightened, but they did their best to reassure us, saying, people could live quite happily with just a section of stomach. He'd be better off.

We all went back and forth to visit him, laden with goodies. He said the food in there was disgusting, and my chicken sandwiches and home-made cake were gone in minutes. He was worried about his job – about my mother – some Income Tax Returns he'd received – me losing the baby – the expense of Bute House – he always worried. But that afternoon he was sitting up in bed joking and laughing with John and his wife Caroline – drinking Coca Cola through a straw in the can. I said I didn't think Coke would do his ulcers much good. But John told me not to worry, the Bacardi he'd laced it with would! No wonder Daddy was so merry. I hung around hesitant to leave, but there was so much to do and organise.

Daddy's operation was scheduled for the next day, and at approximately the same time Mummy and I would be with Kenny at Buckingham Palace to see him receive his CBE from the Queen – and the day after that we were to move into Bute House. It was a time of pressure for me, all those important happenings coming at once. He asked me to talk to the Sister to find out exactly what they had planned to do. I hugged and kissed him telling him there was nothing to worry about and that he'd be in our thoughts. He nodded, put his arms around me and said to tell Kenny he'd be thinking of him 'every stitch of the way!' No visits from John or me, he insisted, not for a few days. He told us to stay away while he had a green tube up his nose. I didn't argue, feeling sure I wouldn't want anyone to see me that way. I walked down the ward, leaving him sipping his Bacardi and Coke and chatting with Caroline and John; they were very close, so alike. I could hear their laughter echo through the grim room and when I reached the door I turned around to wave and blow him a kiss. Thin and pale, but his blue eyes sparkled and he gave me a look I knew so well – happy to have his family around him.

Next day Mummy and I were excited and dressed carefully, wanting to look our best. Kenny looked so handsome in his top hat and tails and I thought I'd burst with pride as he led us into Buckingham Palace. After the ceremony we posed outside the famous gates for the Press and a gust of wind blew my hat off and revealed my hair in tight little pin curls. I tried to laugh it off, but thought why did these embarrassing moments always have to happen to me.

Saturday, February 28th, 1970. John and I worked with a team of helpers from ten in the morning until midnight, for the big move into Bute House. Kenny, it was mutually decided, was best out of it. Miserable amidst chaos, he'd only fuss about trivia, irrelevancies and he'd drive us crazy – *crazy*. So he went to the Garrick for a long – long – lunch, and then he went to see Daddy. 'Send him my love – take him these flowers. Tell him I'll be in to see him on Tuesday.' The house still wasn't completely finished, but we couldn't delay the move any longer. Our bedroom and bathroom, the kitchen and study were habitable – more than. So roomy and beautiful, all the work and expense worthwhile. Kenny arrived, tipsy. He sat in the kitchen agreeing, 'It's a wonderful home, just right for a film star' – but *Christ* why did the fucking fridge hum? 'I can cope with anything in life, John, cancer, *anything* – but I can't live with a fucking humming fridge!' We were *exhausted* – worn out – but still we dashed around humouring him. He was deathly serious – but we thought him hilarious. I suppose it could have gone either way.

The next morning, our first, it all felt so strange. So vast after our little mews house. 'Where are you? – which room – which floor?' But we dashed around so excited. A new beginning. A recent addition to our household was José, a young Portuguese man who was to care and look after us for thirteen years of our lives.

March 2nd, around nine o'clock, we were having breakfast when the phone rang. 'I have a call for you from a Mr McDonagh,' the operator said, 'will you accept the call?'

'*Daddy!*' I was thrilled – he was well enough to call me.

'Ange?' It was John. 'Ange... it's Dad... he's gone.'

He was crying, but struggling to keep his voice steady. I just stood there numb. Kenny told me I had to be the strong one. Mummy and John needed me – I'd have to take charge. Amazingly, I was composed, but my legs felt like jelly. It was almost a blessing to be so stunned with grief. I held it all back. Mummy was crying and Kenny talked about death being as natural as birth, inevitable, nothing to it – and not to worry about what was for lunch, he'd go out and do the shopping. I wanted to scream at him – inevitable for your Daddy or her Daddy, but not *my* Daddy! Daddy, who stood behind me all the way. Daddies are the only men who never let you down, they are always there when you feel lonely and there's no one else to love you. Did I tell Daddy enough that I loved him – and stop going on about your damn *lunch*! I was intensely conscious of the pain in John and Mummy's hearts, and Elaine's too, far away in America. Our sense of loss seemed unendurable.

The night before the funeral Kenny had to go out to an official function. 'Don't worry, Shrimp – I'll explain why you can't come with me.' Black tie – clove carnation – sparkling cufflinks – if fine feathers make fine birds – well he certainly looked a fine bird – wonderfully handsome. In the three days since Daddy had died, I'd lost ten pounds in weight. But I hadn't cried.

I felt a wave of gratitude towards Sybil, who came to spend the evening with me – I dreaded being left alone. Our fathers had been close friends since before we were born, so that gave us a special link. She left me at around eleven-thirty to go home to her small dog. 'Don't worry about me,' I told her optimistically, 'Kenny won't be long now – he won't be late tonight.' Well, I was wrong – usually he came home when he felt like it. He'd said very early on in our relationship, when I'd complained, 'I warned you, no woman is ever telling me when to come home' – I was outraged. But Kenny was Kenny. I curled up tighter, rolled into a ball, clutching my flick rag, the pillow over my head felt crumpled and empty and my sobbing started – grotesquely. I felt so abandoned. The shock had been such that my grief hit me like a tidal wave. *Daddy!* Daddy, I cried, for the love I'd always accepted and lost, and how could Kenny be so callous and stay out all night before his funeral? Had he misunderstood my need for him? Help me – I'm frightened. I lay there hugging my knees, rocking with the primal urge to comfort myself. I lay in the dark begging him to come home. *Kenny I need you tonight*, I felt blinding hurt and anger. *Frantic.* Where was he? Who was he with? My pillow was wet and smeared. At last I heard his key turning in the lock and the front door slamming. I ran to the top of the stairs – it was almost six-thirty in the morning. He was groggy, could hardly make the stairs. I hated seeing him like that – it wasn't part of the Kenny I adored. We didn't quarrel – I was crying too hard and he was too drunk. He reached out for me in the bed and held me tight – repeating over and over, 'Sssh Shrimp, I'm here now – you've got me now.'

The day of the funeral started two hours later. I was shattered on so many levels – and he was full of remorse. He rang up a signwriter and ordered, 'Remember – it's just not good enough!' to be printed in large red letters – which he kept for years in his bathroom. He told Mary Evans, by way of explanation, that he'd been frightened of my grief. Too much responsibility, he couldn't handle it. He asked her, 'When am I going to get my wife back?' She was astounded: 'Kenny, it's only been four days – she loved her father.'

He tried to make me understand that he'd lost so many people he'd cared about, his father and mother, Harry Dubens, Ronnie Squire – during the war some of his friends had been blown to bits literally by his side. He'd had to help pick up their arms and legs, putting them in sacks, so how could he be expected to remember what it felt like to be me – who had never experienced a loss before. He felt I was self-indulgent – and I responded by calling him 'unfeeling'. On this we really were twenty-six years apart. Some processes can't be hurried. For a while after that he was ultra-loving – bending over backwards. I was responsive, needing his love and loving him so much. Soothing noises were made. I didn't make a fuss. But inside me I was saying to myself, it's not as good, it's not as good. I felt, for the first time, that perhaps we had problems I couldn't handle.

My girlfriend Maggie already had two children – Ben and our goddaughter, Olivia. John and Caroline had James, and we still had none. I was becoming so depressed about it. I continued with my visits to Harley Street for more tests and this time I had Kenny tested as well. At first we laughed. Of course it couldn't be true. He was a sexy, earthy man with two daughters – and we couldn't believe it when they said he was sterile. Whether we wanted to believe it or not – it was true. It was the question we'd never asked. He was devastated, more in despair than me. It hit him where it hurt most, feeling it put his manliness in question. On the other hand I felt almost a sense of relief. All those years of craving to be pregnant, now perhaps it would all fall away from me and I could relax and accept that we were going to be childless. Wanting a baby had cast such a long shadow over my life. He clung to me like a child, saying, 'I can't give you a baby – I've let you down.' My effortless tears, leaking at any sign of vulnerability or need, were blotched over his shirt. Hugging him I said, 'You are all I need – all that matters to me.' It was true. I wanted and needed him to believe it.

Cold water treatment might help, we were told, so he'd sit on the bidet as I filled it with ice cubes. But it was difficult to take it seriously. Laughingly he told a chum, who also told a chum and, much to our embarrassment, it hit the newspapers. But perhaps, he decided, it was all right to talk about it – no point in keeping it all to yourself, if you can help someone else who's in the same trouble, who hasn't got the twenty-five pounds to spend in Harley Street. Kenny's life had been about giving and sharing kindness and fun with other people; he had a gold thread running through him. Sometimes it was difficult for me; I didn't always want to be as good as him.

Between '70 and '73 Kenny was intensely active in the theatre. He went into a revival of *The Winslow Boy* at the New Theatre for Binkie. This arose from a promise made years earlier, after Kenny's first theatre success in London in *The Deep Blue Sea*, that he would appear in another play for him. The revival ran for nine months and happily once again he was directed by Frith Banbury.

His next play was *Getting On* by Alan Bennett. For weeks Kenny refused to read it – for weeks saying he didn't want to do another play for a while. So the producer, Toby Rowlands, sent the play round for me to read. We were packing to go on holiday when the script arrived. I loved it – Alan Bennett at his most acutely observant.

'Sorry darling, this one you've got to do,' I told him.

'I was frightened you'd say that… it means we'll have to cut short our holiday, blast it!'

The play was set in the late '60s and was about a disgruntled MP. He gave a marvellous performance and was received with superlatives by a loving British press. Sometimes I'd go and sit in the audience and would marvel at the way he held us all in the palm of his hand, telling us when to laugh, when not to. His stagecraft delighted me, I was dazzled. I felt I'd forgive him anything. I'd listen, my ears flapping, to comments made about him. The public never left the theatre feeling cheated. I felt proud – 'That's my husband!' I wanted to squeal.

Beginnings are wonderful, no matter how late they happen. Jane, Kenny's elder daughter, was now part of our life. They had come closer to each other and I enjoyed seeing the smiles on their faces – an end to their long separation. 'She's a lovely girl – I can't find a flaw in her character,' Kenny murmured as he pottered around the bathroom preparing for bed. I remember that I stood on the stairs outside her room the first night she stayed. I was reluctant to move. In the back of my mind the thought registered that father and daughter had never slept under the same roof before. I tried not to judge, but wondered why, and was filled with resolve: things would now be as they should be. After a minute or two I hurried down the stairs, anxious that if she found me there she might think I was listening. We became real friends – hers is a friendship I treasure.

It was another period of good times for Kenny. He agreed to advertise Mellow Birds Coffee – he felt it wasn't quite the thing to do, but then Olivier, who is without question our greatest actor, lent his name to a series of advertisements for Polaroid cameras in the United States. After this, Kenny, who had always held back, felt the way was clear to follow this lead. It was to be financially extremely rewarding. The money he made from that advertisement bought Bute House for us.

He went on to do a series for BBC TV called *Six Faces*, made on location in Milan. He and I stayed in the magical Villa d'Esta Hotel on the edge of Lake Como. It was another one of our happiest times; I was so relaxed and content. He'd drive to the city every morning – I really enjoyed lying by the pool all day – the lake nestling in the shade of the mountains – who wouldn't. I was slightly bothered by an easily excited Italian – he wouldn't leave me alone, following me everywhere, jabbering away. Such a pest, I thought, and being an easily excited Irish girl, I pushed him, fully clothed, into the swimming pool. He turned out to be an Italian nobleman – he should have known better. I eagerly looked forward to Kenny coming back in the evenings – drinks on the terrace and then dinner. I could hardly wait to get to our bedroom. The thrill had come back. I felt reassured.

Did I love him the way I had when, in desperation to sleep close to him, I'd ripped a telephone and radio out of a hotel wall, in order to push the beds together? Or when one afternoon, out in the cold biting wind, coming across the Swiss Alps, we huddled together in our clumsy ski clothes? We opened our jackets and wrapped them round each other and kissed, standing in the whirling snow, simply knowing we would never be apart from each other. Well, no I didn't. Our relationship was eight years on – and I loved him much more. It hadn't been a candy-coated daydream – we had our problems. But we'd made allowances – we'd adapted – showed our love in different ways. My life was determined by his needs, boosting his confidence when he felt defeated, driving him here and there, sitting up all night hearing his lines, being his mother and a sister and his nurse, and every now and then his lover. This is what we had built together.

I spent my time in a sort of trance, a solitary figure. I'd joke with him, 'You take me out – twirl me round and show me off – then you put me back in my box.' I seldom, if ever, went out. Except for my visits with Jill to the theatre, or to my mother, who was finding it almost impossible to function without my father. My nesting instinct was still strong – I made marmalade, baked bread, pickled onions; worked on our garden, massed now with roses, herbs and nodding delphiniums. When Kenny was working in the theatre, most nights I'd sit alone in the study doing my needlepoint, isolated and protected from the harsh realities of the world. I'd found a facade. I'd learned the art of maintaining a public face – never to be indiscreet and to realise we were always on show. We had one dreadful wrestle on the floor of our bedroom. The whole incident took place in total silence because my mother was in the next room. We were pushing and pulling, then when we walked out, red in the face, hair in disarray and clothes going in all directions, we just smiled sweetly and it was 'Hello Mummy – Hello Marjorie.'

Occasionally we'd be going out together and there would be a quarrel; it stopped dead the moment we opened the front door. We'd appear to be lighthearted and bright. Back home we'd open the front door and pick up the row exactly where we'd stopped.

'I don't like being married to a star any more than you like being one.'

'You're 59!'

'That's not old.'

'It is for an adolescent' – there were a few of those.

'Don't walk away from me – if you are angry, fight with me – I won't fall apart. I'm not damaged goods! – I demand to be able to quarrel.' The Irish in me found it difficult to live with what I think of as the Englishman's vice of refusing to admit his emotions. Whenever he was about to say something that really mattered, he'd stop. I felt if only he'd talk to me, I wouldn't keep raiding the fridge for the comfort of food. I wish I'd had the understanding to realise that Kenny spoke underneath his dialogue. It was what he didn't say, while he was saying what he was saying, I should have listened to.

I was the little Catholic Princess in her ivory tower; materially he gave me everything. I am quite young, I thought, but apart from our wonderful holidays, this is a dull life. And yet when we were together, all this heaviness would vanish. My instinctive reaction to him was one of respect, wonderment and indulgence – loving him was my disease. I'm not arguing the rights and wrongs of our life, everything is subjective and this is my story as I remember it. I'm simply telling it as it was for me.

I was brought up in a very strict household – rather old-fashioned, I suppose. There was nothing avant-garde about our upbringing – I'd seldom heard the words male chauvinism or emotional feedback. Elaine and I weren't encouraged to subscribe to the feminist movement. We were taught absolute loyalty to the men we married.

That was how my life was and I was content. Used to being on my own, I wasn't swamped by my solitude. I accepted that people like Kenny will always attract admirers – hadn't he fascinated me? He was very busy and often late home, but he always took the time to call and let me know whether to hold dinner or not. Sometimes I wished it were different, wished I could be dashing off to the theatre every night to do a show. Sometimes I'd find myself sitting in the study, stitching away, wondering if needlepoint was my lot – would I still be sitting here when the varicose veins started to creep up on me, and would I be hooked on Valium? Occasionally it was difficult to feel I existed, I waited in so much. Where did I begin and end? But I held it all back. I wasn't moving, just taking up space.

John came to see me one evening; we sat talking in the kitchen – the rest of the house was out of bounds to those who smoked. (Kenny once asked my mother to go into the garden if she wanted a cigarette – it was raining and she walked up and down under her umbrella, puffing away. We all collapsed with laughter. But he was one hundred per cent serious. He could spot a matchstick on a rose bed at twenty-five yards – 'Someone's been here, Shrimp!') John felt I should 'loosen up… you're thirty years old and living the life of a middle-aged woman!' he said heavily. It's strange how this failed to annoy me. I was fascinated, was that how I appeared? 'You were a beautiful lively girl – you've become a beautiful *lifeless* girl.'

It became a disruptive visit – we couldn't agree on how my life should be.

Sunday – the great day of rest, telephone off the hook, slumped in front of the fire, in a daze from the long lie-in. Our Sundays were precious and private. He refused invitations for us to be weekend guests, except to the Porters and Evans. 'We have a lovely home and garden – we don't have to rely on other peoples set-ups.' There were no Sunday lunch parties, getting together with chums. 'I need my Sundays to rest – recharge my batteries.' We dreaded the harsh change of gear to

Monday mornings, the discipline and effort of eight shows a week. Sunday gave us time to talk. We discussed my future now that we knew we couldn't have a family. We knew we were deceiving ourselves in imagining I could continue to be content with only staying home. As an actress I'd been a part-timer. I felt I'd had it. Could I come back, having lost years and roles – and my place in the line? I would not be daunted. I was beside myself with joy being Mrs More – but that fact hadn't quite knocked Miss Douglas into a state of unconsciousness.

We sought Laurie's advice: he sat behind his desk, nodding his head as if he'd heard it all many times before. He was sympathetic, saying he'd do all he could to help me, suggesting a junior colleague of his, Michael Whitehall, as a possible agent for me. When Kenny and I went down the stairs after this meeting and headed for Scotts for lunch, I felt quite confident of the future. Some work would be wonderful – it felt exciting with all we had going for us. Exciting to be thirty and starting out again.

I was lucky: Michael was very able and he revived some interest in me and work came along. I did some television and a couple of films. But the theatre was still out of bounds. I felt very fortunate – apart from a baby, didn't we have it all? The actors I worked with always seemed happy to have me around – pleased to see me. I didn't have to hold anyone at arm's length, nobody made a pass. I was Kenny More's bird. I was very attracted to two of the actors I worked with. I don't suppose they were aware – I didn't radiate with adrenalin – I kept my crushes hugged to me. If I did cast a glance innocently once in a while – I was only doing what I hadn't done in my teens. I was attracted towards those two men because they talked to me.

If the twenty-six year difference in our ages showed, then it was my intensity versus his lack of it. He didn't care *passionately* about anything, except perhaps injustice. That was one of his greatest strengths, he thought of everyone but himself. Behind that irreverent, earthy and wicked sense of fun, was a man who stood behind his choices. His moral courage was definitely one of the qualities that made him such a sought-after friend, to men and women alike. I remember on the set of *The Comedy Man*, it was our first day's shooting and Kenny noticed that, unlike him, the actor he was playing the scene with didn't have a stand-in. The actor in question was quite established and, more to the point, elderly. Kenny decided it was poor treatment – 'Either that actor has a stand-in, or I'm getting in my car and going home.' The atmosphere became very strained. 'You can call in the fucking army, but I'm going home!' They knew he meant what he said. I was still in awe of him and was surprised by this outburst, and I never forgot it.

During the years, I saw him fight lots of people's battles – including a couple of mine. But ask him to be passioately interested in Watergate – or the culling of seals – or the Biafran war – he wasn't a man who collected causes. Some students were shot to pieces by the police on the campus of Kent State University in the USA in May 1970. I watched it on TV saying, 'How *terrible* – how *terrible!*' I looked at Kenny and he said, 'It's too awful – what's for lunch, darling?' It *infuriated* me – quite a few times.

We saw the year out in Paris, the beauties of which hardly need retelling... with its gentle light and noble buildings and wide tree-lined boulevards overflowing with cafes and art museums, fascinating shops and restaurants, the food unrivalled. The most romantic city for a memorable New Year's Eve. We dined at Maxim's and went on to dance the night away at our favourite night-club, the Schéhérazade. We laughed so much, the prices were ridiculous, who cared! I wound myself into his arms. 'Oh Morehen – don't let's ever settle for second best... when it's not as good as this, let's part... if ever you meet anyone lovely... do whatever you want to... I want you to be happy... but please love me enough never to let me know...' We walked, or rather tottered back to our hotel, we hadn't any money left for a taxi – dawn was breaking through the mists of the Seine. We were tired out but high with happiness. As New Year's Eves go – it was a rousing success. One to remember.

In February 1973, before Kenny started rehearsals for his next play, *Sign of the Times* by Jeremy Kingston, we flew off to Guadalupe for three weeks' rest in the sunshine. And we stayed for a few days with John and Caroline on the Dutch West Indian Island of St Maarten; he'd been working there for about a year. It was disastrous really – Kenny's face got terribly sunburnt and I nearly drowned during a beach party – but apart from that it was good to see them and catch up on little James. He'd become a tiny golden beach-boy. As I cuddled him, I thought how my father would have adored him.

Kenny came home early one afternoon from rehearsals; they were about ten days in. He said he felt really lousy and headed upstairs: 'I don't want any dinner, darling. No fuss, I'll be all right.' He looked very forlorn and I put my arms around him, whereupon he turned around and put his head on my shoulder. 'I don't want to worry you, Shrimp... but I'm in pain... I'm passing a kidney stone.' I got him to bed and after I'd seen that he had everything he needed, I called the doctor. It was hoped the stone would pass naturally with the help of pints of water. I spent most of the night on my knees holding a potty with a piece of gauze over it underneath Kenny's penis, hoping to catch the stone for analysis if he passed it – but the blasted thing was firmly lodged in his urethra. It was a ghastly night – the pain got worse and worse, and after sixteen hours of this, the specialist said he'd have to operate. Kenny had been through it all years before with an earlier kidney stone, so he knew only too well what he was in for, but the whole medical scene was new ground for me. He was booked into St Vincent's Clinic, the private nursing home immediately opposite us, and I was delighted that he'd be near enough for me to be able to help nurse him.

It was about eight in the morning when he was admitted. I am not frightened, I am not frightened, I tried telling myself, but I was briefly engulfed in waves of negativity. If anything should go wrong I couldn't live without him – wouldn't. I lived in fear that he might die, had a bottle of sleeping pills hidden, and worried, would God let me into Heaven to be with Kenny if I was a suicide? Yes, I decided, God would forgive me, he understands about love. I pulled myself together in an attempt to appear more in command than usual, but my hands were clammy and all that day I trembled inside with anxiety.

After his pre-med injection he was groggy and we held hands as we waited for him to be taken to the theatre. He kept saying he was sorry, sorry to have let his producer, John Gale, and the other members of the cast down, and sorry we had to spend our anniversary this way. It was our eleventh.

I spent the next few nights and days with him, sleeping on a mattress on the floor by his bed. He was in pain, couldn't shave or walk; there had been complications, we were told, and for a day or two he was an awful shade of green, but he picked up quite quickly once the tubes were out of his side. I cooked his food at home to avoid the hospital's menus. I scurried across the road with all the dishes I hoped would appeal to him. I was on the phone continually, all his friends showing concern. I felt exhausted from repeating the same tale over and over. Flowers, books – the presents spilled in daily, it was overwhelming that so many people cared. He was getting better every day. I can still see him standing at the bottom of his bed in his pyjamas, he was bent over and clutching at his stomach. 'Look, Shrimp, I thought this would reassure you,' and he did a little jig for me before I helped him back on to the bed. He then handed me this, written on a page torn out from his diary:

'No one or anything can be perfect – perfection is the dream, never the reality, we can only achieve degrees of perfection in life and love – However, simplicity, innocence and the complete faith of one person for another can bridge imperfection and the dream is brought that much nearer. Your faith and love for me, little Shrimp, is the one and only real truth I have ever encountered. You may sometimes think I cannot match your feelings, or reciprocate your emotions, but it is not so. I am aware, so aware that words and even deeds are a poor substitute, so bear with me in those rare moments when we are oceans apart and we feel the tightening in our chests, they are, and always will be, nothing – nothing, compared to what we have found and nurtured together.'

He asked John Gale to recast and let him out of his contract, but John told him he wanted him for the role and was prepared to hold the production for six weeks: a very generous concession on his part, but it's hard to recover from a major operation to a date on the calendar – an added pressure. But the worst was behind us and we decided that after a few days at home, we would go to the celebrated Cipriani Hotel in Venice for a month of peace and quiet to recuperate. His spirits were good, but he really wasn't strong enough for the journey. He was frail, hung on to my arm. I thought he was just tired, but for the first three days he ran a fever – I was constantly on the phone to our doctor in London. I watched Kenny's face sag against the pillow. I gave him his drugs and saw the glass trembling between his fingers, realising that this vigorous man was vulnerable. There were no more scares like that one and we slipped into a wonderfully gentle therapeutic routine.

Venice was a first for both of us and we absolutely fell in love with the city. The Piazza San Marco is like a vast 17th century drawing room in the open air. We'd sit in the spring sunshine at the little cafe tables, drinking to the strains of music, feed the hundreds of pigeons and soak up the splendour of the scene. We took the steamer and, as he got stronger, the gondola through the waterways to admire splendid buildings; the glittering gold of the mosaics, the pink and white Palace of the Doge, the churches with gothic arches mirrored in the dark rippling canals. We bought some lace and glass – gifts to take home. The shops were fascinating, everything seemed worth buying, but as Kenny was at my elbow, I didn't. We wandered along the paved alleyways on foot in search of the wonderful collection of paintings that Venice displays – into dozens of churches, dipping our fingers into the holy water and lighting our candles. We said our prayers – there were lots of motives at work here.

By the end of the four weeks Kenny felt really good – he'd gained the weight he'd lost and I gained even more. We arrived home and he felt strong and ready to start rehearsals. At this point in our lives I felt our marriage was at a peak. Any anxieties I might have had I pushed back into the dark areas of my consciousness. In our photograph album Kenny wrote 'Venice '73 – a wonderful holiday with my little love'. Life seemed wonderful indeed.

After that glorious holiday he went straight back into rehearsals for *Sign of the Times* and his attention towards me once again slackened. The play, the company, became seemingly very important. He was a wonderful head of the company: untemperamental, and unselfish in his work. And offstage, incredibly generous and fun to be with. He pushed the boat out, always the first to pay the bill. They enjoyed him. As I did. 'If you are a success in our business... you can be eighty-four and have three heads and you can still pull the birds!' Perhaps he said it as a joke, but it worried me. I felt threatened, excluded. Some of the actresses he worked with were friendly towards me, but I found others somewhat over polite and patronising – I was to them 'the wife' and not a fellow actor. It was always the ones with the least talent; or rather that was what I imagined. And did I imagine our hold on each other diminishing during these months? It was, of course, possible, because I was caught up in a BBC television series called *The Dragon's Opponent* with Virginia McKenna and Ronald Pickup. I had a terrific part and was kept very busy, so much to think about. I wanted to be good, get it right. Any problems I had with a part, I always took to Kenny, who better? I remember his gestures rather than what he said, he'd throw up his hands and make a mock grimace of horror and say, 'Not like that, Shrimp! – try it this way.'

I would feel absurd, but anxious to learn. I'd stand next to the Aga in our kitchen and say, 'Sorry… I know what you mean, I think…' He refused to let me off the hook, making me do it again and again. When he thought I'd got it right, his face would crease into his sparkling smile. When it came to work, he always found the time for me.

It was around that time that we attended the Topping Out Ceremony for the Kenneth More Theatre in Redbridge. A tremendous honour, surely the highest tribute that could be paid to an actor.

I think of marriage as being like a river trip – the rapids and the falls and the calm patches… and in the stormy waters – you hang on. I read somewhere that people who love each other, at times hate each other, it's like night and day. Everything is still there, but it's in darkness. The discord and anger doesn't rub out the love, which runs along deeper channels.

'Why do we fight, Shrimp?'

'Because we're alive and human and living together,' I'd say, although I wondered too.

Infidelity happens to women every day, but not to me it doesn't. In a moment of unbearable tension he blurted it out. He told me things that could never be unsaid. I remember the feeling of utter misery flowing out of me – my heart cracked. I remember his face as he left for the theatre, his little half smile, but his eyes full of sorrow. He said, 'I love you, my little girl – and I'm sorry I've hurt you.'

I remember the pain and the tears I cried. *Run*, at first I thought I should run. I didn't know how to take it, didn't know where to go. I was destroyed. Tormented by thoughts of him with who knows who, those faceless women. Faceless to me. I'd built my life around him, tried to be what he wanted, and one sentence had blown apart all we had built together. Would I ever be able to call him Morehen again? How do you deal with betrayal? I couldn't find the answers to the questions that went round in my mind. I felt guilt-ridden, it had to be my fault. At our wedding party someone wished Kenny a happy life. I jumped in with, 'I'll see to that!' – and I'd failed him. I should have been different. He'd fallen in love with my ebullience, how had I become so uninteresting? Almost numb with lack of identity, I was dull and dependent, painstaking instead of impulsive. Of course I was dull with my confidence whittled away. I was an observer – when had I stopped participating? I saw that I had become so dreadfully unconfident that I could only sustain myself as a person through him. I thought that when you married, that was it. But nothing's it – not forever.

I wrote all this down in my diary. I didn't know what the time was, but after that last thought I went downstairs and switched on the sauna and ran the jacuzzi; sitting on the edge of the bath dangling my legs in the swirling warm water, I cried. What was the *matter* with me? Seemingly we had everything. The perfect marriage, but what was the missing ingredient? Were we being torn apart for a hundred vague and tiny reasons that had crept up on us with the passing of the years?

I felt distant from everything – nothing mattered. It wasn't his fault, it's just how he was – how things were. I wished I could be different. I was no beauty – a funny girl. 'She's so funny!' friends used to say of me – which I found dispiriting, like being called 'nice' – of little value. I felt I didn't have much to offer, I appreciated my life was easy, that he spoilt me – that appreciation was conditioned by my experiences in childhood. I was his fan, his audience, his nurse, his wife and his daughter; waiting for him to come home from the theatre, the Garrick Club, his golf, his friends – whatever was so frustratingly keeping him from me. The outside world versus home life – I felt I lost out. I'd panic sometimes, was frightened that this loneliness was my lot. I played the part of the injured wife to the limit – interrogated him all night. It was a wildly unhappy process. I was so tender, the hurt so bad – and I had to be seen to be hurt.

I unburdened my sorrows to Jill. She listened, and I remember at one point she said, if she were me she'd be 'awfully cross'. Well, what would make her 'awfully cross' drove me to the edge of mental sickness. For me it was a real crisis and it had the effect of making me want to withdraw from life. I didn't continue to reproach him – there had to be an end to the questions and answers. If we were going to survive the crisis, there must be no more of that. But I'd always been subject to the blues, and despite taking anti-depressant tablets, it was now more noticeable.

Sometimes a heave of self-pity would engulf me and I'd have to go to the bedroom and stay there until the trembling had gone away. Something was happening to me – or rather something was *not* happening that I hoped or needed to happen. But to the outside world I maintained my bouncy walk, still cracked the jokes. 'Keep laughing – there isn't anybody getting out alive you know.' The smile was strapped on. But inside me I had fallen to bits.

We did all we could in those next eighteen months to repair the damage, to rebuild the trust. We wanted to make a go of it, as we still loved each other and believed we had so much going for us. And I tried to face life more realistically. I found it hard. We talked it out. Sometimes he'd get infuriated with me and say I was crazy: no adult woman would react this way because of infidelity. For most women, he thought, it was low down on their list. I should seek help, go to a psychiatrist. Other times he would be adorable and appealing. We were watching Princess Anne's wedding on TV, and he took off my wedding ring, kissed it and placed it back on my finger, telling me I was the only woman he'd ever loved, the only woman in his life, and the only woman he wanted to live with. No one else had meant anything, 'ships that pass in the night'.

Slowly I was coming out of it. I cared so much about him; the only difference now was that I had started to care about myself too. And believe me, that was all the difference in the world.

To our delight and relief we were back on an even keel. Elaine came home for a visit bringing Lynette and Allison with her – and John and Caroline had another son, Joe, and there were many exciting things to do. We were invited to receptions in Downing Street, to Buckingham Palace garden parties – our social life had never been grander. We appeared together in an episode of his TV series *Father Brown*. Wearing his priest's costume, complete with flat black hat and little round wire glasses, he looked in the mirror and chuckled. 'Blimey O'Reilly, Shrimp – I'm really going to pull the birds looking like this!'

I appeared in my first play: Harold Pinter's *The Birthday Party*. Lulu is a small part and it was an out-of-town production, the Gardner Arts Centre at Sussex University. It was not a very distinguished affair, it didn't go to my head. I just about got on and off the stage without bumping into the furniture – but the feeling that I'd actually made a start was so stimulating. Kenny came to see me and afterwards, backstage, he called my performance charming – charming isn't a very strong word in the theatre. But he had tears in his eyes and told us that we'd taken him back to his early days as an actor; playing in a small theatre, miles from the West End, to a couple of dozen people on a hot sunny afternoon, and doing it for no other reason than we wanted to.

'Enthusiasm is what the theatre is all about!' Between us, enthusiasm was a very important quality. And we had it in abundance.

We went to the South of France for Kenny's 60th birthday, and spent another happy Christmas with Brother Cyril and Pat, before leaving for a month's holiday in the Seychelles. There was peace, plenty of time to read and visit some of the other islands – Praslin, La Digue, Silhouette; in tiny aircraft we'd take off through bright skies. It was tremendously exciting – a unique holiday. It was a month of complete and unforgettable happiness. We'd survived our hiccup.

The magazine *Punch* published a number of letters from husbands to wives for their St Valentine's Day wish and asked Kenny to contribute. He wrote:

> Darling Shrimp – Shrimp, I call you, and nobody else is allowed that privilege. Living with you is an experience, never dull, never predictable, always unusual. You can be Old Mother Riley, or the Impossible Dream. When St Patrick planted the McDonaghs in Galway, he must have had me in mind. Who else but you could ask me, 'How do you spell…?' fourteen times whilst writing one letter, and keep me smiling? Who else but you could look at me with big blue eyes, standing in the High Street at Mahé, in the Seychelles, and in reply to my 'What would you like, darling? I'll buy you anything you want' come out with 'I think I'd like a paw-paw milk shake…' You could have had a gold bracelet, I was in that kind of mood! Only she could confront her husband, who'd come home with the milk, by picking up something to throw at him, then, realising it was something of hers, put it down and pick up something of his! I love you for that… and only a 'Shrimp' could go out and buy her fella a fur coat with her entire earnings from a gruelling television show. What unbounded joy is your innocence. Heaven protect me from the woman who knows it all, I want no part of her! You have given me your youth – you were twenty-one when we met and I was forty-seven. With that youth you have also given me a golden bonus I had no right to expect, the priceless gift of love. You are, in a way, totally innocent, not of life, but of everyday things that can happen in life; an original innocent in the purest meaning of the word.

It would be plain sailing from now on, I thought.

That was a serious miscalculation on my part. Six months later I found myself in the grips of an almost uncontrollable sexual passion. It was, to a girl like me, a crippling excitement. It impaired my thinking, unsteadied me. I had never been in such a turmoil. He was a six-foot-three, green-eyed heavy drinker. He wore blue jeans and cowboy boots. My friends said, 'You're crazy' – no one need tell me that I was doing wrong. I turned him on, I was sexy. He said so, and when I was with him, I could believe that. He saw something in me that Kenny hadn't for years, or, if he had, he'd neglected to tell me. For five months it was all so crazy, I almost felt sane. He lives in America now – and I'm older. Our short-lived and passionate intimacy matters to no one. There had been some tremendous moments, he said. I agreed. We never saw each other again.

In my life there is a large uncharted area of regret; the password to it is – 'If only'. I wonder how my life would have evolved if only I hadn't had that affair – if only I had done this instead of that. An unanswerable question that fills me with pain. If only I could rub my life out and start again.

Whenever I hurt him, I hurt him *honestly*. Kenny – this is what I'm going to do, am doing, have done. Your honesty's a killer, impossible to live with, he'd tell me. A piercing pang of remorse goes through my heart at these words. It was all out in the open now. I had cried, of course, stomach-twisting wrenches. For a while there was so much empty space and ache between us. It had all been so horrid for Kenny; at first he was distant and angry at the hurt to his pride, and the disruption in his life. That was only to be expected, and it was natural too that he'd feel let down and humiliated. But his emotional outbursts were soon over. It seems a lifetime away, as though it never happened, except when I wake up hugging my pillow, my blankets in a heap, wishing it hadn't. My memories of our long conversations at this time are rather shaky, they run in twitches and jumps, rather like a home movie. I was young and healthy; a reasonably happy vegetable, bored rigid with being cooped up in that lonely house with my depression – the curse of the leisured classes, creeping all over it. While I sat plucking the hairs out of my legs, one by one, life was what was happening to me, and it was passing me by. Starting my affair, I was alive again, I told myself. I was fed up with being married to a man who was seldom there to make me feel I was married. I felt I was loving somebody who didn't want to be loved. I wanted a husband like any other. I wanted Kenny as my husband – we had so much left and didn't want to chuck it all away. I wanted to love him and be loved by him, but as time had gone by, we seldom made love; the tension had mounted and, inevitably, I suppose, I found myself playing the old game of infidelity. It had come to that. He was relieved, he told me, that my involvement had only been on a physical level, the word 'love' never mentioned. There was no emotional entanglement, no heartbreak and misery at the end of it.

'I'm going to fight very hard to keep you,' he said as he handed me two first-class tickets to Kenya. We flew off for four weeks in the sunshine, cherishing the hopes of picking up those precious old threads.

Getting away was a heavenly process of healing. We hadn't been prepared for a Kenya of such wide protecting sky and vaporous existence, of brilliant sun and starry nights. It was surprisingly very green. Emerald rolling hills and snow-capped mountains ahead of us, as we lumbered around the bush in our Land-Rover, the dust from the wheels closing in around us as we headed for the long grass ahead of us. I kept having to take deep breaths – the raw beauty of the country was staggering – Kenya had cast its spell on us. The locals call it 'the Kenya-high', and we were on it. The silence of the bush is in itself a sensation. This wasn't a holiday, it was much more a rich and unforgettable experience. We slept under canvas, ate our food beside camp fires under the magical baobab trees, as Africa sprawled around us. The animals leaped and scampered past our eyes – at night the hippos rubbed themselves on the guy ropes of our tent. One unforgettable night I woke to find a giant monitor lizard trying to climb through the small window flap – I was flabbergasted, but kept my face expressionless, so that it wouldn't be frightened – *it* wouldn't be frightened? My heart in my mouth I slowly put out my hand to prod Kenny awake, but nestled into his pillow, this proved impossible. He continued to snore – I was aware that it might have been this awful noise that had attracted the lizard. Oh, *please Kenny*, I prayed, stop snoring and wake up. He didn't, he slept through the whole adventure – but that didn't stop him turning it into a very entertaining after-dinner story. He told the story so well and often, he began to believe it really had happened to him and not me!

We finished our trip with two weeks on the coast at Malindi; we sat on the balcony of our hotel room, looking down towards the noise of the exploding ocean. Sitting in the cool air we talked about going home the next day.

'Funny, for the first time we can't be sure what's ahead of us,' he said, picking up the threads of wool from my needlepoint. 'Funny' isn't the word for it, I thought. My heart began to pound and my mind raced. It was a new experience for me to be uncertain as to what would happen next. I had always had, and wanted, the security of being sure of tomorrow. We had problems, they were admitted now – open to debate. We weren't going to smooth things over, we would make adjustments to keep things going; because that's what we wanted. We would make a new life for ourselves. It was not impossible, but we couldn't go on as if nothing had happened. I was grateful he hadn't made the big gesture and walked out on me; he wanted nothing more than to forgive and forget. Not once did he behave like the wronged husband – love is more than words he told me. But I was frightened at the thought of an open marriage with its 'smart arrangements'. We accepted it might not always be pleasant and hoped that, between us, we could keep our troubles contained within our marriage. Praying for harmony, we huddled together trying to sleep on the long flight home. We didn't talk very much – but the quiet between us was brimming with more than we could express.

Once we were home, I was offered a play, *The First Mrs Fraser* with Anna Neagle and John Clements. It was to be a twelve-week tour and would then, hopefully, come into the Vaudeville Theatre. It was a creaky play, but mine was a terrific part. Kenny was certain I was right for it. I wasn't certain at all, but happily agreed. I asked Kenny if he was sure that it was all right for me to go off on tour... of course I could get home weekends... and you'll come and be with me, won't you darling... I couldn't do it without you behind me.

Of course it was all right... this could be a turning point for you... but he wouldn't be able to be with me... he wanted to use the time to go on his longed-for Amazon trip. He wanted to do it the slow way, getting there by train and ship – he'd be away for the entire twelve weeks.

I was stunned. I couldn't believe it – I couldn't believe he'd leave me alone for twelve weeks at such a crucial point in our marriage. I was upset, angry, but most of all desperate. Don't say you are going to fight hard to keep me and then leave me for three months! You need your head examining! I felt unimportant to him. Okay – if you won't stay with me – take me with you. I'll be a good girl. I'll turn the play down – I'll do anything – but *don't leave me alone. I need you.*

No, he wanted to go on his own – he needed time to think, away from me. And anyway, I'd ruin the trip for him with my horror of insects: 'The bugs up the Amazon are *that* big!' he said, waving his hands around to emphasise his point.

'I'll get used to them – just give me the chance… put me in your pocket, Morehen.' I pleaded and begged and cried. All to no avail. He was adamant.

Through all this, as if things weren't bad enough, I went down with pneumonia. The designer, known affectionately as 'Bumble' Dawson, had to come to the house to fit my dresses; I wasn't allowed out.

I was at my lowest ebb – emotionally and physically wrung out. The shadows had come to stay. He was due to leave for Brazil on the very day my rehearsals started – I was distraught, fell on the stairs. But even my best performance wouldn't make him stay.

The changes I felt I had to make at this time, in order to cope, changed the rest of my life.

February 16th '76, the first reading of the play, was a nightmare for me. Preoccupied with my own part, I didn't give too much attention to the other actors; their voices seemed to come out of a haze. For a moment, that morning after Kenny left, I contemplated suicide, looking at the bottle of pills sitting on the shelf in front of me – their brilliant fascination almost seducing me. But not quite. The misery flowed from me. For fourteen years there had always been Kenny. Now he'd gone. I felt I'd lost a limb. To survive I knew I must be positive. Positively right or positively wrong. But positive. So fuck you, Kenny, for leaving me.

Those rehearsals were for me a unique experience. I was a beginner in the world of the theatre, and I had the luck to land a really good part in a star company. Rehearsals were a serious business. Under a dismal working light we'd feel our way round the marked floor, and stumble through the text, searching for interpretation, or sit huddled in corners clutching paper cups of vile-tasting coffee while we dolefully learnt our lines; and cautiously putting out feelers towards each other in the name of friendship. Susie, knowing I was unused to touring, started to teach me the ropes. We exchanged telephone numbers... that began our close friendship.

I arrived at the Yvonne Arnaud Theatre, Guildford, for the dress rehearsal. I looked at the dressing room list – No. 1, Dame Anna Neagle; No. 2, Sir John Clements; No. 3, Angela Douglas, which made my heart miss a beat – and I climbed the stairs to my little room to set out my bits and pieces of make-up and photograph frames. It was all so frightening/thrilling.

Final technical rehearsals, and then the opening night. As I settled at my dressing table making my face up, I went over all the final notes that darling Charles Hickman, our director, had given me. I looked at my telegrams and flowers, and at the photograph of my father. My face went all hot – this one's for you Daddy.

First Jeremy, then Susie flashed in and whispered the traditional 'merde'; Ian and Al too: so much goodwill. Fifteen minutes, please – and another dash to the loo. Oh, God, I asked, do you know how nervous I am? I walked slowly down the stone stairs and waited in the wings trying to remember Iris Warren's lessons on deep breathing. From beyond the curtain came the excited chatter as I paced up and down. The whisper came, 'house lights out' and the animation in the auditorium settled to a hushed silence. A sweep and a swoosh – sounding like the rustle of a giant ball-gown – and the curtain was up. I walked on stage to a smattering of applause and murmuring. I was terrified, but I *loved* it. I was on the edge of a wonderful adventure. The endless summer of '76 and one of the most glorious happy times of my life had begun.

I began to feel a new energy, a new confidence, and younger. I was out in the world and taking a hard look at the ways of others of my age – how they lived their lives. Now I could take the initiative and begin my own. It was such a release – I'd found new territory and I suppose what followed next wasn't surprising. I took a lover. He and I were very attracted to each other, the physical relationship we had was potent – he answered my need. We made love whenever and wherever we could – I'd plunged in without any hope of getting out in one piece. For both of us it was an incredible time, new fun, new madness. 'Do you love me, Ange?' he'd ask – but my heart cried out for Kenny. My lover was great fun to be with, but love is a strong word. It's Kenny I love, I'll only ever love Kenny.

I was learning how to tour – how to test beds for damp and, worse still, bugs. One bleak morning at about 3 a.m., I woke in my digs, and sitting on the end of my bed I looked around me at the old black gas-meter standing humbly in the corner by the dismal cupboard, which was my kitchen, back to back with the crude partition which separated the even smaller grotto which contained the rust-stained bath. There were two hooks on the door for me to hang my clothes. The woodwork in the bedroom had been bright green, and the dim yellow distemper was crazed and smudged with stains; paper was peeling from a damp patch in the corner of the ceiling. There were faded curtains at the windows, and they didn't fit – the windows themselves were grey with filth and not to be touched with bare hands. The design on the linoleum round the edge of the floor had almost disappeared with time, and the rug by my bed was threadbare with a wide hole in it. I'd never in my life lived in such dingy conditions. Where was my lovely home? What on earth was I doing here in this dismal hole? But when I got on the stage at night, I knew the answer – I *loved* it, loved the work. Every night you have the thrill of maybe getting it right. I'd been bitten by the bug. I wanted to live on my salary, be like my new friends. I wanted to be me, and not the privileged Mrs More.

Duncan Wheldon, our producer, extended the tour yet again, replacing John Clements, who'd taken me under his wing, with Michael Denison. With my friends I was off again in my little Mini – Paul Simon and Rod Stewart blaring on the stereo – to stay in cottages in the wilds of Wales and Scotland – apartments on the beach in Sussex – we were fortunate to see

Britain from tip to toe in all the glorious sunshine of the now legendary summer of '76.

Kenny's letters from his Amazon trip were full of detail and colour – the cockroaches were *that* big, the butterflies the size of tea plates – and vivid descriptions as to the difficulty he had with his ablutions; all in all, he thought, he'd been right in going on his own, it being too primitive for me (if he'd seen some of my digs he might have thought me hardier than he gave me credit for!) – and he said he missed me, felt we had so many reasons to stay together and that he'd never, willingly, leave me again for so long.

He crammed so much into his letters that I didn't feel it strange that his handwriting had become smaller, somewhat difficult to read. I do remember we joked about it, saying that from now on perhaps he should use the phone. It was all dismissive, just lightly remarked on. His letters, waiting for me at the stage door, made me light up like a Christmas tree. My core of happiness still depended on him.

When he returned from Brazil, he too was off on the trot: Spain – Italy – Australia. He was there for just over two weeks and my spirits went into decline knowing he was so far away. I wasn't happy until he came home. I had to have constant contact with him – phone calls, letters; our weekends at home together, or when he came up to be with me.

Towards the end of the summer he was making a film in Lanzarote and he slipped on the volcanic rock, badly bruising three ribs. Thankfully it was on the last day's filming, so he could come straight home for me to look after him. I was in my element again – needed by him. He sat on the edge of the bed with his back towards me and asked me if I wanted to leave him, so that I could have a baby. I kissed him on the back of his neck and told him not to be silly, the only baby I wanted was his. 'It's all right between us, isn't it, Kenny? There's only one thing that's wrong... I mean, underneath, it's still as it was.' It was another of those times when we were very close, and we believed we had things licked.

My next few months consisted of looking after the house and Kenny while he was working. He played too – but with great discretion. I never knew the details, didn't want to. I was still wildly jealous of him and easily hurt. I couldn't be indifferent to him, everything he did continued to affect me deeply, so he protected me from that, never humiliating me. He was consumed by his work and was so full of energy and raring to go, and with his knowledge and blessing I continued to see my lover. I'd never had the opportunity to spread my sexual wings, and Kenny had the understanding to see it for what it was.

Duncan Wheldon asked Kenny to appear in Frederick Lonsdale's *On Approval*, with the delicious Geraldine McEwan, playing at the vast O'Keefe Centre in Toronto, then for a limited run in London. Simultaneously the director, Stuart Burge, cast me in *The Scenario* by Jean Anouilh with Trevor Howard and Helen Cherry. It was a very good part for me and I'd be playing opposite Gary Bond. It was another production for Duncan, and the marvellous thing was that I would be in Toronto at the other theatre, the Royal Alexander, at precisely the same time. What luck!

Our time out there was tremendous fun – Gary, Sue Lloyd and I would go dancing or to dinner, and after the show there always seemed to be a party in somebody or other's room. I'd get all ready for bed – into my nightie – when Sue would come in telling me I was missing a lot of fun, yank me out of bed, throw my mink coat over my nightie, and off we would go. I'd get some very strange looks in the lift from the other residents. There would be company parties in Duncan's suite when the two productions got together. There were trips through the snow covered countryside to Niagara Falls – I can see Kenny quite clearly standing with the Falls behind him, his eyelashes white with snow, and the icy wind whipping the skin from his cheeks – it was well below freezing. He hopped from foot to foot banging his hands together, saying, 'God almighty, Shrimp – it's brass monkey weather – but aren't we having a lovely time!' Yes, we were.

Kenny flew home and I travelled to Washington State to visit my sister Elaine and her family. Nothing had changed simply because she lived so far away from the rest of the McDonaghs – we were still a close family. My nieces, Lynette and Allison, were seventeen and eighteen and divine to me. They took me everywhere with them. 'Mom – she's wonderful – she dances like she's eighteen – she ice-skates like she's eighteen.'

'Yeah!' my sister told them, 'and she gets exhausted like she's fifty!' She was quite right – they'd run me off my feet. I *was* exhausted, but didn't want to admit it. After a memorable three days in the Rockies, there was a tearful farewell as they saw me on to the plane. 'Y'all come back now, y'hear,' my brother-in-law told me, doing his best to make us laugh, as Elaine and I dabbed away at our eyes with what was left of our damp and shredded pieces of Kleenex.

Bute House glowed its welcome home. Everything looked wonderful – and for the millionth time Kenny and I asked ourselves what would we do without our faithful José. We were very dependent on him – he looked after the house and garden as though they were his own. We couldn't have lived in that large house without him.

Poor Mummy was under the weather. I mentioned a visit to the doctor, and she bristled, but she went. She had tests and, when she got the results, I remember she sat in the kitchen and said very matter-of-factly, with no build-up:

'I've got a shadow on my lung, Angela – promise me you won't worry, darling, but it's cancer.'

I was standing at the sink and I felt my legs buckle – I was stunned as I listened to her – all I could understand was that she needed an operation. She is a very practical person, not given to dramatics, and didn't appear frightened. I was frightened enough for both of us. To lose her I felt would be unbearable.

In the middle of this terrible time, when Mummy was at home with us resting and trying to recover from her operation, Kenny left us for a two-week holiday on the Greek island of Paxos. He said, 'Don't make me feel a shit, darling': he had to go and I couldn't. Mummy needed me; he said he needed some sunshine before he started rehearsals for the London production of *On Approval* with a new cast. Could I cope without him if Mummy died? She was down to six stone and vomiting water. She looked so bleak and frail – oh God, help me.

My mind was everywhere. I was so distracted I accidentally drove through a set of red lights and almost wrote my car off. I shudder to think how close I came to injuring the family in the other car and I remember how kind and concerned they were for me: they didn't utter a single harsh word.

My relationship with my lover had lasted a lot longer than perhaps it should have done. He'd said he loved me, maybe he had, maybe he hadn't, and I suppose you should never remember anyone's promises. Anyway, his love changed like the wind and suddenly, without warning, it was over. He told me he wanted someone of his own, someone to make him tea in bed on a Sunday morning. Of course he did, but it wasn't going to be me. Not much was said, it was just over. After a shaky start, we are good friends again – delighted to see each other whenever our paths cross, which is how we promised each other it would be.

Thankfully, Mummy was out of the woods. She was stronger than she looked, the specialist told me. She was going to be all right, so that was one anxiety less.

I did everything I could in those next few weeks to pull my life together. I went to a hypnotist; I don't know how I thought he'd be able to help me, but I was so worried about my situation. I tried meditation and mind-control classes and I went to a psychiatrist – three times – but it wasn't my scene. The silences embarrassed me, and I found myself heaving around with the boredom of simply talking about me. I needed a two-way conversation – someone to help me find an alternative way to think about my problems. I couldn't relax – still cracked the jokes – 'super little trouper' – and when I found myself handing out advice about the house plants on the psychiatrist's window sill, I realised the answers to my problems couldn't be bought by the hour.

I needed some time alone with Kenny, one of our cherished holidays. But no chance of that: his play was a moderate success and the run wore on – and our marriage with it. Once again, with all the pressures and demands, we were living apart – together. I had no direction.

How are your feelings, Kenny? – mine *hurt*. I started not eating, getting thin and crying like a child, hoping he would pity me, scoop me up. It was ridiculous really, because he was a child too. Everyone is, we're all children, always.

It's staggering how your life can change – it can change just like that. If I manage to get it down on paper this morning, and pray that my words don't appear to be clever phrases – then maybe it will make some kind of sense. I was struggling for the right to be thought of as I was, not anybody else's image of what I ought to be. I couldn't give in, and if today I have regrets and guilt in the way I handled the situation, then I must do my best to accept that there isn't a thing I can do about it now: unfortunately what's done can't be undone. And to torture myself further would be a form of self-indulgence I can't afford. Sometimes I think I must have been mad – I'll never ever have again what I had. So much time has been wasted – why does it take such a long time to understand? Why does understanding come too late?

This was the day in the spring of '77 when everything came to a head. He was walking across the bathroom. He was going. A hired car waited outside to take him to his committee meeting; the chauffeur took his briefcase and umbrella from the hall. I kissed him on the cheek and put my arms around him, touching lightly the well-recognised, almost unavailable figure that I felt I was losing.

'See you at one o'clock, Shrimp... Wheelers in Old Compton Street... don't be late, love.'

My first surprise of the day was that he didn't react to my affection, not at all. He just kept on walking. I found myself trailing behind him – if I'd been made of silk, I'd have floated! I felt like a butterfly-catcher and he was the elusive one – always at the tip of my finger, tantalisingly just out of my reach. Of course at first I smiled and thought, I ought to have known better, he was already thinking about his day's work. I turned it into a joke, and then I pretended it hadn't happened.

Later I met him outside Wheelers; it was raining slightly and he went through the first set of double doors, leaving me to follow. He let them swing back into my face – then through the second set of doors; and he let it happen again. *Whoosh!* And not a trace of apology. I was utterly amazed. But he'd already walked to the table and the head waiter was hovering around him, so I shot over and sat down next to him – remembering where I was and who I was with. For a dreadful and yet superb moment I thought about leaving. But from long experience I knew better than to lose my temper. It's no good, it's no good. I didn't say much, just a few comments here and there and he made soothing noises as the food and wine arrived. Kenny became engrossed and my thoughts began to drift, and my heart ached. If I'm going to be this lonely – wouldn't it be better to do it on my own?

That afternoon we were sitting in the study with the curtains drawn back; it was still light, and it was a pleasure to see our glorious garden. I received a letter by the second post from a theatrical producer, in answer to mine asking him if he had a play for me – could he help me? He'd answered almost by return, and I was flattered by his prompt reaction and encouraging words. I babbled on excitedly until Kenny said, 'Well, he would say that, wouldn't he…? I mean, darling… he wants to keep on the right side of me… he'll probably want me to do a play for him one day.' *It might be you*! *It might be you*! – but leave me my hopes! At that moment I couldn't accept such harsh realities. The whole scene now seems like a fantasy; and he would never remember saying it – and I would remember always. In my heart I realised that his words made some sort of sense, but nevertheless I felt my timorous belief in myself ebbing away, and that all too familiar second-hand sensation begin to take possession of my spirit. How long could I last?

'Angela, love, just serve the cheese… let Kenny tell the jokes… he's so marvellous, isn't he?' One of our guests at dinner that evening interrupted me with that remark. His words went through my mind and heart like an arrow, and quivered there. I got myself into the kitchen and closed the door behind me. As if in slow motion I sat down at the kitchen table. I could hear them talking on the other side of the door. I heard the talk turn to, 'Darling Ivor – Darling Noël – Darling Gertie' – the animated conversation filled with so many 'darlings' – and I felt like a spectator in my own home. It's all hopeless, I thought, the bottom of my world is dropping out. I remember, too, looking out at the garden and feeling it reflected my loneliness: it was weeded, watered and empty. I had illusions, lots. It was an illusion to hope I would stay, and it was my illusions – not the lack of them – that were destroying me. Possibly that insensitive remark was the jolt I needed. One final reminder that I was slowly being swept under the proverbial carpet; albeit beautiful and soft. But one that was becoming increasingly uncomfortable when experiencing the sensation of being trodden on.

To tell the truth, it's got to be the whole truth and nothing but – that's difficult. I am an actress – we watch ourselves go by. We see ourselves making love, laughing, grieving. What is real? Somewhere along the line, the spectator and the participant inside us have to go side by side; you have to stop pretending to be someone else and worrying endlessly how you are coming across. Some people grow up by rejecting and denouncing the children they were last year, and certainly I had behaved in a way I didn't respect. I'd reached a point where there wasn't enough time left to waste; believing that the saddest words in the English language are, too late. Staying with Kenny because I was frightened to go, frightened to stand on my own two feet, wasn't a good enough reason. If I was the fool, if I was the loser – I'd have no one to blame but myself. There would be problems and loneliness and sadness, but I wanted to determine my life, be responsible for my own happiness.

There were many heartbreaking decisions to make. Life is curious; we lay in bed in each other's arms talking until we were tired out, wrung out; discussing our trial separation with our hearts full of love. His mask slipped and I saw his vulnerability: he wasn't saying one thing and meaning three others, he wasn't bottling up his emotions. We agreed we'd been running around trying to find certainties and they didn't exist. We examined much of our life together. The pluses and the minuses; it was obvious that I had wanted more of a one-to-one relationship than he could handle, and that I had taken on a relationship that was twice my size. I told him that apart from a few exceptions, his friends were too old for me. Smiling that still ravishing smile, he assured me, 'I do understand – most of them are too old for *me!*' I couldn't put my sexuality into a separate compartment as he could. I didn't want a marriage of 'sophisticated' arrangements and discretion. I wanted to walk down the street and hold my head up. And he looked forward to being able to come and go as he pleased. No excuses to make – no guilt.

He told me then that he'd made a will in '73 leaving everything to me and that if we had died together, then my mother and his daughter, Jane, would share the estate between them. Sarah had already been well provided for under the terms of his divorce settlement. I was very touched that he felt that close to Mummy. Nothing would change, he said, you'll always be my heir, everything will be for you. I argued that if I wasn't going to be his emotional responsibility, then I didn't want to be his financial one. He refused to discuss that subject further – he was adamant. He was also insistent that we tell no one, except our closest. This was a trial separation: divorce was never mentioned – not ever. We'd put Bute House on the market: 'It's too big for us anyway – we rattle around in it like two peas in a colander,' he said, 'and we're so dependent on José, we couldn't cope here if he leaves – and Christ, Shrimp! just look at the paint on that window sill, it's peeling, we'd have to move anyway!'

That made me laugh: he hated workmen in the house, to the extreme. The next few days were mournful; our hearts were in misery, but we tried to be matter-of-fact – resolute. I called Bernard Walsh, our estate agent, and asked him to come over and talk. We wanted to sell and we wanted a small furnished flat for Kenny while I did up a small house which we were sure he'd find for us. If he read between the lines, discreet man that he is – he didn't let on.

I thought, I'll be joining the 'I want to be alone with my boiled egg and yogurt' syndrome, and I pictured myself in my small house, somewhere in Chelsea. Nothing special, nothing that would be too much of a responsibility. I'd had my fill of burglar alarms and the daylight blacked out by the grilles on my windows. My life had been so cushioned, so regulated and I didn't want to live like that any more. I was concerned about living on my own – could I do it? He'd always been my first thought in the morning. I'd be out in the world on my own – with no status. It wasn't a thrilling prospect, but I intended to cope. To my relief I had begun to realise that I had an amount of grit in my make-up and that it must always have been there.

Handed down from my parents, something I'd retained, a lingering relic of our hard times.

I could scarcely believe my good fortune. Duncan Wheldon offered me another play, two weeks in the north of England, and eight weeks in Bournemouth. It was an old Agatha Christie, but we regarded it as a stroke of luck, feeling it was best not to be under each other's feet, having once made our decision, and I could come home each weekend to do my house-hunting. This was how my new life started, my new insecurity.

The prospect of total upheaval in our lives filled me with an inner sadness, but by the time rehearsals began I had arrived at a state of composure that resembled a facsimile of the Angela Douglas people thought they knew. Sharp – bubbly – my nervous disposition under some sort of control. And my sadness didn't vanish at the prospect of a new temptation. It appears to be second nature, almost essential, to some actors to appear jokey, flirtatious, provocative – but Peter wasn't like that. It started very slowly; we would bide our time.

Within a month we had sold Bute House, but that sale fell through because I wouldn't include a few fixtures that had sentimental value for me. I remember Kenny and Bernard looking animated and cross with me and I realised it was only natural. '*Angela*,' Bernard said, waving his hands about, 'we're talking about a sale of a quarter of a million pounds! – surely you won't risk losing it for a few Victorian brass door handles!'

'I'm selling our house, not our home.' And I wouldn't give in.

At this stage, of course, I was frightened by the speed of it all – I felt pressured, it was all happening quicker than I could cope with.

'Can't we compromise, Kenny?' I asked.

'What does that mean?'

'I'm not sure, isn't that what people say at times like this?'

Two weeks later Bernard found another buyer for Bute House, and this time the sale went through without complications. I never met the new owners, I couldn't face it; I didn't want to be able to picture them in my kitchen, barbecueing in our garden and sitting by our fireplace – I just hoped they'd love it, as we had.

I found another house. A small house like lots of others in a tree-lined street – and it had potential. But I began to feel removed from it all, as though all these traumas had nothing to do with me.

We flew off to Barbados for Christmas, not foreseeing that being together would be so heavenly. We seriously wondered what the hell we were doing going ahead with our separation. Under the influence of a beautiful tropical island, we brought out the best in each other. We wanted too much – each other and our freedom. Wishful thinking. No life could be built on that premise. Kenny was adorable to me on holiday and when he was adorable, he was very adorable and hard to resist; he was everything I wanted. The sun shone and we were by the ocean and we talked and talked, agreeing to take things step by step, and to stay as close as possible to each other – 'Neither of us must be left crying,' he said. We relaxed and laughed on our daily walks along the beach. We used to pass Engelbert Humperdinck who was on holiday with his young family.

'Morning Hunkernink,' Kenny would call out.

I'd nudge him in the ribs, '*Humperdinck*, darling, get it right!'

He pronounced it a ridiculous name. 'Humpernink – dink – shmink – what's the difference!'

We went deep-sea fishing, snorkelling, sailing and even parasailing. For that you wear a harness, rather like a trussed chicken. A line is attached to you and the other end to a motor boat; and from a small platform, about a mile from the shore, you take off and glide around for about ten minutes, getting a stunning bird's-eye view, hopefully landing back safely into the arms of two burly attendants. Things didn't go smoothly for Kenny. As he came in to land a gust of wind took him off course and he was dragged along the edge of the landing stage, the jagged wood cutting into his thigh – I saw, to my horror, blood all down his leg. He wasn't badly hurt, but we were both shaken, although he repeated over and over to the attendants, 'My fault, old boy – so sorry – don't worry...' I was tight-lipped and upset. 'No fuss love... you can baby me when we get back to the beach.'

'They *should* have caught you – it *was* their fault!' I muttered through clenched teeth, as the boat got close to the shore. His trunks in tatters, but still wearing the inevitable dark glasses, he vaulted over the side to help push the boat in and to prove the British really were made of sterling stuff – only to find that we were still in about fifteen feet of water! He surfaced, spluttering and spewing seaweed, his glasses falling from his ears and his hair plastered over his eyes – but he was laughing, and so was I – fit to burst! His sense of the butch Battle of Britain hero abroad was sometimes taken to ridiculous extremes. I found him hilariously funny. His attempt to communicate with a six-foot Masai warrior, out in the African bush, as he swatted flies with his safari hat – 'Frightfully hot here, isn't it, old boy?' – had me rolling about. He'd laugh too: 'Silly arse, aren't I – I know I'm quaint!'

Back in Barbados, we had to try and walk the length of the beach, in full view of prying eyes and pointing fingers, trying to hide all the blood and nearly naked hip, and doing our best to pretend he hadn't nearly lost a leg – and his trunks. We put our arms round each other's waists – me holding his trunks together – and did a 'joined-at-the-hip-three-legged-walk' back to the bungalow, passing Engelbert on the way. 'Christ! Humpernick – don't go up on that thing!'

To which he replied, 'Don't be silly, Mr More, I want to live!'

We flew home to London feeling apprehensive about our emotionally undefined future.

After a few days at home, the director, Freddie Carpenter, asked me to go to Hong Kong to appear in a musical. A musical! My *dream*! However, I didn't feel I could accept because of all the organising that needed to be done with the move from Bute House. But Peter offered to move into my new house to supervise the builders in my absence – and Kenny was equally adamant that I shouldn't miss this opportunity of seeing the Far East, telling me to fit the house move around my work schedule. 'Hong Kong is a shopper's paradise... don't worry, I'll pay your income tax... everything so cheap... you'll go broke trying to save money!' He saw me off at the airport along with the other members of the cast, which included Barry Justice, George Cole, Virginia McKenna and Peter Gale. Old friends and new. And off we went on a wonderful adventure.

I was installed happily on the eighteenth floor of the Hilton Hotel where baskets of delicate fruit sat side by side with a pot of jasmine tea, set out on the coffee table. Two orange chocolates lay on my pillow with a note wishing me a happy stay in this, the year of the horse. Wrapped in the fluffy pink towelling bath robe, I emptied into the bath the little bottles of gift-wrapped cologne left beside the taps. I had daydreamed about the East since I was at school, when it was only a space on the map in my geography book. From my window I looked out at the deep green hills dotted with jagged skyscrapers and felt elated at the prospect of venturing out and embracing Hong Kong. I became enchanted, loving the river of bobbing black-haired humanity. Bicycles everywhere, weaving in and out of the trolley cars, and the bumper-to-bumper traffic. I loved the bustling and the hustle, the rickshaw men touting for business through 24-carat smiles, the billowing laundry which hung from the junks in the harbour, and from bamboo canes in so many windows. I'd escape for a while, the smell of hundreds of meals drifting through the air, accompanied by the clatter of chopsticks and ping-pong dialogue, to the ocean. Standing on the deck of the Hong Kong Star Ferry, I'd look back at the staggering skyline, taking deep breaths of the crisp air, trying to absorb it all, and I felt that the experience of Hong Kong was quite unlike anything that had ever happened to me. Ginny McKenna and I became very close: she has such a capacity for understanding and is so tender-hearted.

The show was great fun to do – someone had the line, 'He smiles a lot', and one night he said, 'He *smells* a lot.' I heaved with laughter and had to go upstage and stand with my back to the audience until I could stifle my giggles. Later George said, 'You've got talent, it's all there – but you must try and do something about your concentration.' I could hear Sister Veronica's words ring in my ears as she told mother thirty years earlier, 'Angela has a mind like a grasshopper! – her concentration is all over the place!' I want to be a good actress, I told George, almost more than anything. Arriving home with half of Hong Kong's best bargains in my luggage and tenpence in my purse, I was determined not to lose sight of that.

For quite a while now Kenny and I had shared an agent, and for me it proved to be a psychological mistake. When he rang, my heart would beat faster, but mostly his calls were for Kenny, so I chose to go to a new agent.

Home again, and so many distressing decisions to make. It was an agonising feeling – our sixteen-year-old relationship in shreds. Kenny left all the practical arrangements to me and I don't know how I'd have coped without Peter's help. He and I were becoming more involved with each other, and I discovered what a good friend he was to have in a time of crisis. He was straight and honest and took great care of me.

I found Kenny a furnished flat a few streets away from my new home, Peter and I working round the clock for two days, moving in all his favourite possessions, to make it as familiar and as welcoming as possible. Late at night I drove back from the flat to Bute House where he waited for me to collect him. He got in the car without looking back. It was all settled. It was while we drove through Hyde Park – the familiar route of so many happy walks, past our 'sparrow flats west' – that I felt my first wave of hysteria, my control going with the suddenness and impulsiveness of a skid. We got into the flat and he sweetly thanked me, saying he appreciated all my work – '*No, no*,' I cried, when he spoke with love. My tears flooded my eyes and poured down my cheeks, my neck and all over his shoulder. They kept coming and I didn't bother to wipe them away. '*Please, Morehen*... I can't... take it,' I wailed. 'I can't... I *can't.*' I heard him over the noise of my sobs trying to reassure me, his arms around me trying to bring me some measure of comfort. Spasm after spasm of grief washed over me; I was inconsolable in my despair. Couldn't we stop it, now? What was going to happen to us? Drooping mouth and howling eyes, I cried unashamedly, *I feel like I'm dying, Morehen*. It was the first time I had had real hysterics. 'Let the old boy look after himself for a while,' he whispered. I reeled down the corridor in an aimless daze – *please don't let me go*.

I got rid of my evening clothes, my furs, thinking, these days are over for me. I sold our silver – gave away half our home – I didn't really know what I was doing. It was all so painful. I dug some favourite plants out of our garden and took them to Peter's parents' house; and when the removal men arrived, I was ready for them. I'd done my homework, all I could, the rest was up to them. They had come to us highly recommended – 'They are used to moving fine art – one of the best.' Well, they proved to be *disastrous*. The foreman cheerfully informed me on arrival that he hadn't done it before. A happy amateur in Gucci shoes and Cartier watch. The whole three days' experience was a disgracefully inefficient fiasco.

Leaving Bute House on March 30th '78 was a little death. Thank heavens for Peter, what would I have done without him? He gave me a large brandy and the worst of my reaction was over by the time I banged the front door behind me for the last time. Hang on, Ange, hang on, and I did. It was just that I felt there was very little left of the girl I thought I was.

Everything hurt. I liked the house I'd bought, it was pleasing enough, but I felt it had nothing to do with me. Get it the way you like it, Kenny told me, have everything you want, to compensate you for leaving Bute House. I had no offers of work, and so focused all my energy on redesigning the interior. It was a channel. Our friend Maria once told me that there were seeds of great efficiency in me and on a visit to the new house she exclaimed, 'Darling! The seeds have *flowered*!' I felt as though a huge chunk of me was missing; and to keep going, to be busy, was just what I needed for my sanity, my health. I told one or two people; but Kenny, even to his most intimate friends, wouldn't admit that we had separated. Nobody really knew where they stood with us. Last year Maria told me that she'd met him at a dinner party during this period, and she'd said things to him like, 'Are you sure? – Won't you be sorry? – What are you playing at, Kenny?'

And he'd reacted with, 'You don't understand – we love each other – I'm going to need her one day and she'll be there.' He knew, if I didn't, that one day I'd be back in his pocket. It was just a matter of time.

It was perfectly reasonable that our friends found it difficult to understand our way of handling things. If you love each other, then that's it – you are together. 'I know what you're up against, Angela,' 'Brother' Cyril told me in front of Kenny. 'Just give the silly old devil another couple of years – then he'll settle down, be the way you want him.'

What about me? Another two years of my life? *Don't you care about me too*? In another two years I'll be almost forty! I *could* be a mother – I *could* be a full-time actress – I *could* find somebody wonderful who'd be wonderful to me – I *could* lead the normal life of a young woman. I *could* get away before he dies – because I could honestly say, how would I ever live without him; my one essential existence. Get away now, build a new life – love him, give him all he wants – but, Angela, *protect yourself*; quite simply you love him more than life itself – I guess that's what's called a mid-life crisis.

I walked round the park talking to myself a lot – I walked and walked – and felt very much alone. I doubted my capacity for independent action. It's difficult to describe my emotional contradictions. I sat on a bench brooding, and feeling depressed to a degree I couldn't adequately explain, or comprehend at the time.

Mummy's reaction to our separation was sympathetic. She loved Kenny, but I was her daughter. She saw what our love had given me and what it hadn't. 'But darling,' she said, 'you're still in love with him – you cry whenever you talk about him.' She knew, of course, I was in misery and why – and I told her I wished he loved me in a way I could understand.

The first few weeks were peculiar – Peter and I sleeping on mattresses on the floor in the one small room that hadn't been ripped apart. We had a bathroom, but no kitchen, no floor-boards, no heating and, for part of the time, no roof. Miserably uncomfortable months; driven mad by the erratic behaviour and unreliability of our builders.

I leaned heavily on Peter – he saw me frightened, exhausted, depressed – my emotions poured all over him. Some days he'd be locked into a furious silence; he could say nothing in a very aggressive way. I'd sometimes see his face fall into a despairing expression when I left to lunch with Kenny, which I did at least twice a week – but he never abandoned me.

At first Kenny was irritated when he was advised to go into hospital for an operation on his prostate gland. He felt perfectly well and had no discomfort, but was, however, getting up two or three times during the night to pass urine. He hadn't had an unbroken night's sleep in three or four years. He made a grimace, 'It's an old man's complaint… we'll tell everyone I'm having another kidney stone removed.' He found it necessary to put up a front and I understood. The doctor felt it was to Kenny's advantage to have the operation at the age of sixty-three, rather than leave it until he was older, because the process of recovery would be easier, and if he could get a decent night's sleep it seemed to be sound common sense. We didn't dither about and a room was booked at King Edward VII's Hospital for Officers in Beaumont Street. I packed his suitcase and took him in – I spent every moment I could with him. The nursing staff there were faultlessly kind and sympathetic, and made no comments on the large paper mobiles I hung in his room to amuse him. Standing on the pavement and looking up at Kenny's window, you'd have thought it was a nursery! He enjoyed the silly things I did. I tried always to have stories for him; he'd positively beam as I arrived, rushing in with food and goodies. Some flowers arrived from a woman I didn't know and a box of chocolates from another. The messages on the cards were affectionate, private, and I said perhaps I shouldn't be opening them.

'They don't matter do they, Shrimp?' he said screwing up his face, and looking out of the window he made comments on the weather. I cuddled him – he smelt of baby powder, and possibly ten seconds went by as I thought of Peter and making love and how safe he made me feel that way. I felt clean, empty of jealousy – finally it had washed away and this gave me strength. I told him, no, they didn't matter anymore. I read the cards twice and left them on the side, behind mine. We began to talk in whispers, our conversation threading together – it was in a way the best visit of all.

All thoughts of the house and its problems left me – Peter would tell me the saga of his day and I couldn't seem to take it in, and when I think back at those weeks, I don't remember anything other than looking forward enormously to being with Kenny. I'd get on to the bed with him and there was peace, and plenty of time to talk. We'd talk into the night and he'd still say, 'Do you have to go, darling?'

Take him to the sun, the doctors told me, it's what he needs. It was imperative to get better as quickly as possible, because he'd agreed to do a film for Disney, for a great deal of money. We decided to go to Corsica, feeling sure we'd find the sunshine there. We flew off, he was weak and he couldn't stand or walk without my help, and looked pale, but he was cheerful and psychologically in a good state – behaving sweetly as usual, never complaining.

It was a difficult journey and we were tremendously relieved to arrive at our hotel. I can't remember its name, but it stood in beautiful gardens, its terraces leading down to the sea, which we could see from our room. We'd come away quickly, the journey had drained him, and for the first three days he sat quietly on our terrace. Little by little, to my relief, he gained strength and his colour improved. Our stay there was as peaceful as we could have wished, and as sunny. He was, as ever, impatient to hurry the process of recovery and we decided to have a gentle swim in the pool. He found it difficult to swim, and we just paddled around. He'd always been a physical person who enjoyed swimming, deep-sea fishing, golf, skiing; and his confidence was shattered, I believe for ever, that afternoon when he felt his legs buckle under him as he tried to pull himself up the steps out of the pool.

I was right behind him, pushing his hips. 'Christ, my legs have gone...! I've no strength.' And his face looked haunted with disbelief and panic. *Walk, walk* – we must walk a little bit more every day, and even if his heart did sink at the prospect, he'd hold my arm and we'd religiously make our way to the village and back every afternoon, and if we passed anyone en route, he didn't look them in the eye. He had determination and courage, and I look back with such admiration.

When the day came for our journey home, Kenny was so much better. Although it tired him, we weren't worried. When we went to see our doctor, the next day, he expressed surprise that Kenny had found the operation such a trauma. He told us of patients of the same age who were back at work in two weeks – for some, he said, it was a piece of cake. I didn't take it as a bad omen.

The next few months passed with Kenny gradually getting stronger. He hasn't really been ill, I told friends – only recovering from surgery. He went to Alnwick, outside Newcastle, to make his film for Disney. From there he completed work on his autobiography, *More or Less*. We talked daily on the telephone; I couldn't visit him, I had to stay and get this house built. It was proving to be such a nightmare. My nerves were stretched.

After the months of emotional pummelling, a numbness took charge of my brain. Everything was hazy around me. It was misery living in a house that was a building site; no heating, no hot water. The whole place looked awful. Such commotion, such noise.

'Who's this bird with the keys?' yelled a cockney bricklayer, hanging from the scaffolding.

'Shut up, you berk! – that's madam!' which made Peter and I laugh. A thing we hadn't done for a while. Hammers and drills clattering and whining. A bulldozer in the garden churning up more rubble – such a din. At one point there wasn't a single room that hadn't been pulled apart and, seeking privacy, I had to dress outside in Peter's van. The house was filled with the heavy footsteps of Irishmen and cockneys shouting to each other. I got bits of their conversation and they'd hastily apologise to me for their language. They should have heard mine sometimes, as I sat in bed, papers and plans all over the duvet. Before I went to sleep, I'd swear that I'd never, never go through this again.

Peter and I talked – we had so much in common. But we didn't say anything too deep, or too tender. It was difficult to know what to say. Suddenly and unplanned, 'Do you love me?' escaped from my lips. He didn't flinch, he went on looking into his tool box as if he hadn't heard. But he had, because later he put his arm around me and held me, making me know I'd asked a silly question. What was he thinking? Looking at him I felt full of qualms and sadness – and guilt.

Kenny became a fairly frequent visitor, coming to the house most Sundays, arriving in his little MG, carrying champagne. In his smart suit and shiny handmade shoes he'd stand amidst the rubble, and exclaim, 'Blimey O'Reilly, Shrimp, how do you stand it here? – God, Pete, I couldn't live like this!' I knew everything he was going to say before he said it. 'What are you doing, Pete?', and when he was told, he still didn't know. I'd take him around the house with me; 'Listen, did you hear that!' he'd say in whispers every time a stair creaked, or the boiler snorted. He was glad once the tour of inspection was over and, changed into more comfortable clothes, he'd happily supervise the barbecue; lunch was his department and priority. Nothing changes. The three of us would sit out in the garden, which looked like a bomb site – buckets, rubble, ladders, bulldozer and cement mixer – chewing on our chicken legs and drinking champagne, and wonder what the hell the neighbours thought of it all.

Late one night after dinner, we drove him to the tip where we used to illegally dump our building rubbish – in the headlamps he could see the rats scuttling around – he sobered up considerably and began to laugh and curse in an astonished way – a really strong volley – 'You're in your element aren't you, Shrimp?' *Yes! Yes!* and at the same time, *No! No!* – but I felt it was useless to tell him he was always on my mind.

We all three went out to dinner a few times; Kenny was worried about us not eating.

'Look at you, Shrimp – you look about fifty!'

Was he trying to be funny? I was on my feet in a flash looking in the mirror. I saw that I had black roots and no make-up, and being so thin, I looked weird.

'Jesus,' I said and burst into tears. Peter said he'd get me brandy for my nerves. I was glad of it.

He wouldn't admit publicly that we were living apart, for reasons other than my rebuilding our house. He'd give interviews to the press:

'Angela has a passionate interest in everything, but I don't share all her enthusiasms. She's doing up the house now and it's going to be marvellous when it's finished, but I've deliberately kept out of it because I like instant trees. When I open the back door I expect to find a garden there. I can't stand the noise of builders, but she can. She'll spend a week choosing just the right handle for a door. There's always been something of the father figure in me for her, it's something I like. She needs a strong pair of arms around her and I feel I give her the security she seeks. Love has developed, you see; what was once all sex has become lasting affection. One advantage she's always had from our relationship is that I've been able to give her an older man's experience. She values my advice and always has done. We share a sense of humour and can tune in on the same wavelength, she's as quick as a whip. She wears her heart on her sleeve – a crazy creature of moods, very Irish in the way she swings from intense sorrow to intense joy. She is exciting to be with and the one unfortunate thing is that she has not had a child. I would like her to have someone to remember me by. I took her when she was very young, and I regret I wasn't able to give her a child – I failed her there. She has a real maternal instinct – she would make a wonderful mother. I know that if ever I became ill for any length of time, she would enjoy looking after me. After my last operation she took me to Corsica, and she walked me like a baby,' Kenneth More smiled; 'just like a baby,' he said.

I wished he wouldn't give these interviews at this time. You couldn't say it wasn't true, but as I scanned the lines I was relieved that Peter hadn't seen them. The silence between us would be shocking if he had. It was common knowledge that Peter and I went everywhere together – the press on our heels. I'd sought a level of self-respect, believing there was a pretty world out there if you wanted it badly enough. People asked, how are you and Kenny? They asked every time they saw me, but he'd sworn me to silence. And I felt like a two-timer when Kenny talked to the press in this way. Which left me nowhere.

I used to wonder how it would all end. I had such mixed emotions. It would take me ages to write, my problem being not what to say, but how to say it. We'd always believed that when a marriage fell apart, you separated, made a clean break. But it wasn't like that for us. We'd lunch together a couple of days a week. I did his food shopping and laundry, and José looked after the flat. Kenny paid my bills – continued to make sure that in that area at least I had no worries. 'We're all right, aren't we darling…? I mean we see each other all the time… and we have our freedom… being separated isn't so bad!' But when I asked him whether he'd made up his mind – did he want me to find him a cottage in the country, where he felt he could do some writing, or a flat in town so that he could be near me – he'd dismiss the subject and say, no, he hadn't made up his mind, and anyway he didn't want to hurry things.

I received an anonymous phone call from a woman telling me she was in love with him. And a couple of letters – and once a photograph of him taken in a nightclub. What did I feel? All the expected responses flooded back – jealousy that ran like melted butter over toast. Inside me I was a tiny mad girl, and I clung to Peter. With him I forgot for a while the terrible anxiety which gripped me when I thought about the desperate condition my life was in.

It was about eleven o'clock on a lousy autumn morning. Rain was coming in the window – one of those that either won't budge at all or closes with a thud taking your knuckles with it. I had two jackets on so at least I would be warm until Peter could get the central heating going again. I'd asked him nicely – using wheedling words. He'd said okay, okay – but didn't stop smiling. He set me tasks to give me something to do. It had seemed to take for ever, eating our energies – and our plans to drive to India, sleeping in his van, would have to wait until next summer. In our mind's eye we'd seen a beautiful little house, and now when friends came, they didn't leave muttering and calling us crazy – they emerged with words of praise falling out of their mouths.

That morning, or maybe it was another morning – all those mornings were exchangeable – Kenny's voice from downstairs called, 'Morning Pete – okay?' – excitedly and with energy, 'Shrimp…? Shrimp?' as he roared into the room that would be a study. I noticed his lovely tan and wished I'd combed my hair – it was all a tangle. He waved a copy of his book to me, saying not to tell him off if he'd got bits wrong… it's a bloody good yarn… I only want you to read this…this piece about you… it's my favourite. He seemed shy of me and stood over me waiting as I read: 'A day without her is like a summer without the sun – she was born to give happiness and laughter and she has given me both. Of course we have disagreements and bleak days as well as sunny ones, as all couples do after years of marriage. But we share a tremendous bond which no one could ever destroy.' He'd signed my copy 'Joe' – harking back to earlier days. Together we nodded and cried. As a way of easing the pain it was ineffective.

The night before his 64th birthday I went over to his flat. We were going out to dinner after I'd done his packing; he was leaving for Canada the next day on a promotional tour for his book. I gave him a cushion for his desk chair, my girlfriend Veronica had knitted it for me. I'd asked her to put 'Darling Morehen, always in my heart. Shrimp'. For my birthday, five weeks later, he gave me a gold safety-pin with a golden heart hanging from it, and he'd put – 'Shrimp, the name on my heart'.

'We're supposed to be separated' I blubbed as he pinned it on me.

'That makes no difference to how we feel, in here,' he said, tapping his heart. 'The love hasn't gone from our marriage. I want you… and I want my freedom… I know I can't have both.'

This morning I look back with wiser eyes and I can see it all quite clearly and feel, if only…

Our lust for travel never lay dormant for long. We would spend hours with our Reader's Digest Atlas, happily planning journeys. 'I long to take you up the Nile' or 'Why don't we go and see the Grand Canyon this spring?' Some of these dreams didn't come true – however, that year, '78, we spent Christmas on the French West Indian island of Mauritius. The flight was uneventful, but very long; Kenny let exhaustion take over and slept most of the way. We had a bungalow on the beach with a heavenly uninterrupted view of the ocean. We woke to bright sunshine and blue skies, and lots of time to talk and think about the future. The need to communicate was very strong. On impulse one day while we were lunching I gave him the new house. There was nothing tangible to go on, I sensed his insecurity and need to be settled. We agreed I'd be the one for a cottage in the country.

We hired a car and had a few trips to other parts of the island, but we spent most of our time sitting under the Makuti beach umbrella reading. Kenny hardly left its protective shade, only to swim in the very early morning, or at dusk. He'd found for the first time that he couldn't take the sun, and despite the precautions we'd taken, his face had burnt badly. To walk from the umbrella to our bungalow I had to wrap his head in a Kikoi, leaving only his eyes free, and carry a sunshade closely over him. We'd walk as quickly as we could, and still he'd burn. We'd been damn careful and it didn't seem to make sense.

One morning, as he emerged from the shower, I told him to straighten his shoulders – hold his head up when he walked. We made a game of it, played at being soldiers. I was the sergeant major shouting instructions – *shoulders back*! – *head up*! – *arms swing*! – we giggled a lot. Even though he said, 'I can't, Shrimp – I can't, I'm doing my best!' I'd watch him amble, his arms not swinging and shoulders sloping forward, I'd never seen him walk in this strange way, and I thought, oh dear, he must be getting old, my Kenny, of all people. I'd never stopped calling him mine.

Before leaving for the airport and the long journey home, I covered his face in thick white pain-relieving cream. He looked a sight and I kept him away from all mirrors. In the departure lounge, people came up for autographs; everyone wanted a few words. At one point a young Indian said, 'Are you really Kenneth More? My God aren't you small... and so old... wait here don't move... I'll get my mother, she'll back me up!' I was blinded with anger, wanted to spring to his defence. Kenny said nothing, except 'When did you last see a film of mine...? *Genevieve*...? that was twenty-six years ago... so yes, I expect I have aged.' All said with such dignity, his painfully red and pulsating face covered in what looked like whipped egg whites. Given enough time, would I ever be as tolerant as him? He winked at me and gave me a smile and a squeeze as we walked on to the aircraft.

I hadn't been home three days when my new agent rang to say that I'd landed a really marvellous part in a new series the BBC was planning. I was delighted, positively beamed down the telephone, even though she couldn't see me. I rushed round to the flat where I found Kenny in bed with the inevitable script in his hands. I'd never seen him so happy for me. I had something to talk about again, other than the house. I'd feel interesting again. I climbed on to the bed and told him about the other actors, and the director; I went on telling him everything, it was always absolutely necessary for me to tell him every detail. I cuddled into his arms and they felt clammy. I felt the back of his neck, his chest – 'Morehen, are you feeling all right?'

'Absolutely.'

'I think you're depressed. Is everything getting you down? Will you see the doctor...? for me please, promise?' my words running together. Holding my hand lightly, he protested, but eventually he gave me his promise.

Clamped tight in the grip of fear I crept into bed, my hands feeling in the dark for my flick rag. I huddled there with the pillow over my head, feeling paralysed with terror. Suddenly something broke loose in me and I began to cry oozy tears into my pillow.

'Don't be frightened, Shrimp,' he'd said, 'but I've got a touch of Parkinson's... very mildly... only a little.' Standing in the bedroom of his flat I couldn't do anything but look at him helplessly, my knees wobbling beneath me. I'd open my mouth to say something, but nothing came out – I just opened and closed it like a fish. I was stunned – we both were. He gave me a brave half-smile and we were calm. Undramatic. He took down our medical dictionary from the shelf. What we read looked threatening. Still we didn't panic. I didn't cry at all.

'Morehen... I want you under my wing.'

'I want to be there.'

My years of adolescence were over.

Part Four
Wife

Today I can recall the heartache I felt that summer evening in '79, standing at the window feebly attempting to wave goodbye to Peter, leaning against the radiator, my fingers scrabbling at the curtains and not being sure if I could or couldn't accept – if I was *resistant* enough to accept – a life of celibacy and with no hope now of holding a baby of my own in my arms. Whatever his feelings, Peter had always been supportive, there when I needed him. He was one of the few people with whom I didn't feel the need for a mask. With him I could be myself. I remember talking to him and the fun we'd had together. I remember when he said he loved me. Did I love him? Yes, yes, I did, and I had shattered our relationship beyond repair. My tears fell stubbornly and there were plenty of them as I felt the suck of despair. I can remember thinking, it's back – that feeling of loneliness, worse than before.

Of course, there would be many adjustments, changes to be made, and it was probably the next afternoon that I called Caroline, my agent, telling her in my tiniest voice I couldn't do the TV series, or any other work in the foreseeable future. 'What do you mean? What's happened?' she said, horrified. I wanted to tell her, tell someone – but Kenny had been insistent – 'No one must know.' Understandably she sounded exasperated with my reluctance to answer her questions. My behaviour must have appeared extraordinary: I was being difficult, distant, and I half expected her to sack me. Mad at me she might have been, but she didn't cross me off her books, for which I'll always feel grateful.

I bathed and chose my clothes with care. Bright, happy clothes – my baggy red dungarees and my red and white T-shirt. I moved restlessly around the house, plumping the cushions, drawing the curtains, switching on the lamps. The familiar sound of Kenny's MG pulling up outside put an end to my fussings. I stood by the front door and watched him crouched into the boot reaching for some wrapped bottles, a housewarming present from Brother Cyril and Pat. I could see myself – I didn't look young or old – and as he walked towards me I thought he looked a little dishevelled and hot and I felt eager to hold him in my arms. He was overwhelmed by what we'd done with the house. His eyes moist, he said, 'It's lovely, Shrimpy... a film star's house' – and for a few minutes we were a little shy with each other, but he talked to me, the words dancing out of his mouth. 'I'll be all right as long as I have you... I want to be a proper husband to you. I hope we can have some happy times together – I want us to be husband and wife. Just give me a chance... you'll get me the way you want me – I feel I know now what you need to be happy.' I think it was then that I resolved to have the courage and strength to fight this devastating blow that fate had dealt us. If the days ahead were to be filled with fear, if we had to face months and years of uncertainty and heartache, if this was the price we had to pay for being together, where we belonged, then it was a price we would pay. We were in this together.

I'm sometimes embarrassed by confessionals and I've often in the past resented intrusion into areas of my life I hold most dear to my heart. Talking about something that means a lot, and yet feeling I have to make it more interesting each time I tell it, in some ways denies my sincerity. But one of the reasons I've written this book is that I hope, by talking about how it was for Kenny and me, to be able to reassure those who have had their independence taken away through ill health, and perhaps feel they're a burden, that they aren't. I hope to be able to convey to whoever reads these words, a little of the joy it gave me to care for him. To make it possible for him to live in his own world, however confined, to be in his own home, lie in his own bed – that brought untold rewards. Admittedly the strain placed on both of us was tremendous: sometimes it almost seemed as though both of us had the illness. He continually thanked me, saying how lucky he was to have me. But I was the lucky one – the dimensions of our relationship were endless. In many intangible ways he gave me so much in return. It worked both ways.

Unless someone you love suffers from Parkinson's Disease, you cannot be expected to realise fully the heartache this affliction brings. If by describing what happened to Kenny I can bring a greater awareness of the problems of Parkinsonism among the public, and if through the Kenneth More Memorial Fund, which I support with pride and love, research can bring us closer to a cure, then Kenny's career and his suffering will together have given his life even greater purpose. As one of the foremost actors of his generation he had a rage to live, a life full of energetic creativity, which won him fame and friends the world over, until this insidious disease crept in behind his carefree facade.

We read all we could about Parkinson's Disease, wanting to prepare ourselves for what might lie ahead. We learned that it is a disorder of the central nervous system, its cause not definitely known. That no two patients are exactly alike nor does everyone suffer to the same degree, there being a very wide spectrum in the severity of the disease. We learned about the symptoms, what to watch out for. We went to see our special friend and doctor, 'Mac', who gave us almost two hours of his precious time. He examined Kenny thoroughly and he talked to us, explaining what we could and couldn't expect out of life. He said we could, with a little luck, look forward to growing old together, that this disease does not kill. He was adamant that Kenny should be protected from stress. His life from now on must be quiet and calm; the effect of anxiety and trauma could have disastrous results on his nervous system, causing irreversible damage.

The next few months were very hard, almost too hard. We were struggling to keep our bearings. We had to relinquish so much – how did we keep going? Undoubtedly it was made more difficult for me because Kenny found it necessary to pretend to the outside world that things were all right. He was the one with the illness, and I believed he had to be allowed to handle it in any way that was best for him. Friends and family weren't fooled and they rallied, but he gradually froze them out. I found it very difficult keeping such a stiff-upper-lip front. I needed to confide in someone. But perhaps if we didn't talk freely about it, if we hugged it to ourselves, didn't admit it, perhaps it would go away. I was consumed by him: looking after him was using every part of me – we were living day to day and refusing to think about the future.

Each passing month seemed to bring new problems. Another kidney stone formed – the same kidney. For about forty-eight hours he was in great pain and our sympathetic new doctor came around to give him pain-killing injections. Kenny continued to drink pints and pints of water, trying to flush the stone out. Neither of us slept. I kept getting up to kneel under him holding a jug, both of us willing with all the power of positive thought for that damned stone to be on the move. Had he been younger and fitter it wouldn't have been such a worry; but at sixty-four and suffering from Parkinson's no one wanted to put him under the knife again – that was considered a last resort. The very thought set our hearts in a panic.

The gods were with us and he passed that jagged stone into my jug at around four in the morning. We were so relieved – we hooted like cowboys and Kenny, exhausted with the long hours of pain and with no sleep, still made the effort to do a little dance for me as he hummed to the tune of *When You're Smiling*. We sat up in bed and celebrated with mugs of hot chocolate. Silent for a minute he looked up at me, his eyes brimming, and then looked down.

'I know it isn't fair – now I'm sick, I only want you.'

I protested: 'I'm here because I want to be – I don't look miserable, do I?' – and hushed him up, but I know it was a sentiment that continued to prey on his mind.

One disaster quickly followed another. One night Jill came round for supper. It was a Saturday, and Kenny had his on a tray in front of the television while Jill and I sat in the kitchen. We were always happy to see each other, picking up where we left off. Sitting at the table talking and talking and then she very gently dropped her bomb. As sweetly as she could she told me she had cancer. It was totally unexpected – I was speechless. I heard what she said, but for months I couldn't accept it.

About a month later Mummy suffered two heart attacks and on the drive to the hospital I began to talk out loud, pleading, sobbing to God, 'Oh no, God, please don't let her die.' I was terrified and my legs were trembling as I entered her ward. She was propped up in bed waiting for me. Pale and thin, she raised her hand, insisting there was nothing for me to be scared about. But I still was. And two days later her little dog Timmy died. Our Christmas present of all those years earlier, he had been a sunny, brave dog, loving us all without reservation. We were frightened of breaking the news to Mummy now that she had heart problems, but she was very brave in her distress.

When I was alone that night sitting in the kitchen, I became very emotional. It seemed to be a certainty that, given enough time, I'd lose everyone I loved. I gave way under a wave of self-pity.

Life was further complicated, in May 1980, by Kenny being sued in the High Court by Daniel Angel. When Kenny's autobiography, *More or Less*, was published in 1978, it was widely acclaimed by critics and readers, and serialised in the *Sunday Express*. One of the happiest results was that so many people we had once known, and who had somehow dropped out of our lives, now wrote to congratulate Kenny on his book and to tell him how much they had enjoyed it.

Unhappily one reader, whom Kenny had always held in the highest regard both professionally and as a friend, thought otherwise. This was Daniel Angel, who had produced what many considered to be Kenny's greatest film, *Reach for the Sky*. Danny claimed that Kenny had libelled him. Nothing, of course, had been further from Kenny's intention, but try as he might the matter could not be resolved and eventually came to trial in the High Court.

Before it was heard, there had been weeks and months of legal letters, meetings and other deliberations, and all this time Kenny's health was deteriorating. This was happening very slowly at first. So slowly, indeed, that outsiders hardly noticed the slight slurring of his speech, or a certain unsteadiness on his feet, almost instantly corrected. But Kenny noticed. And I noticed. To both of us, these were serious signs.

Finally, the day came for our appearance in court. The nervous strain, added to the effects of his illness, was so great that he could barely will himself to walk the few steps into the dock. We sat on the benches listening to the evidence, literally trembling with fear. That sounds dramatic, I know, but if you've ever been unfortunate enough to be involved in a lawsuit, you'll understand what we went through. His hand resting on my leg was icy cold, and I kept wanting to be sick. When the court adjourned we would walk to the nearest gentlemen's cloakroom and wait for it to be empty, then we'd slip in and take the brandy I kept in my bag, drinking it neat from the bottle to try and steady our nerves. We couldn't go to the restaurant for lunch with our solicitors because Kenny found the stone spiral stairs too hazardous and the effort would only have exhausted him further. So I made a packed lunch and brought it with us – we ate it in the corridors, sitting

297

on a window ledge and trying to be as inconspicuous as possible. With the illness his hands had started to shake slightly, and he would put his food down whenever someone passed in case they noticed.

'Good God, Ken, what are you doing here? Why aren't you in the Bahamas?' Even though his heart was full of doubt and gloom, for each well-meaning but misplaced remark he found a joky retort and a smile. Only we knew how ill he was. Only he knew how ill he felt.

He was very anxious that when he went into the box to give his evidence, if he slurred his words and couldn't stand up straight, he might give the impression of being drunk. So before our QC, Anthony Hoolihan, started to examine him, Kenny had to admit the truth publicly for the first time in court – which wasn't the way or the time he would have chosen. Without going into specific details, he said that he was ill and was giving up his career because of increasing ill-health. To many outside it seemed inconceivable that he could have played his last part. He was being so courageous, and I knew that he was playing not only his last, but his greatest part.

The case went on for several days, and finally the jury retired to consider their verdict. I can't remember how many hours they were out, but certainly long enough for us to make a couple of furtive visits to the gentlemen's loo for our swig from the brandy bottle.

Finally the result was declared. We had lost.

'Oh my God!' Kenny muttered, with a look of immobilised horror, his hand gripping my thigh. 'We're ruined, Shrimp!' And for a minute or two that seemed to be the case, but the jury considered that three hundred pounds damages would be adequate compensation for Danny. Because we had been advised to pay five thousand pounds into court, and as the damages awarded to Danny had been less than that figure, he had to pay most of the costs.

So to that extent Kenny had won, but in a deeper sense he had lost. So much had depended on the case – if Danny had been awarded high damages and if we'd had to meet all the costs, we could have been destitute and might even have been forced to sell our home to find the money. And with Kenny's public announcement that he was not able to work again, the future would have been bleak.

On the evening the verdict was announced, there was no celebratory dinner for us – we had dinner quietly at home in front of the television. Kenny's announcement of his retirement was featured in the news bulletins. They made it sound very dramatic. 'Christ!' he said, 'they normally only do that when you're dead.' Friends rang up to congratulate him on the result of the case, and he was thrilled that they were so relieved for him, but talking on the telephone had become difficult, so he asked me to thank them for him and send his love.

Something made me wake at dawn next morning, to see the grey light over London filtering through our bedroom curtains. I had been awakened by the sound of sobbing. Kenny was weeping uncontrollably beside me. I held him tightly in my arms, making hushing and soothing noises, feeling that perhaps it was a good thing for him to let it all out, all the bottled-up and repressed emotion. I made him herb tea, ice packs for his eyes, but on and off his crying continued through the day and I recognised the signs of a nervous breakdown. The strain of months of fighting to appear normal and healthy and ebullient, as the public knew Kenneth More, plus the pressures of the court case, had contributed to the deterioration of his health. From then on, he began to go downhill.

Within reason, we tried everything – driving all over the labyrinth of London. Homeopathy – hypnosis – acupuncture. Looking back over it, that summer seemed to have been a period of doctors' surgeries – neuro-surgeons, urologists, pharmacologists and psychiatrists. We struggled up staircases to talk to men with serious faces and quiet voices. They did tests and made copious notes, Kenny's life written down on white slips of paper. I'd watch him sitting there on the edge of a chair, a true child of his times: straight-backed, willing to please, he'd describe the wretched symptoms with such brave candour. I was so proud of him – still impressed by his polished manners and his consideration for others, his dignity. My mind was in turmoil. I found it difficult to resign myself to the fact that he'd become the victim of this degenerative and incurable disease. The emotion I felt was akin to grief – it was all so hard to believe; in my anguish I grasped at straws. One specialist promised me: 'Your husband will never be in a wheelchair' – a rash prediction.

One night, as I helped him prepare for bed, Kenny reached out and touched me; smiling his faint smile he pressed the knuckles of his hands gently together: 'I'm so sorry, Shrimp… that we've lost me.' He was hurt and melancholy.

'We'll get you better than this darling… I promise you.'

He let out a deep drawn-out sigh and the expression on his face was full of despair despite his effort at a smile. I put my arms around him, giving him an enormous squeeze, and kissed him. For the merest instant our eyes met and the love that flowed between us was marvellously intense and intimate. If everything happens for a reason – then the reason for this illness was us. The difficulties certainly got to us, but they strengthened our relationship.

Kenny often said that it was unmitigating hell – but wonderful too, for all it had given us. The great love we shared bonded us together and gave us solace which helped us get through the relentless heartache we woke to every morning.

Who hasn't known everything, their share of pain and joy, and we tried not to regard this experience as a tragedy. It's about the process, not about arriving, and if survival is at least a matter of will, then Kenny had what it takes. 'I'm fighting it, love… I promise you I'm fighting it.'

Later that summer, I came home from the dentist to find him waiting for me, sitting at the kitchen table – a bit nervy and excited. He'd been offered the part of Jarvis Lorrie in *A Tale of Two Cities* – could he do it? What did I think? – if he didn't take this he would probably have to accept the fact that he might never work again, ever. I shall never forget his face, alight at the prospect of working again – and the look of hope in his eyes – life for Kenny equalled work, it always had. Naturally he was terribly apprehensive. The doctors thought he could do it – should do it. With his heart in his mouth, Kenny told his agent to go ahead and fix the deal.

I went with him for his wig and costume fittings, standing just close enough for him to rest his hand on my shoulder. No gesture of apparent affection was ever more studied. His balance was becoming affected and to steady himself he had to be holding on to someone, something. If someone called his name and he turned quickly or looked sharply over his shoulder, he could lose his balance and fall. So the silver-topped cane that had belonged to the celebrated C. B. Cochran, and been given to Kenny by Evelyn Laye, became a more or less permanent prop. We went to Cumberland to visit Jane, and Kenny's enchanting granddaughters. Her medical qualifications were of invaluable help and support to me – she explained everything to me in a language I could understand. In the privacy of the country lanes Kenny practised his dialogue for the film – working on his pronunciation – where was that wonderful voice, it was very distressing. 'This fucking illness has hit me where I work!'

A chum had given us a religious book to read, assuring us it would help; and after we'd read it, I would drive us through the countryside en route to the Miller Howe or the Sharrow Bay hotels, the car humming under us, calling out, 'With God on our side there isn't anything we can't do – please God, help us.' Please God – words so easily said. Please God – if you make Mummy buy me that doll I'll do my homework every night. Please God, if you'll let me have a baby, then I'll stop being so jealous of Kenny. Please God, if you'll make Kenny just a little bit better, then I *promise* I'll never ask you for anything else. I'm sure it's wrong, but all of my life, whenever I've prayed I've asked for something.

Looking back on that final performance of Kenny's, I try and console myself with the fact that even though the pressures and strain were tremendous, at least he was 'having a go' – for two weeks he was with creative people whom he admired and the unit was such a happy one. I remember it as a time of tremendous insecurity and, paradoxically, of laughter. We were on location in the picturesque village of Senlis about forty miles outside Paris. We didn't attempt to go out to dinner with the others – and sometimes I longed to, it would be silly of me to pretend otherwise; after a quick drink in the bar of the hotel, we'd go straight to our room, into our pyjamas and bed. It must have been evident to the others that Kenny wasn't a hundred per cent fit. It had been in the papers and on TV, but still we played a game of half truths to our friends and the press. We had to, to keep going. How could we have done otherwise? But no one on the unit made any comments to us.

One hot sunny afternoon I was sitting in his canvas chair behind the camera and watched Jim Goddard, the director, set the next scene up with the actors and crew – I loved being amongst the organised chaos. Kenny, and I think two other actors, had to sit in a coach driven by four horses and head in the direction of a small wood. On the word 'action', the horses gently trotted off, but, unforeseen by anyone, a rein had become entangled between the back legs of one of the horses and it bolted. I heard the commotion, the sound of alarm – and saw the carriage begin to sway violently. I remember springing from my seat mindless of my book and handbag spilling from my lap, running towards the coach shrieking, '*My Kenny…! My Kenny!*' For a moment I think I blacked out completely and then I remember shaking violently and sobbing like a baby, clinging to the comforting arms of two friends on the unit. They held me tight, telling me, Kenny's all right – Kenny's all right. I felt as though the top of my head had blown away with nerves – he'd been so close to being hurt. I wanted to wrap him in cotton-wool – I couldn't take risks with him, he was too vulnerable now, and so was I. The incident had looked more dangerous to me as an onlooker than it actually had been. And Kenny never knew I'd been so frightened.

Much as I didn't want to, when we came home I made an appointment to see our GP. I was sure something was wrong with me, surely I'd overreacted? I told him everything; I was finding my nerves so difficult to handle. I sat across from him in his tastefully decorated surgery and he didn't look at all surprised with my breakdown of symptoms. He talked kindly to me: all very understandable, he felt, considering the strain I was under. He regarded his list of drugs thoughtfully and put me on a short course of tranquillisers. We both agreed that this was a long-term situation, and that neither of us wanted me to wake up at forty-five with the menopause racing towards me hooked on tranquillisers.

One by one Kenny was being deprived of his greatest pleasures in life – lunching with his friends at the Garrick, playing golf, driving his car – although, with my arm or his stick to steady his balance, he could still walk, so we were able to keep up with quite regular visits to the movies. Occasionally he'd feel ill during the film and would want to leave and, because of the increasing difficulties he had walking, that wasn't easy in the dark – so now, in my spacious handbag, along with the bottle of brandy for panic attacks, I carried a torch.

After some discussion we decided to go to France for a holiday. We wanted to go to the south, back to our beloved La Pinade Hotel, but I'd never driven in France and was nervous at the responsibility. I suggested Monte Carlo as it was only a taxi ride away from Nice Airport. Kenny was less than enthusiastic at the idea – 'Too many unhappy memories'. 'But

Kenny...' I protested. And won. Off we went to stay at the Hermitage Hotel in Monte Carlo for three weeks. The hotel was unbelievably beautiful – it was bright and sunny – the very last word in luxury. We'd sit on our terrace which overlooked the harbour and while I read or did my sewing, Kenny looked through his binoculars: lovers roaring around on scooters, the private yachts bobbing about, water skiers, were all subject to his scrutiny. So amazingly generous, he really pushed the boat out: 'You can have anything you want' – I *had* everything I wanted except the most important thing, his health – you can't buy good health. Sometimes, in the afternoon, I'd leave him sleeping and I'd go into the small public gardens and sit on a bench, and I'd remember how things used to be. How eighteen years earlier he'd sat in these same gardens reading my secret love letters. I'd open my eyes wide – endeavouring to stop the tears – but down they'd come and I'd hurry back to the hotel, hiding them as best I could.

In October I had my fortieth birthday. He took me to our old friends Armour and Winston in the Burlington Arcade and chose for me a small pair of diamond earrings. Being forty was no trauma for me – no fuss.

Christmas 1980 was both wonderful and wretched. We made it to the Berkeley Hotel for our traditional Christmas lunch. We were the first to arrive and the first to leave. At home in front of the fire we hugged and kissed and said quiet loving things – that was all wonderful. But it was wretched watching him trying to open his presents; the muscles in his fingers had begun to stiffen and he fumbled with the ribbons. I quickly cut the strings and bows – and then he said he just didn't have the energy to open the boxes – it was all too much for him. So I opened them, oohing and aahing – overreacting like a child – as though they were a complete surprise and hadn't come from me... we laughed about that. I looked into his sad eyes as he smiled at me – that bittersweet smile said it all.

That New Year's Eve he fell over in the kitchen. Thankfully he didn't hit any sharp corners – but his elbow was badly bruised. 'You don't want an old thing like me falling about the place… I can't be enough for you like this.' He was wrong.

On January 23rd '81 Kenny was admitted to the private ward of St Thomas's Hospital for tests. The doctors were confused, and so were we. No one could understand why he felt so ill. The side effects and symptoms of Parkinson's can be ghastly, but it shouldn't actually make you feel ill. He always tried to sound better than he felt for the doctors. 'I'm okay really – I just feel bloody.' I'd get angry and demand he be more honest with them.

'I don't put an act on for *you* – I tell *you* how I really feel.'

I kept trying to make him see sense by saying – 'I can't make you better – hopefully *they* can, you *must* level with them.'

He found it difficult to stop being the good patient – feeling conscious-stricken about being a nuisance, a burden. In hospital he never rang the bell, never complained. Months later one of the doctors sent a memo round to the nursing staff: 'Remember Mr More is an actor – do not be taken in, he is a very sick man.'

Kenny's room on the twelfth floor was a good size, with a staggering view over the Thames and the Houses of Parliament. After we'd got him into bed, I busied around arranging his flowers, putting my teddy and our photographs where he could best see them, and I hung the by now familiar mobiles, wanting him to feel secure – if only I could do more. We didn't know how long he would be in for. They wanted him there to take him off all his drugs, so that they could assess him properly, see what possible side effects they were having. And they wanted to do another brain scan, X-ray his kidneys and check up on his prostate gland. He had been having worrying experiences with his bladder over the last few months – during the film and on our holiday. Sometimes he couldn't pass urine at all, and would be in severe pain until the spasm passed, or, occasionally, he would lose control completely. The boxes of pads in my handbag and the towels in his bed at night became routine. It was distressing and unnerving – a trauma for both of us. I can't recall how many different tests were conducted, but it was discovered that the muscle that controls the bladder, the sphincter, had, because of the disease, lost some of its elasticity, and this was the reason for the spasms. We were told by the urologist that Kenny's bladder probably hadn't been emptying completely for ages, possibly causing infection and that perhaps was the reason he felt so 'bloody'. And now there was another problem. The brain scan had shown slight atrophy of the cerebellum. 'My fucking brain's shrinking, Shrimp!' He still refused to give in. I was upset and frightened, but tried my best to hide it – I was bright and cheerful, overly so. But he knew me too well, and put his arms out towards me, pulling my head on to his chest to comfort me. I exploded into tears – tearing into his pyjama jacket.

During the three weeks that he was in St Thomas's I spent every day with him, arriving at about two and staying until late at night. It was a precious quiet time together. I'd lie on the bed with him, my head on his shoulder, or I'd sit with my shoes off so that Kenny could hold my foot for comfort. The hours flicked by. Talk. Silence. Talk. When he slept I used to look at his face on the pillow and think how handsome he was. He looked younger: his weight loss and the fact that he had stopped drinking probably had something to do with it – and his still marvellously thick head of wavy hair. And I'd remember some of the good times. I could recall vividly, perhaps too vividly, how he'd looked in his shorts and the bright red T-shirt I'd bought him in St Tropez. I'd had his nickname 'Mabel the Maid' written across the chest. I called him that because he was so tidy, and fussed about in the kitchen putting things away before I'd actually used them. He liked to wear it when working in the garden – as he meticulously flicked the lawnmower clean of grass cuttings with a feather duster, which he kept especially for that purpose – and then having hosed the dustbins out, he'd hang them in the trees to dry! To see him – and he was so serious about it – made me roar with laughter, and I seemed never to have a film in my camera when I needed one.

I thought too about how when we'd first met, he'd set to work on my vowels. 'Noël Coward will never employ you with that flat "a".' He held Noël Coward up to me as a figure of discipline. 'Noël would have a few words to say if he saw you sprinkling your salt over your chips.' I'd barely heard of him then, and would want to say, 'Noël *who*?'

Inappropriate thoughts of our life together returned to me. My images and memories were deep inside me and I realised how lucky we were to have all this time together now, to say it all, feel it all – the time to see it all afresh – I treasured every moment.

The urologist decided to nick the sphincter muscle – a very minor operation and after three days Kenny was allowed home. We'd been counting the days. I filled the house with flowers and lit a log fire – I wanted to give him a hero's welcome. Such excitement! No more hospitals, no more tests. It was suggested by the head of the Pharmacology Unit at the hospital that we should go away for a few days to find some sunshine. He was one of those rare doctors who immediately communicate their sympathy, dedication and skill – he inspired our complete trust.

So we flew off to the Hermitage Hotel in Monte Carlo. Same glorious suite – but it was a very different holiday. It poured with rain, almost non-stop, and Kenny's appetite had definitely decreased. We had lots of books to read, but it was all so quiet, and we decided that Monte Carlo without sunshine is as depressing as anywhere else, and we'd rather be at home. By this time he wasn't strong enough to deal with the hand luggage, passports, or anything; but he'd taken care of everything for years, and now it was my turn.

By the end of the month Kenny was still unable to control his bladder, and on several occasions he'd call out in the middle of the night. 'Shrimpy I'm sorry… I can't be brave any longer… *I'm in agony…* my bladder is in spasm.' We'd hurriedly stumble around, not bothering to dress. I'd just wrap him in his dressing gown and a blanket and, as quickly and as carefully as I could, I'd drive to St Thomas's Casualty Department where a doctor would draw off the urine. Still Kenny didn't complain. He submitted to all the indignities without protest. He was trying so hard to be brave. When the sphincter wasn't in spasm, it hardly worked at all and some days I'd have sixteen pairs of underpants on the line. Finally it was decided that he should have another small operation, and this time the sphincter would be cut completely through. He made no attempt to hide his despair, as he turned to me. 'Shrimp, I'll be incontinent… I'll have to have a permanent catheter up my cock,' he said in a quiet voice. 'That's the worst news yet.'

It was arranged for him to enter St Thomas's again, but this time as an NHS patient. Our specialists told us simply that medical insurance might not cover all the staggering costs and 'we don't want lots of little brown envelopes slipping through your letter box.'

Kenny was docile, a little quiet, as we drove there. He said he was worried about being in a public ward – the lack of privacy, the stares and pointing fingers, the autograph-seekers. Not being in perfect shape he dreaded being looked at, now more than ever and, as if to illustrate his point, as we made our way towards the lifts a woman nudged her companion and gave us a penetrating stare.

After several floundering sentences, she peered into his face for a few seconds, then announced loudly, 'I know you, don't I? You're Harry Secombe.'

'No, silly,' retorted her friend, 'it's Kenneth More… I wondered what had happened to 'im…'

We did our best to remain impassive. Kenny, however, favoured them with a wry smile.

'Hello Ken... wot you doin' 'ere...? Why aren't you on the telly?'

'Actors get ill too,' he told her, 'I've retired.'

'Wot did you say, Ken...? I couldn't understand what he said... could you?' she asked her companion.

'*He's retired... He's not well...* my husband doesn't work any more...' I could feel my face flushing with anger and I leaned over his wheelchair trying to protect him from their questions. *Leave him alone* I kept thinking, can't you see how ill he is? And as the doors opened, we scuttled away.

'You wouldn't think he'd let himself be seen like that...'

Thankfully, their voices trailed off out of our hearing.

Dear Sister met us at the entrance to her ward and she wheeled Kenny into a private room – a similar room, same view, only this time he was on the tenth floor, and on the NHS. From the delighted expression on Kenny's face, you knew what relief he felt. He couldn't stop thanking her. I helped him to bed and then sat on the edge with him just holding his hand. We weren't in the mood for idle conversation, we were quiet and I stayed there until he fell asleep.

During '81 Kenny spent five months in St Thomas's Hospital, for stays of two or three weeks at a time. Bladder infections, chest infections, catheter rejections, low blood pressure. Depression. Reassessment of drugs. With the exception of the occasional 'good day', he continued to tell me he felt 'bloody'. I was at the hospital with him every day. I couldn't keep away. Every day I'd arrive a little earlier, stay a little later. Sister allowed me to use the ward kitchen so I could take his food for him – homemade soup – pureed stews. He found that less than appetising, but I wheeled him into eating it. I'd bath him, wash his hair, go through the mail with him: the letters were pouring in daily, a great pile of letters sat waiting on my desk staring at me. Extra difficult for me to cope with, being a dyslexic speller. I'd read to him or curl up on the bed and we'd nap together. During this time our routine seldom varied. I hated saying goodnight, hearing the lift doors close. At home I had too much time to think, and in my emotional state I became desperate and found it difficult to control my thoughts. In front of him I was bubbly and optimistic. 'You're so positive… you raise my spirits more than anyone,' he'd say, but alone, I found it still a piercing shock to realise that he was suffering almost daily deterioration, and that so little could be done for him. 'If love could make me better, I'd be all right, wouldn't I darling,' he said as we bade each other goodnight – you'll be better than this, I continued to promise, but the words had an empty ring to them. At home in bed I'd feel lonely and forsaken. My commitment to him was unconditional. I'd waited all these years for him to need me – and I loved him almost more now than when he was self-reliant.

Kenny was now more or less confined to the house. Nevertheless, with the help of our friend, Toby Rowlands, I was able to take him to a matinee of *Amadeus*. The Royal Box in Her Majesty's Theatre is on street level with no awkward steps to negotiate. It was a glorious afternoon in the theatre, and one neither of us would forget. As the curtain came down, he turned to me, his eyes moist, saying, intensely, as he punched his clenched fist into the palm of his hand, 'Thank God, I didn't do anything else with my life!'

I made a pillowcase with the words 'I love you' written on it and filled it with presents for his birthday, his 67th. I asked all our closest friends to come for champagne that evening, wanting to make September 20th a happy day for him. Flowers, telegrams, presents arrived, it seemed so many people were thinking of him that day, and even though his mood was gentle and quiet, I know they certainly lifted his spirits. Because he'd slept most of the day, he was able to sit in his chair for two hours that evening, trying his best to be a good host. His friends gathered around him, leaning over to kiss him warmly on the cheek and he clasped their hands – there was so much love and affection in the home that evening, you could almost touch it. If it was painful for him to watch everyone drink and laugh the way he once had, he didn't show it. As I helped him to bed later when everyone had gone, he asked, 'Did we make it the best party ever, darling?' I told him I felt it had been a very special evening in many ways. We kept our talk light, but underneath there was a feeling of penetrating sadness.

On our way back from the hospital one afternoon, I found it difficult to resist visiting Bute House again. It was almost as we had left it. The roses, the curtains and blinds, the brass door handles, all as before. For a minute or two, as we sat in the car in front of the house, we were each lost in our own images of the past, so many memories – I saw the life we'd had, a different life. And as I looked at the house, I remember thinking, I had to come here again with Kenny and lay the ghost. From the look in his eyes I felt sure he was feeling the same.

November 1981 – late on a grey afternoon I remember snow starting to dance outside the window. Mummy and I, sitting side by side in our kitchen wrapping Christmas presents. I needed to look at her face, hoping only for an expression of delight, corresponding to my own.

'Mummy, I've been asked to write my autobiography... about me and Kenny... how it's been', and I paused for a significant effect.

'But what about your spelling?' she laughed. That was all I needed to hear.

'Don't laugh at me...! I've got an agent and a publisher... they've given me an advance!'

'Well, I know you can talk freely... but out loud, in a book...? for everyone to see, Angela, how can you do it?'

She stayed silent and went on wrapping her gifts as if I were not there, making me feel flustered.

Three days before Christmas Eve, I brought Kenny home from the hospital after a ten-day stay. The tree was lit and the drawing room looked pretty and festive with its gay decorations. Supporting him on my arm, I watched his face as he looked around our home – I'll always remember his sweet reaction, it brought tears to my eyes. We hugged; we loved Christmas. Before Kenny's illness we'd only ever had two at home – our first and the one after Daddy died – but it's a time of exaggerated emotion. Pain, joy – all doubled. It was difficult for us to feel other than sentimental and tender, not knowing what the next year would bring. Or perhaps being conscious of the fearful possibilities: we were frightened of what we might have to face – life as it really was, not as we wished it could be.

During the next two days, our friends came by – Mary had made us a cake; Ginny had bought and wrapped the Christmas presents for me that Kenny had asked for: Wendy, Dee, Hawkie and Maria all brought gifts. Sarah arrived to wish her father a merry Christmas and, as it was obvious he wasn't feeling well, she left early; leaning over him she kissed his forehead and I heard her whisper, 'I love you, Daddy.' I wished she were nine years old again, and ours.

Jill was coming to spend Christmas Day with us. She too had just got out of hospital and was feeling well enough to get up and around; seeing the marked improvement in her was almost the highlight of the day. I'd prepared all our favourite food, turkey and plum pudding with all the trimmings, and they ate quite well. Kenny insisted on opening a bottle of his best claret, and he managed to sit at the kitchen table to decant a bottle of port, even though he'd hardly be able to do more than sip it. He was trying so hard to give me a good Christmas. Wendy had made up stockings for us, and he got a big kick out of opening all the little packages. He couldn't open the rest of his presents – 'We'll save them for tomorrow' – he was tired, it had all been too much for him. Jill hugged him, put on her cheerful act. She'd been with us for our first Christmas together, we had all shared so many happy times; as I helped him upstairs, she and I exchanged a look that said it all.

'I often look at your face, and wonder about your wants,' he said quietly as I plumped his pillows.

I tried telling him that just sitting in his chair, he was enough for me. 'I need you to be there, Kenny,' but he found it difficult to accept. I was a healthy young woman, full of energy, and I channelled it into him. I was very protective, paying unhesitating attention to everything to do with him. I didn't feel deprived, I felt grateful that he loved me and that my life had been touched by his. I loved him, absolutely. And nothing could compare with my memories of that Christmas.

'Darling, I'm in agony!' awakened me. 'Mama's here – Mama's here!' and as I groped for the light switch, my eyes flickered towards the clock; 4.20 a.m. 'I'm so sorry to trouble you... my catheter is blocked.' Spilling out of bed, I pulled on the clothes I'd heaped on the floor the night before, simultaneously wrapping him in his huge white towelling dressing gown, helped him downstairs into the night and our car. She started first time, no middle of the night temperament, thank heavens. It took only seven minutes to get to St Thomas's and we were greeted warmly by Sister, who surely must have been harassed. There were policemen all over the place; apparently a man had been found shot in Clapham. 'Very dramatic,' she said grinning, 'we've never had a shooting before... forty pellets... I thought that only happened in New York!'

The doctor arrived and with great speed made Kenny comfortable again. 'No wonder you were in pain, Mr More, sir... we've just taken a whole litre of urine from you.' After the catheter change, he rested for a few minutes and we heard, from beyond the curtain, Sister say to another patient:

'Now Patrick, you've had seven stitches in your head… so be careful… off you go home now.'

'Home? Oh, Jesus, Sister… what time do the pubs open?'

Kenny slowly shook his head, 'That poor bugger's on the butt end of our society, how can he get it to work for him.'

Dawn was breaking over the Thames as we hurried home. I bundled him through the front door as speedily as possible and picked up the newspaper from the mat.

'Can you take a joke, love?'

'Try me.'

'It's Friday the 13th.'

Another drama over.

It was around this time that the specialists came to see us and advised us on the advantages of an Ileal Conduit Diversion – an operation whereby the bladder is bypassed and rerouted through a valve on the stomach and the urine flows into a bag. They spoke for a while and showed us the appliances. We discussed the pros and cons – no more blockages, possibly no more bladder infections. Kenny was lying back in our bed when he said quietly, pointing to his urine bag, 'Is it true that I could get a kidney infection with this catheter…? And that a really bad one could take me in three days?' I think the doctors thought he was being dramatic, but had to admit that could happen. At that point he turned his head towards them and said, calmly, 'Then leave me just as I am, that could be my passport out.' I couldn't believe what I'd just heard; my legs started to shake and my heart started to tumble. I moved in closer – he held my face between his hands and told me, 'Shrimpy, I don't know how much longer I can go on – I feel like falling down in a heap… how long does it take to die?'

I felt so scared and lost. I've never found it easy to keep a tight rein on my emotions, and that night after I'd put him to bed, I slumped into his favourite chair and let the self-pity pour over me. On my own? No Kenny? I don't want to live if I can die… what will become of me… don't leave me alone

314

Kenny... I can't take any more... I sat there in a daze, sobbing. I wished I had someone to run to, but who? The feeling of desolation was, at times, unbearable.

Ill as he was, he remembered St Valentine's Day. A van pulled up at the door and I was handed the most beautiful bouquet of red roses I'd ever seen. I hurried to the bedroom: 'Morehen... how did you manage to order these?'

'How do you think? Ginny of course; she did it for me... but I wrote the card myself.' His spidery unsure handwriting was proof to the effort he had taken to write, 'Darling Shrimp, you make up for the pain of living.' I struggled to keep hold of my composure.

One evening about this time Jill came for dinner. Her effervescent personality didn't give the slightest hint of depression. Towards the end of the meal, as she bent down and retrieved her napkin from the floor, she said, 'My guess is, Ange, I'm riddled with it.' I went hot all over, in a blaze. 'Well... I've had a good life,' she said almost indifferently.

'You have?' I heard my voice falter, realising the extreme inadequacy of my words. I had been so taken off balance my wine glass slipped out of my hand.

At the beginning of March he was admitted once more into St Thomas's, this time with a virulent chest infection. Protesting all the way, he insisted on walking the length of the entrance hall to the lifts, not wanting to be too often in a wheelchair – he had to prove he wasn't a complete invalid yet. He apologised for hanging on to my arm; he was supported on his right side by his stick. In my other hand I had his luggage – all those things you take with you to compensate for not being at home – and each time the suitcase got bigger and heavier. With great effort we very carefully negotiated the swing doors, moving slowly down the corridor towards the lifts. There was the usual traffic with the usual remarks: 'Hello Ken... what – you here again?' Kenny, ever approachable, would reply jauntily, 'Yes... I'm crazy about Matron.' Kenny briefly becoming the old Kenny. I'll never forget a tall black man coming up to us just as we'd made it to the lift gates. He became so excited at seeing Kenny – he couldn't believe it: 'Is it really you, Mr More?' – on and on. Obviously desperate to shake him by the hand, and seeing no hand available, he suddenly made a grab for the walking stick, and furiously pumped it up and down. 'How wonderful – my wife won't believe me when I get home,' and Kenny and I tumbled down like a pack of cards, he falling on me as I fell on to the luggage. 'The British public... God bless 'em,' I heard him mutter weakly, as a man came to our aid, saying, 'You are a good sport, Ken' – I'll say he was.

Once again the deluge of get-well wishes started pouring in, and most of the correspondence he received was from people sending love. Some requested photographs, and a great many were from fellow sufferers of Parkinson's disease or their relatives, people wanting advice or encouragement. I gave these special attention. We also received our share of begging letters; and some were so pathetic, poignant, that, typically, Kenny would say, 'We must send them some money.' One man wrote that he was a young actor in desperate straits for money. 'Poor sod,' he said, quietly turning the pages, 'he hasn't got a suit for auditions... that breaks my heart... his wife needs a new dress... let's send them a couple of hundred.' Kenny was the old Kenny. We received a few hate letters. He'd have been very hurt if he'd seen them – they certainly bothered me.

When Jane and Sarah came to visit, he tried to smile and be happy, and seeing us together seemed to be a positive comfort to him. One afternoon we were sitting round his bedside. 'How lovely,' he said lightly, his hands smoothing the sheet, 'look, I've got my three daughters all together around me.' Laughing, we all looked at one another. Nothing needed to be said.

We had no idea how long he might be ill and no idea of the horrors that lay ahead, but over the months, the disease had begun to bite and we had become increasingly aware of the seriousness of what we faced. And with little hope for tomorrow, he was sometimes so sad, so quiet. I started to realise that the disillusion of ill-health had begun to take over.

'Shrimp – I'm losing my nerve.'

'Try and keep hold of it – we're not through yet.'

'It's such a shock being ill – in my dreams I'm still a boy running around.' Sometimes he'd have violent hiccupping spells throughout our conversation. But even so Kenny didn't complain, although, physically, he seemed to be melting away. I was continually bending the doctors' ears, asking endless questions. They talked to me, but they couldn't give me the answer I wanted to hear. I'd plead with them, knowing that these kind and dedicated men held the life of the man I adored in their hands.

Our friends were tremendous and I found it impossible to thank them adequately. The one lesson you learn through this kind of experience is whom you can, and whom you can't rely on. We found that friends came from where we least expected them. I'll never ever forget the ones who turned up trumps – and the ones who didn't.

On March 29th early in the morning I was in the study writing when the call came. Elaine has been killed – in a car crash. I stood there and shook – I couldn't stop. My sister is dead, I said to myself. My poor lovely sister. I was destroyed when I hung up, it all seemed impossible – she was only forty-four and hadn't had her full share of life. I sent my thoughts and prayers beaming towards her – hoping to catch her spirit. God bless her – God help Mummy and Lew – Lynette and Allison – and me. How could there be a world without Elaine – I'd always had a sister. My family is shrinking, I thought, and that realisation would become more acute.

317

I tried to pull myself together as I went upstairs to Kenny. He knew something was wrong the moment I opened the door. I put my arms around him and told him as gently as I could. He looked quietly straight ahead of him and said, 'She's been spared the misery of old age.' Mummy came to stay – we needed to be together – her pain was unimaginable. We made long phone calls to America and to my brother John in South Africa. When a member of the family dies, it draws everyone even closer. We all needed to talk about Elaine – remembering so much from our childhood. She would leave a space in our hearts that couldn't be filled. We would all always have her in our thoughts – always miss her.

I was in a terrible state of nerves and tiredness, hardly knew what I was doing, what I was becoming. But in front of Kenny I was on my toes, saying whatever I had to say, making it warm, funny. I'd feel him relax and a little of his sadness would pass. With him I was cheerful. Surface cheerful. But I could cope, would cope, because I *wanted* to, determined he shouldn't glimpse a look on my face which might give him a disheartening doubt.

I'd started having nightmares: seeing him bedridden, the room in flames, calling to me for help. Burglars breaking in and hurting him. I'd scream, 'Don't hit *him* – hit me, *me!*' And one that kept returning, picturing him dead in our bed. I'd wake up in an icy sweat, tears covering my face. Sometimes I felt myself skidding despairingly downwards into a morbid depression.

Time crept on and I remember putting him to bed one night – by this stage he needed to be lifted, pulled and pushed into position. His muscles were stiff, and he'd be unable to move from that position till I woke in the morning. Kenny waved an arm at me as I tugged at the sheepskin undersheet. 'Shrimp,' he said tightly, making an effort to control himself, his voice sounding deep and faded because he seldom used it, 'the only reason I don't want to die, is that I'll miss you.'

Later, in bed, as I hid under the covers, I heard those words over and over again. My mind was full of sad and bewildering thoughts. 'Prepare yourself, Angela, get the right attitude,' friends said, 'it will happen.' On my own. No Kenny. I'd form the shapeless words in my head. They'd frighten me, and contemplating that filled me with a special loneliness. I'll think, I'll think, I promised. But don't ask me to now.

At this point, our GP turned his attention to me. He stressed with some urgency that either I took a two-week holiday, or the offer of a job. If I didn't have a break of some kind, he said, he'd have an additional patient to contend with. It amazed me that I was still occasionally offered work, but I was caring for Kenny – work wasn't contemplated. Then some TV work came along, a small part in a comedy show. It was a good part and the rehearsals would only be in the morning – I knew I was lucky to be offered it. But I protested: I felt guilty and anxious about leaving Kenny to work. Around-the-clock nursing was arranged. I knew he'd hate that. Mummy very kindly came to stay and help. He would be all right, everyone told me. He will be fine, the doctors comforted me. All the arguments were worded intellectually, carefully. But the words were easier for them to say, than for me to believe. My heartstrings tugged as I accepted the job. To relieve my guilt, I told myself that it was doctors' orders. Kenny made no secret that he wanted me constantly with him – it was enough just to know I was near. But he told me he was happy for me and that I mustn't judge by his lack of facial expression. 'My face can't smile any more, darling.'

Oh, how I hated being away from him. I got through the show, I don't know how, but I did. Looking back at those times I can't remember a lot about it, except coming home with my daily reports. It felt good to have something to talk about again, and he enjoyed my stories. When sitting in his chair became too much of an effort, he held court in bed. I talked – I bubbled – telling him about the other actors, my clothes, everything. Did I talk too much? Maybe. But life for Kenny had always equalled work, and he was still interested in everything, his eyes amused, alive. Actors call it 'Doctor Greasepaint'.

We lived day to day. Admitted once more into St Thomas's, the doctors informed us they were going to put Kenny into intensive care for twenty-four hours to be able to decide if enough oxygen was getting to his brain. If necessary, we were told, he could have a tracheotomy operation to create a hole in his throat and a plastic tube would be inserted in the hole to keep it open. The mucus that accumulated would have to be sucked out as he couldn't cough like a normal person. If it were not sucked out, they told me, his lungs would become waterlogged, and he would drown. I tried not to show my alarm. God forgive me, I said helplessly. I love him – I thought I could do anything for him... but I'm not certain I could do *that*. 'You'd find it repellent?' they contributed. Aware of the need to tread lightly, I phrased my answer as delicately as I could – but, in so many words, I told them I was scared of swallowing the mucus. They laughingly reassured me that I needn't worry: there was a small electric pump for that.

I arrived at breakfast time the next morning. Kenny made no attempt to conceal his distress: 'That was my worst night ever... no sleep at all... tubes... wires... frightening machines... I felt like a trapped animal, darling.' It was then decided the operation wouldn't help him.

Even though he was weak and listless, he submitted without protest to my request that he walk the short length of the ward corridor. His walk, now reduced to a shuffle, was the daily challenge. He'd lean on my arm and on the other side there would be the ever-present urine bag and trailing tube. Those walks exhausted him, but he wouldn't give up.

One afternoon a short, plump chaplain wandered into the room. 'C. of E. aren't you, Mr More?' he enquired, fidgeting with his tight collar. The brief and aimless theological discussion ended abruptly with – 'Tell me, Mr More, what is your purpose in life?'

'To do a pooh every other day,' he replied flippantly.

'That's not what I meant.'

'I didn't think it was.' And then to stem the hurt look, he added, 'Don't worry, I say my prayers every night... and my little wife's always on top of the list.' I don't have to wonder why I loved him.

Because by now it took a tremendous effort on his part to manage the stairs, I decided to convert his study into a summer day-bedroom for him – it led on to our large terrace which I'd fill with tumbling geraniums, fuchsia, roses and marguerites. It would be perfect, so at dawn one morning I went to Nine Elms market to buy all the plants I'd need. The eager faces of some of the dealers greeted me. 'How's Ken?' they would ask sadly. He's very ill, but beautiful, I told them, my voice sounding as if my head were in a barrel. I felt a great wave of gratitude, not just for the bunches of flowers they pressed into my arms for him, and for the nurses. It was also for the affirmation that he had originally become a star almost by public demand. It was the British people who had noticed him, not studios or agents. On the stage and in films Kenny was usually seen as a debonair Englishman who could meet any crisis. This was perhaps the quality that his public loved most. In private he could be insecure, less resilient – but during his illness he was an amalgam of all the qualities he'd ever portrayed. Courage. Warmth. Integrity. Little boy lost. Humour. Kindness. Pride. The British public responded loyally to him in these last years, as he coped with this crippling disease, acknowledging the fact that he was generating a courage far beyond mere film heroics.

And I remember all this because I need it now, cherishing it because it comforts me to know he was so loved.

I'd talked to him about my plans for his study and I suppose it was foolish, but I found it painful telling him his desk, his clock – his things, would have to be sold. Another ending. I remember he turned his head on the pillow and, looking at me, he said, gently, 'Oh, darling... selling your beautiful things.'

'You are my beautiful thing.'

He was desperately ill, yet he still cared about whatever he knew mattered to me.

Jill was now a very sick girl and losing ground. Whenever she felt up to having visitors I'd go to her before dashing off to Kenny in the hospital; they were concerned about each other. Almost every day he'd ask, 'How's Jill?' I bought a card for her and asked him to sign it, and I'll never forget the sad expression on his face as he hesitated for an instant before struggling to sign his name.

On May 31st I brought him home from the hospital. He was nervous and tearful – so delighted to be back in his own bed, said it was like being handed the moon. I promised him that from now on he'd be nursed at home, no more hospitals. 'You can't promise me that... supposing I have a stroke... or another kidney stone,' he said with one of his shatteringly straight looks.

Days went by, the weather was glorious. Our routine at home had been the same for months, only now he couldn't manage the short shuffly daily walk to Edwards' flower shop on the corner, and now we had to have a nurse. I knew he'd hate having a nurse around; so would I. I was possessive, wanting to be all he needed. But from Monday to Friday Anne came for four hours in the morning. She was buoyant with merry Irish eyes, and easy to be with, capable. Between us we did everything that was necessary for him. And at the weekends, he was all mine to look after. Some days there was a haunted and hauntingly sad quality in his brown eyes and he was weak and listless, not wanting visitors – except for a special few who sustained us, each in their own loving way. Generally he found being visited debilitating, needing such a concentrated effort. He felt inadequate and ashamed to show his infirmity – he was deeply embarrassed. 'I don't want my friends to see me this way – they know I love them – I want them to remember me the way I was,' he'd say in a very quiet, but firm voice.

'Can I have a dog, darling? Surely now's the time to have one while we're at home so much... I've always wanted a dog.'

'No, Shrimp. When anything happens to me, I want you to be free – a dog is a fifteen-year commitment.'

I whirled round. 'Oh, please!'

'No, love, in important matters... I'm still the boss.'

After that last sentence I moved to the bed and lay down beside him. I put my head next to his and I could feel his faintly fevered cheek. His muffled voice said. 'Darling... don't ever stop being the girl I know.' He fell silent.

'Oh, Morehen,' I protested in a murmur, thinking despairingly, what will I do without you? I didn't say anything for fear of sounding hopelessly banal.

Sometimes he would ask me practical questions – did I understand about insurance? Would I remember to have the gutters checked? Any problems you have, he'd say, go to Laurie, he'll look after you. I told him not to worry about me – he was leaving me full up with love, I was strong now, I could cope. I felt we'd finally both grown up and I'd say how silly it was for him to be dying now – now that we were perfect for each other. 'You never taught me to spell!'

'Too late now,' he murmured.

He was lying back in bed with his eyes closed – doing his leg exercises had exhausted him, I thought. Then suddenly he said, 'I want to be cremated.'

'Your ashes scattered at sea?' I asked hesitantly.

'No... No!'

'Or, with me? Do you want to stay with me?'

'With you, I want to be with you.' I groped for words that were properly tender and he was almost smiling – as we held hands, he closed his eyes again and a few seconds later he fell into a peaceful sleep.

Although he was up to very little physically, his brain was as alert as ever and, fortunately, we had a diversion: this manuscript. Kenny was characteristically enthusiastic. One day while I was shaving him and telling him about the ideas the publishers had for the jacket of the book, he said, 'Do you want a picture of us together… would that make you happy?' Then looking at his image in the mirror, he added, 'Let's do it soon.' I understood he'd found a positive way to express his love, his appreciation, but I wasn't convinced that it was fair to put him through the trauma of a photographic session. I protested, but he was emphatic. He wanted to do this for me. And it was wonderful seeing that this lovely gesture meant so much to him.

I knew I had to be light-hearted and started to smile even before I entered her bedroom. But as I looked down at Jill in her bed, I had to will my anguish not to show. She was, of course, watching me and she met my eye. I was smiling brightly, but all to myself I was saying – don't die on me Jill – *don't die.* I was allowed to stay for half an hour and it was wonderful to see her awake and able to recognise me. She was alert: we could hear the twenty-one-gun salute in Hyde Park, in honour of Prince William's birth – we counted them together. She showed no pain – her blue eyes shining. I didn't want to leave her although I knew she must sleep. I caught sight of myself in the mirror, seeing my small alert face, my alarmed eyes, and as I slowly bent to kiss her, she gently stroked my cheek, lowering her eyelids sadly, whispering, 'I'm sorry, Ange.'

As I closed the door behind me I stood on the top of the stairs for a moment, not wanting to leave, but I couldn't trust myself not to cry. That humour – that perception – that friendship. And then I was alone, out in that empty cobbled mews street. The silence was intense; there was only the evening's darkness to hold me.

Jill died a week later on June 30th, ten minutes after I left her bedside. I wanted so much to stay with her, but another of her friends said, 'Jill's got all of us – Kenny only has you.' I drove home, almost from memory. I felt numb – a great emptiness – so many losses – so many irreplaceables.

July 1982 – My emotions of the following few days were so complex and abundant that they were, and still are, impossible to individualise. Life was closing in on us. We were living day to day. I felt I had to ask the doctors the burning question I'd tried not to ask for months – terrified of the answer. But now I had to face the harsh reality – God give me strength! – 'How long can Kenny go on being this ill?' They talked – I listened. I heard them say, 'I'm sure you know already Angela, the drugs aren't touching his Parkinsonism – the disease has savaged his central nervous system – his brain will be affected next – it's galloping Parkinson's... a year, perhaps eighteen months.' I didn't cry – I just felt a caving-in of my stomach.

I didn't ever tell Kenny – even though we often talked about his dying.

'Who will I care for?'

'*You.*'

'Where will I live?'

'You stay *here.*' I'd had my orders.

The dimension of time seems to disappear when you know that something has got to happen. I'd found it didn't help, crying all night into my pillow and talking to God, please God, just give me another chance... don't let him die, God. I struggled to face the fact that he was dying, slipping by notches. We were rock bottom – our life never worse – our

325

love never better. Kenny so brave and uncomplaining – so
tender and affectionate. How had we ever been unhappy
together – we couldn't remember.

I have only my bizarre reasons for remembering Kenny lying
on the bed, flicking through a book Ginny had given him on
Buddhism – me squatting alongside repeating how I thought
Buddha's philosophy would help him. After a few moments he
snapped it shut, and growled weakly, 'Oh, bugger Buddha!' He
could still make me laugh.

It must have been in the middle of the first week in July that I
asked him to read a section of my writing. I fumblingly drew
the worn pages from the envelope. 'There,' I said, flourishing it
in front of him, spreading out the pages; then, self-conscious, I
turned away and busied myself with his drugs – I had my work
cut out. Eight small dishes – four pills in each to be given at set
times through the day. I'd drawn up a chart and pinned it to
the kitchen wall, along with the daily details of liquid
intake/output – how many sweats – colour of urine – enemas
– coughing fits – all the grim details. He called from the
bedroom, 'This must be good, love… it comes from the heart.
That's all that matters.' I couldn't get back into the room quick
enough. '*Do you really think so…?* are you proud of me?' I
blurted.
    'If I die… promise me you won't cool off on it…' That
brought me up short. 'Don't cool off,' he repeated.
    I clambered on to the bed. 'Oh, Kenny, Kenny,' I
whispered, wanting to say, but unable to say, don't die, not yet.
    He broke in, almost brushing me aside. 'Look at this
passage… words jump from the page…it's really good stuff,'
he assured me.
    Encouraged, I teased, 'Well you would think that, wouldn't
you. I mean, I've made you look the greatest lover in the
world!'

He hardly let me get my words out. 'Remember when you come to making me a shit... make me the greatest shit in the world!' His eyes were gleaming and on a level with mine. His mouth twisting in an effort to smile, he half choked on his throaty giggle and made weak dabs at his eyes. With my heartache momentarily in abeyance, at that moment I thought – we couldn't be happier.

July 7th was a bright sunny day for Lord Snowdon to take the cover photographs. There was an instant rapport between the three of us and it was exciting, even though I was worried sick knowing the effort Kenny was making, in every way. And two days later when I looked through the rough prints it came as a shock to realise that we both looked at the end of our tether.

I sat beside his bed in the dusk watching him – he was sleepy now. Outside the sounds of the birds squabbling in the trees and of a birthday party in full swing in a neighbouring garden: 'Happy birthday – ha-pp-y bi-rth-day'; then I remembered that tomorrow was July 12th, the date of my miscarriage thirteen years before, and I began wondering about the son he and I never had. Lying there, Kenny looked terribly vulnerable, I thought – the bag on its stand and the disconcerting pulley hanging overhead – and I felt a rage erupt in me like a bubble. God, why did he have to go like this? to suffer so? – who had he ever harmed? – God? – no answer. It was an awful feeling. His eyes still shut, I nuzzled his neck. 'Thank you precious... thank you for everything' – this said with enormous tenderness in a voice I could hardly recognise – crickety and hoarse – his breathing ragged. I couldn't answer, I just smoothed his hair and murmured in a voice I could barely hear.

The party music was in full swing when I went to bed and I lay there for quite a while. Doubtless it was exhaustion and distress that helped me sleep that night. But I slept restlessly, chaotically and woke just after dawn – everything so still. For a moment I stared straight at the wall – my heart was thumping and I had the strangest feeling, understanding quite clearly that we were now living minute to minute.

Wanting to be with him, I crept into his bedroom – I can see it as clearly as if it's happening now. He was awake, alert. Hearing me, he slowly turned his head towards me and held out his arms: 'I love you – I love you – you won't ever forget how much I love you,' his eyes implored urgently as I got into bed beside him. During the preceding weeks emotion had entered into the most ordinary situations. However, there were no tears that day; we were tranquil as we talked quietly.

At nine o'clock José arrived – he'd been away with flu and came straight upstairs to see us. 'Good morning… how are you feeling today Mr More, sir?' Kenny replied, 'Don't worry about me, José… how are you…? you're the one that matters.' Then Anne came on duty and gave us a boiled egg breakfast in bed together.

After breakfast Kenny fell asleep again and I went downstairs to give Anne the information she needed for the daily report book we were keeping. I told her that during a prolonged and distressing coughing attack he'd brought up some nasty black blood again, and I'd thought his urine looked murky – could that be anything to do with the drenching sweats he'd been having? 'He's getting so weak,' I told her.

I said to Anne that I wanted to do everything for my husband that morning, but would she change his sweat-soaked bedding and prepare his favourite smoked salmon sandwiches for lunch. And not to forget his craving for chocolate.

It was a warm and gloriously pink summer's morning and while Anne made up a bed for him on the terrace I shaved him and got him into the bath. While I washed his hair, his words rushing together, he pressed me again not to forget how much he loved me. I promised him I wouldn't.

He slept for a while on the terrace, surrounded by the lovely garden which had given us both so much pleasure. As he slept I returned Douglas Bader's call – I had to tell him I felt it would be better if he didn't come and see Kenny that afternoon as he was feeling sleepy. When I went back upstairs, Kenny asked me to help him into his own bed and I curled up beside him while he napped again. By one o'clock Anne and José had gone home and for the rest of the day he slept for short periods – waking – sleeping – waking. At one point he reminded me that Wendy was coming to supper tonight, and told me about the special programme on the Falklands that he wanted to watch.

Just before six o'clock he fell asleep again and I lay there with him waiting for Wendy to arrive. I was watching his face when he opened his eyes and said softly, 'Don't grieve, little one... have a long holiday... I'll be waiting for you.' These were the last words he spoke. Gently gripping my hand he closed his eyes and shortly after he slipped into a deep coma and died. My head was on his chest – I heard his last heartbeat.

I'd been told of all the emotions you're meant to feel. I felt overjoyed that he was free from his misery and at peace; hadn't he suffered enough? And I felt – alone. The room became unnaturally silent and before Wendy led me out, looking back over my shoulder at Kenny's face on the pillow, I kissed him and, for the first time, there was no response from him. I blessed him for all the love he'd left behind. And I told him, over and over, Kenny, mine is with you.

Grey skies,
blue skies

Lives end. Hearts are broken. How do you mend a broken heart? How do you stop leaves falling from a tree? 'Time heals,' friends said to me with genuine kindness. I'd say it's like a scab over a wound: if you start to pick at it, the pain can feel like day one. For several years after Kenny died I was tangled up in sorrow. Emotionally bruised beyond anything I could imagine, I felt as though I was falling through darkness. Despair beyond despair. There was no 'Band-Aid' for my grief. I talked to God down on my knees by my bed, asking: 'Help me, God... show me how... I can't do this.' Many days the thought of my own death was dazzlingly attractive. My love for him was the core of my life. There is peril to love like that. When the loved one is lost to you, the life is lost. It crumbles to pieces. That is what happened to my life. As the days passed, more and more things happened and I wanted to tell him, so whatever I was doing I was always writing him a letter in my head.

It's not as though Kenny could exactly be described as being the perfect husband. Never around on house-moving days. Came home at seven in the morning on the day of my father's funeral, having spent the night drinking at his beloved Garrick Club. When my mother was diagnosed with cancer... when my brother, the father of two tiny boys, had a serious breakdown because his marriage had collapsed... when I was barely recovered from double pneumonia and he felt it an appropriate time to book a three-month cruise up the Amazon!

So where was he when I needed him most? Feminism? I don't think he'd ever heard the word. He was a child of his time, brought up in the twenties. I was a child of *my* time, brought up in the fifties, and I left the shelter of my parents' home to live with him when I was barely out of my teens, to be sheltered from the harsh realities of life for the next twenty years. I was to learn that he was far from faithful, always with an eye for a pretty girl. He was also intelligent, charming, very brave and had a great sense of fun. If you had met him you would have been struck by his abounding love of life. Loving him was my disease, as I was his. He wrote: 'A day without her was like a summer without the sun... she was twenty-one when I met her and I was forty-seven. With that youth, she has also given me the priceless gift of love. I've never loved another. When I die they'll find her name "Shrimp" engraved on my heart.'

Like most bereaved people, it was at home I felt safest and yet most desperate where the void left by daily closeness is at its deepest. Forty-eight hours after his death I switched on the television and there he was. I leapt from my bed, thrilled, calling 'Hello darling!' Tears flowed like rain, exhausting me with grief. After his memorial service at St Martin-in-the-Fields, friends came back to the house. Lauren Bacall stood with her arms around me in the study and said: 'Look at that painting. It will always be a lovely painting. One day, though, you'll hang it on a different wall.' Remembering her tenderness from three decades away, her words to me were wise and proved to be very true.

Alone now. Close the door. Close the curtains. Close my eyes. Residue of dust from my past to be sifted through. You can never appreciate what your memory is until you start trying to ease open its door and form it into sentences. I took to my bed. My world was a fearful place. When kindly friends asked me out, I had the perfect excuse to hide away. I had to finish my book. I'd promised him I would. I found it at times almost impossible, tossing screwed-up balls of paper at the wall, shouting: 'I don't know how to do this!' But finish it I did and I'll be forever grateful, because when it was published two years after his death I was launched back into life and on a level I hadn't been since the years before the illness. Suddenly I was hot. Life by the tail. However briefly, this was my moment. Theatre and television work came my way. Designers sent me their beautiful clothes to wear when being interviewed on television. Sent to America to write for the *Daily Telegraph*, I became a regular contributor to the *Female* pages of the *Sunday Times*. Quite extraordinary for someone who'd never put pen to paper before. 'You have a voice,' or so I was told. Apparently it was said: 'Don't teach her how to write or she could lose her natural talent.' Well, whaddya know, I have a voice!

When the book was published, I remember the actor Derek Nimmo saying to me: 'I've just read it… I'm ashamed to say I didn't know there was so much *you*!' I wanted to tell him it was always there but no one ever talked to me or asked me about my thoughts or opinions. I was completely in my husband's shadow. All my conversations were held in my head. I was constantly asked: 'How is your husband? What does he think of this and that? Is he filming?' I complained to him that even when buying the tomatoes, I was made to feel like his PA. Small price to pay for a wonderful home, two great holidays a year and no anxieties as to where the money was to come from to pay the bills. Very fortunate. Did I appreciate it enough? I hope so.

Friends – mine, his, ours – were astonishing. After all the dust had settled they didn't abandon me. Friends have their own lives, they move on. Our special friends didn't. I think I must have been half mad. However erratic my behaviour, however unreliable I became, they seemed to understand why.

Derek and Pat Nimmo had a villa in Turkey and invited me to stay with them for a few days. Among my fellow houseguests was the actor Edward Duke. One blisteringly hot morning we were in the sea up to our necks in the water, trying to stay sure-footed in the waves while clutching our glasses of white wine, when he asked me: 'Do you want to stay on your own for the rest of your life?' Usually I would have brushed his question aside with some smart remark but this time, startled by his directness, I suddenly felt very small. He'd hit a raw nerve. I muttered a soft 'No'. No discussion. A candid: 'You'd better go home and stop talking about Kenny. Open the window. Life's a one-shot thing. Get yourself out there... it's a playground!'

You have to kiss a lot of frogs before you find your prince. Certain times stand out. The first time I dipped my toe into the water was with...

The Fashion Designer.

To me an obvious homosexual. A walker. Safe. After only our third supper he announced: 'Angela Douglas, you are a delight. I can change my lifestyle. I want to. Let's buy a house in the country. Time is running out for you to get pregnant so we'd better hurry up!' Irresistible offer? I don't think so.

Three days passed before he called me. 'I must see you today. Can you come over to the workshop?'

'Yes, but why?'

'I need reassurance. There's a picture of you in the *Daily Mail* this morning. I've got to see that you don't really look this old.'

I didn't feel obliged to respond. A couple of days' silence passed before I received his note dumping me. Apparently thinking about me was interfering with his creativity. He sent the note over by courier bike. Such style.

Then there was...

The Lawyer.

Always on the go. 'What are you doing tonight... tomorrow... the rest of your life?' Always saying: 'How lucky can a man get?' I was told he was famously tight with money.

'So tight,' they said, 'he can peel an orange in his pocket.' I was to find out.

In a supermarket he could do the weekend shopping for pennies. I offered to make an apple pie, so I picked up three cooking apples and some flour. When we got to the checkout, he put the divider down between his goods and mine. I said nothing. He took me to stay with friends in the South of France for the weekend. I wonder if it was paying my fare that put him into a huge sulk the moment we arrived. He gave me the full silent treatment. The only kisses I got were from Aristos, the adorable British bulldog puppy who'd taken a shine to me. Licking my face, he seemed to care that I was crying. You'd cry too if you felt as vulnerable and isolated as I did. On the third morning, alone in the bedroom, I was angry as hell. I wanted to yell at him: 'Look at you! Overweight and losing your hair! Making one teabag last for three cups! What did I ever see in you? What am I doing here?'

From my window overlooking the courtyard, the smell of his cigar wafted up as I listened to him and the others talk about which beach to take the yacht to for lunch. Desperate to be at home and not wanting to be there for a moment longer, I scooped up the few clothes I'd brought with me, stuffed them into my Mulberry wheelie case and crept down the dark, stone-floored corridor lined with identical doors. I tiptoed down the marble stairs to the huge front door where fat little Aristos scraped at my legs with his paws, begging to be allowed to come outside with me into the garden. 'Shush,' I whispered, 'not play time. Kissy kiss, little love. Thank you for being my pal.' I pulled the heavy door softly behind me. The garden was very still. I stood there for a moment before running down the drive, past the mimosa, the pink velvet poppies, the blue plumbago and heavily scented trumpet trees, and was gone as suddenly as I'd arrived. No looking back. 'Taxi! Oh, anywhere, driver, anywhere! It doesn't matter. Just keep driving!'

The Film Producer.

It was my birthday. 'Let's have a celebratory supper,' was his suggestion. How generous of him, or so I thought. He brought four of his office staff with him. Strange, but I suppose okay. As he gave me my present, he reassured me. 'I charge everything to my productions – including presents!' Ouch. I'd just blown out the candles on my cake and made my wish when he stood up from the table, leaving the restaurant – and me to pay the bill.

You'd have thought by now I would have learnt my lesson. Wouldn't you just!

It doesn't get any better.

The Politician.

It isn't an everyday happening for a letter to drop through my letterbox bearing the seal of the House of Commons. It came from an eminent Member of Parliament. He had heard that I was President of the Kenneth More Fund into Research for Multiple Atrophy Syndrome and Parkinson's Disease. He wished to donate £10,000, saying that it would be his pleasure, as he had met Kenny on several occasions while lunching at the Garrick Club. It would also be his pleasure if I were to be free to have lunch with him at the Connaught Hotel. How could I refuse, or even want to? Such an amazingly generous donation to the Fund. And who was I to turn down the offer of such a lunch? A girl has to eat.

A discreet corner table had been reserved. Tall and elegant, I instantly recognised him from television with his thick head of curly hair and hugely unruly eyebrows. He stood to greet me with a kiss on the hand.

Champagne was offered... caviar ordered... he placed the cheque for the charity neatly by my napkin. Conversation flowed, mostly from him. His work took him all over the world. The people he knew and liked and those he didn't. He was full of ideas and full of life. On about my fourth glass of champagne I was beginning to find him very attractive, hanging on his every word. The flirting was mutual. As he swallowed an oyster he said he'd seen me in a play and had spent the evening just admiring my 'delicious' legs. Well, a compliment like that could keep me happy for months!

As with the champagne, the conversation flowed. Secrets were spilled, his discretion slipping. He told me that he'd been married for too many years to remember and that his wife was a 'sensible woman' who let him out on a long leash, turning a blind eye to his peccadilloes. He believed that life was a great big canvas, 'throw all the paint on it you can'.

With that he leaned forward, looked me straight in the eye, and asked in a soft voice so no one else could hear: 'What do you want from a man, Angela?'

My God, what a question! 'Nothing... I've never thought that way.'

'Well, when you marry again, marry for money!'

Almost choking on my words: 'I don't like rich men... I've seen how some of them treat their women. And I'll never marry again... that's my fidelity to Kenny.'

Those famous eyebrows rose in a zigzag of polite surprise. 'You might find yourself in a relationship where marriage was a condition.'

I shrugged and flicked back: 'Then he would be the wrong man!'

He shook his head. 'I'm sorry. I never should have said that.' For a few awkward moments he toyed with his glass. He took a sip of wine – champagne had been followed by 'red of a good year' – wiped his lips carefully and smiled suddenly at me. Placing his hand gently on my arm he continued: 'I'm going to Russia next week on business... come with me, Angela. I'll arrange for a private viewing at the Hermitage. I'll give you my credit card; you can go shopping while I have my meetings... Use me, Angela... use me.' Seeing my astonished face, he put his finger to his lips and added: 'I'm very discreet, you know.' He brushed the tablecloth, cupping a pile of crumbs into his hand, spilled them onto his plate, snapped his fingers and asked for the bill.

The light was going as he hailed a taxi. Neither of us wanted to hurry away as he suddenly hugged me, whispering: 'I always get what I want and I want you.' It certainly was the longest, sexiest lunch I'd ever had. In the taxi I felt intoxicated and not only by the wine. By the attention, the compliments. I was certainly tempted to accept. Oh, be naughty, Angela. Just for once... say yes.

Only that was the drink talking. It was no good, I couldn't go away with him. Oh, how I've yearned to see the glorious treasures of the Hermitage. To be astonished by the history of it all. But – and it was a big BUT – he was a married man. Feminism? What does the word mean if it doesn't mean Sisterhood? 'Do as you would be done by' – my mother's words. No such thing as a free trip to Russia. Nothing else to say. The next day I wrote him a polite and regretful letter.

Onwards, Angela! Forever the believer in true love. The hunt goes on.

The New York Park Avenue Surgeon.

I met him first at a dinner party in New York. Back home he called me, inviting me to return and stay at his condo on the beach at Long Island. I checked first with my darling stepdaughter Jane. 'Should I go?' She gave me her permission. Picture it. Tall, good-looking in an Italian sort of way. A top flight surgeon. Out on the beach with blue skies and glowing sunsets. What's not to like? You might guess what's coming.

He didn't want romantic walks along the beach in the sunset. He was an alcoholic. From dawn to dusk he drank, anything that was going. A mean-spirited, maudlin man. His secretary said: 'Oh, I never let him do surgery the day after a party.' Those were the words that were supposed to reassure me? Once again I found myself yearning to go home. One very early morning, I crept out and along to some neighbours, an elderly Jewish couple. We'd never spoken, just nodded a 'Good morning' or two. Knocking on the door, my small voice whispered: 'Damsel in distress!'

'Did he hit ya, honey?'

And with that, they scooped me up, took me in, booked my seat on the Jitney, and got me the hell out of there, bless their hearts. We remain close friends, often laughing together at the memory.

I arrived back in the city in the middle of an electric storm. Torrential rain lashed down as I got off the bus, just as the strap on my hand luggage broke, sending the contents swirling down the gutters and into the drains. I stood on the sidewalk clutching my purse and passport, a drenched figure listening to Kenny's voice in my head. 'Get home, little Shrimp, take better care of yourself!' 'I will, Kenny, I promise.'

On the way to the airport I asked the taxi to stop off at David's Cookies shop, where I bought at least twenty-five cookies, and by the time I'd landed in London I'd eaten the lot. If being pretty meant attracting these troublesome men, I didn't want to know any more. The dating game was not for me – I didn't know the rules. I threw in the towel. As I drew up to the front door of my lovely house, I sobbed and sobbed and then sobbed some more.

I got back in my box. I worked in the theatre and wrote some more features and concentrated on what I hoped was being a good friend to my friends, nephews and stepdaughters, and giving my mother the loving attention she so deserved and yearned for in her later years.

In today's world, it would seem that if you want to find someone to love, it's down to electronics of a sort. Internet dating or speed dating, chat roulette, singles nights. What courage it must take to get up the nerve. Back in the eighties our stepping stones were links in the chain.

A close girlfriend of mine had a huge crush on someone she had to keep secret, because she was married. If they wanted to go to a restaurant for a romantic lunch and not be seen alone together, they needed a gooseberry – me. Before dessert I escaped to the cloakroom so that they could whisper a few sweet nothings to each other for a moment or two.

In the loo, a woman with a small daughter said: 'Hello, I'm Linda Thomson – I know who you are, I've read your book, couldn't stop crying!' She pulled out a card. 'My husband is the head of the William Morris Agency in London. If there is ever anything he can do to help you, please call.' Grateful for her kind gesture, I scrabbled around in my bag for a scrap of paper and scribbled my number down before going back to join the lovers. By the time I got home, there was a message from Linda on my answering machine asking me to supper the next Saturday. She mentioned the names of the other guests. One was Bill Bryden.

Like many people in my profession, I knew of Bill Bryden long before I met him. He had an enviable reputation as an inspired, award-winning director, an associate of the National Theatre and Head of Drama at BBC Scotland. That's all I knew. Linda had seated us next to each other. I remember him saying complimentary things about Kenny's work, his voice a soft Scottish accent.

There was a pause. Momentarily, my eyes bounced off his. The look between us was there. Butterflies. He's the one. Too good-looking. I thought: 'He's bound to be trouble!' But it was trouble I wanted. Same age. Same profession. Both exuberant, me blonde, he dark-haired. But we both came with heavy emotional baggage: me in love with my dead husband, he going through a traumatic, lengthy divorce. He was living on a boat on the Thames at Chelsea. He said to me: 'You are the rescue from the rocking boat I'm on.' He had a teenage daughter and son. Mummy assured me: 'You can handle that, you love young people.' When I introduced Bill to her, she exclaimed: 'Oh darling, he's got the lot!' Approval. I wasn't now going to be alone forever.

Love in the midst of chaos. Nobody has the perfect life and at times my life was emotionally intense, but with tenderness and respect we rode the waves. Our enduring love and the need to be part of the profession we share in our different ways is the glue in our relationship. Whatever we might be doing gets dropped if there is a movie to be seen and discussed, a play or an opera up for debate, or disagreement, and non-stop ideas about casting. I've always understood that actresses 'of a certain age' (of which I'm now one) find good work incredibly scarce. If at some point you've been in demand, it's almost painful to now play the little wife left behind in the kitchen asking: 'Want another cup of tea, dear?' Not even a little rewarding. Of course the money is lovely and it gets you out of the house, but even so, it's a bullet you have to bite from time to time. I've been lucky quite recently working opposite the charmers Tom Conti and Frank Finlay. The thing I miss most when not on a production is the laughter among the cast and crew. You can come home from a long day's shoot and be exhausted from the fun of it all. Bliss. But if work is slow, it doesn't have to mean the end of creativity. Who was it said: 'Don't hurry, don't worry. You're only here for a short visit. So be sure to stop and smell the flowers.'

And we do. After twenty-four years we are now deeply in love. Perfect companionship, involved in all aspects of each other's day. Nobody has his interests at heart more than me, and vice versa. We are each other's Number One. Three years ago we 'eloped' to New York and, in a hilarious five-minute ceremony at City Hall, we were married. A long larky lunch with three of our closest friends at our favourite Italian restaurant followed. No name change for me. Liberated woman at last!

I read this somewhere. I'm paraphrasing a little:

> Love is a temporary madness. An illness of the brain. It erupts like volcanoes and then subsides. And when it does subside, you have to make a decision. You have to work out whether your roots are so entwined together that it is inconceivable

that you should ever part. That is what love really is. Love is not breathlessness and a quicksilver beating heart. It is not excitement. It is not the promise of eternal passion. That is simply being *in* love, which one can experience possibly more than once. Love in truth is what is left when the flame of being in love has flickered away, and this is a most fortunate blessing. Those who truly love have deep roots that grow towards each other. And when the decorative blossom falls, as it surely will, they find that they are one tree and not two.

My second one and only. I'm told that if you deeply love, when you die you live on a cloud as one conjugal angel. Well, there will now be three of us on that cloud. A bit crowded. But love is love and we'll be very contented. Secure. Kicking our heels up without a care.

No one knows what the future may hold. My prayer is that my Scottish director and his Irish actress may live happily ever after.

Amen to that.

Angela Douglas
London 2012

Acknowledgments

My book has been a long time in the making, and many of the people who have encouraged me on my journey have undoubtedly forgotten about it. Nevertheless, in lieu of an Academy Award acceptance speech and with more time and space, I wish to thank my agent Vivien Schuster who believed I had something to say before I ever had an inkling to write.

I benefited beyond measure from the critical eye of Felicity Green. Penny Perrick has always been a source of unstinting support; and I received invaluable aid from Douglas Rae, Nicky Ryde, Richard Mangan and Louise Stein.